CHICAGO QUARTERLY REVIEW

Volume 27
FALL 2018

Cover art: "Self-Portrait" by Eleanor Spiess-Ferris, Gouache, 8" x 10", 2011

The Chicago Quarterly Review is published by The Chicago Quarterly Review 501(c)3 in Evanston, Illinois. Unsolicited submissions are welcome through our submissions manager at Submittable. To find out more about us, please visit www.chicagoquarterlyreview.com.

TABLE OF CONTENTS

NONFICTION

POETRY

ART

EDITORS' NOTE

We take pride and joy in producing this magazine. Next year, we'll celebrate our 25th anniversary with a special issue as well as readings and receptions to be announced. We could not have enjoyed this continuity without our dedicated staff and the growing number of submissions we receive from writers, new and established, all over the world.

When our contributors are recognized, it's all the better. We're proud to announce that Dounia Choukri's story "Past Perfect Continuous" from CQR #23 has been included in *The O. Henry Prize Stories 2018*. *Best American Essays 2018* includes "Five Famous Asian War Photographs" by Amit Majmudar, *CQR #24*. And our South Asian American issue, guest edited by Moazzam Sheikh, was named a Notable Special Issue of 2017 by *Best American Essays*.

In this issue, we would like to call attention to a personal essay by beloved former CQR editor Natalia Nebel. "Lazarus" concerns a harrowing personal ordeal that we've observed Natalia bear with dignity and grace. Our pride and joy extends to all involved.

MY BOOKS AND I
Isidra Mencos

If you could have lifted the roof of my house when I was growing up, you would have often found twelve people in the living room, each with their nose buried in a book, and nobody talking to each other.

Sometimes when my cousin Sylvia, who was also my best friend, came to visit, I hid in the bathroom. I wanted to play with her, but if she arrived at a bite-your-nails twist in my book's plot, I couldn't have gotten the story out of my head even if an angel had descended from heaven. I stayed in the toilet, holding my breath, hoping that one of my siblings would keep Sylvia busy for a tiny little bit while I sneaked in a few more pages. After three or four minutes, the syncopated bangs of what seemed a machine gun would startle me. I'd look up from the page and see the door shaking. "Get out right now!" Sylvia would demand. "But I need to go to the bathroom." "No, you don't. You're just reading a book. What did I come here for?"

I'd sigh, close the book, get up from the toilet cover, and unlock the bathroom. Sylvia would be standing right outside. "See? I knew it!" I'd have to leave the book on a table, with a longing sideways look, and spend the rest of the afternoon playing.

When I went to Sylvia's house, the first place I visited was the bookshelf in her family room. It wasn't as big or as full as ours, with its double rows of books and the spines ruined from so much use, but sometimes I'd find a treasure yet unread, calling me like honey to bears. "If you keep reading, I won't invite you again," threatened Sylvia, exasperated.

On the *Día de Reyes*, each of us ten siblings got a book, on top of the toys, costumes, and board games. A Christmas without a new book would have been as sad as a Nativity without Jesus. I couldn't wait to start reading. Mine was usually part of a series. *Los siete secretos*, *Los cinco*, *Guillermo el travieso*, and Karl May's Wild West novels were early favorites. I soon graduated to classics, from Dickens and Jules Verne to *El Lazarillo de Tormes* or *Little Women*. Jo was my role model, because I wanted to be a writer.

Since I was the seventh of ten, I had the advantage that, as I grew up, I could read my older siblings' books. My tastes matured in quickstep.

As a teen, I started on the Latin American Boom authors. My childhood's collector fever reasserted itself. I had to read all of García Márquez's books, not just *One Hundred Years of Solitude*. All of Vargas Llosa's, each five-hundred-page tome. All of Borges, whose short stories I reread a dozen times.

I majored in Spanish and Latin American literature, with a minor in French. My favorite class was an overview of Spanish poetry with Professor José Manuel Blecua, a revered researcher who had been friends with the poets of *la Generación del 27*. He peppered his lessons with anecdotes of his time with them. One was a memory of him, Lorca, and Salinas riding a cable car, hanging from the doors into the street and shouting poems at the top of their lungs.

Blecua was in his late sixties. Although half deaf and with a visible tremor in his hands, he hadn't lost an ounce of his youthful passion for beauty. He often interrupted his loose lectures by reciting poems by heart or reading them from a book. It was a sight to see, that brittle old man, his face brightened by a resplendent smile, his whole being overtaken by the poem he was reciting. I sat in the first row so I wouldn't miss a word. Through him, I fell in love with the Golden Age authors: Fray Luis de León, San Juan de la Cruz, Garcilaso, Góngora, Quevedo.

"What kind of trees flank the university sidewalks in Calle Aribau?" he asked us once. When nobody could answer, he scolded us: "How can you appreciate poetry, even less write it, if you don't know the names of the things that surround you?"

La Biblioteca del Carmen became my second home. There I spent hours copying my favorite poems by eleventh- to thirteenth-century troubadours in a sheaf of blank pages. I decorated the corners with elaborate and colorful garlands, replicating an illuminated medieval manuscript. Sometimes I fell into a trancelike state, transforming the sheets into modest jewels. There was no other purpose to my copying than honoring the work of those long-ago poets who brought a piece of heaven to palaces and town squares when war, famine, and illness ravaged lives. I wish I still had that handcrafted anthology. Like so many other precious objects, I gifted it to a now bygone friend.

The first man I lived with, in my early twenties, was as hopelessly in love with books as I was. He first piqued my interest when he offered me homemade chicken soup after a night of dancing salsa. Since he didn't have sofas or hardly any furniture, we sat on the blue-and-white bedspread of his twin bed, eating the comforting soup and talking about Carpentier until five in the morning. Then came the sex, but that wasn't as important.

Soon we were living together. Our library grew in unison with our relationship. With him, I explored the classics of European and American literature. Our shelves filled with Proust, Flaubert, Joyce, Woolf, Faulkner, Steinbeck, Flannery O'Connor, Calvino, Milan Kundera, Kafka, Thomas Mann.

When we broke up, two and a half years later, the only possessions it was hard to part with were our books. We didn't have the heart to separate *The Sound and the Fury* from *As I Lay Dying* or *El Aleph* from *Ficciones*. It would have been like tearing siblings apart. He kept British and German authors, me French and Italian. He fought hard for Latin American writers. I kept Spaniards and was able to hold on to a few Latin American books that had traveled with me from my childhood home.

I had to rebuild my library. Luckily I lived in Barcelona, a city dotted by artisan bookshops, with clerks who knew as much about literature as any PhD. My favorite haunt was Documenta. It was a little store in the heart of the Ramblas, close to my home. It had a great selection of foreign literature, classics, and off-the-beaten-path novelties. I could never resist buying several books when I went perusing.

There was also *la Diada de Sant Jordi*, my preferred Catalan holiday. The streets burst with stands of books and red roses. Men were supposed to buy roses for women and women books for men or for themselves. Screw the roses. Give me the books any day.

I had a controversy going with my best friend at the time, Enrique, who insisted that you shouldn't traffic in quantity but in quality. According to him, it was better to read one book a hundred times, and really understand it, than one hundred books one time. I didn't quite agree. My thirst for new stories was insatiable. But I respected him so much that his opinion weighed on me.

I decided to give it a try during the next *Diada de Sant Jordi*. I went down Rambla Cataluña, carefully picking up dozens of books, reading the back cover, the author's bio, the first few lines, trying to choose just one to treasure. I bought Cortázar's *Rayuela*. It was 635 pages, so the fix could last longer. I met Enrique later that day and told him proudly that I had just bought one book. He approved. But my restraint couldn't last. I had half a library to fill up.

My books traveled with me through seven homes and three live-in boyfriends. But when I moved to the U.S., I couldn't afford to bring them.

My mother paid to ship four boxes by boat. I chose part of my Spanish and Latin American literature collection, since I was going to study a PhD on the topic. The fat two volumes of María Moliner's dictionary, with its out-of-whack organization, also made the cut. I loved that she had listed words conceptually instead of alphabetically. Every time you looked for one, you fell into a delightful rabbit hole. You emerged twenty minutes later with new ideas swirling in your brain, wondering where the time had gone.

I boxed the rest and moved them to the playroom on the third floor of my parents' summerhouse. They formed a precarious tower five stories high, two rows deep, and six rows wide. I said good-bye, thinking that I would be back in a couple of years to rescue them. I had no idea a PhD lasted six years, and I couldn't foresee that I would marry and rebuild my life in California.

Ten years later, during a visit to Spain with my four-and-a-half-month-old baby, I faced reality. I would never come back. I would not have a home in Barcelona again, with a sparkling new bookshelf. I went up two floors, to the playroom I hadn't entered in years, to find my hidden friends. I planned to pack up a few in my suitcase and ship a box with essential keepsakes. I would donate the rest. It wasn't fair to leave them buried.

As I opened the first box, a whiff of mildew rose from it. I picked up a book. It was *Letters to a Young Poet* by Rainer Maria Rilke. The pages felt stiff. Brown spots mottled the back cover. I brought it to my nose. The moldy scent was faint, but unmistakable. A wave of panic surged through me, but I pushed it down. I took out ten or fifteen books and placed them on the floor. I started sorting.

After a few minutes, my fingers felt sticky and the tips were black. My nose itched. I sneezed.

I went downstairs to pick up a dust rag. Going up, each step felt double the height than before. I forced myself to continue the climb.

One hour later, with only three boxes open, mounds of books surrounded me. Most of them were to the right side, which was the group for donation. In front of me, three pillars of "ship, maybe" nagged me.

I had abandoned the idea of packing some books in my suitcase. Their dusty pages and rancid odor were deterrents, but the coup de grâce came when a spider crawled off the pages of a British poetry anthology.

I was holding *Siddhartha*, by Hermann Hesse, in my right hand. I had to make yet another decision. A thousand more still remained. I felt exhausted.

The face of the friend who had gifted me this book rose up in my mind. Every time I went to Barcelona, I met with him, just as I met with all my other friends from childhood onward. My vacations had become a frantic bumper car ride, one swift collision after another, trying to hit as many people as I could before the bell rang.

This trip I had decided not to call a few old friends. It was a relief. These loyalty visits were like quickies without orgasms, the kind of lovemaking that checks the still-happening relationship box and drags a marriage beyond its prime.

The truth is, I had changed, but these friends had remained the same, and we didn't have much in common. Like *Siddhartha*, underlined, reread, and treasured at eighteen, they sat forlorn on a shelf, an occasional dusting bringing up their scent, but never deeply read again.

I still felt guilty. I feared running into them during my day trips to Barcelona. How would I explain myself?

I realized right then that what I was doing didn't make sense. Shipping a few books would be more expensive than buying them again on the other side. But what really got to me was the slow process of digging out my past. Coming to terms with the fact that a part of me would stay behind forever. It hurt.

I picked up the books from the floor and shoved them back in their boxes. I left out a stack of photo albums that had also been hibernating for a decade. I rushed through their pages, choosing a handful of photos, a token image of each person who had meant something in my life. The rest went into the recycling bin one street away from home. Eight albums. All those places and times gone in scarcely five minutes. Anything important enough would stay imprinted in my mind, I told myself. I didn't realize yet how fickle memory is and how merciless time.

When I came back from throwing away half my life, I scrambled up to the playroom to get the dust rag and pile the boxes back up. Even looking at them was excruciating. They stood like a straitlaced governess, dressed in black head to toe, wagging her index finger and shaking her head. I rushed out and plunged down the stairs, two at a time. I barged into the living room and announced to my nephews and nieces that my books were theirs to pillage.

Back in California, my new library kept growing. Contemporary literature stuck to my hands like hot wax. Becoming a member of a book club focused on Caribbean voices opened unmarked territories, the cadence and rhythm of their prose matching the steps of my feet dancing salsa.

I amassed again a whole wall of books, which traveled with me through five houses, the last being the one where I sit now, writing about them. But our cozy arrangement was not to last.

A few months ago, I rented out my home office. Writing took more space in my life, and making money took less. I needed another source of income. The rest of the house, with its open floor plan, didn't have room for bookshelves.

I had just finished Marie Kondo's *The Life-Changing Magic of Tidying Up*, the latest in a string of books about simplifying that I get into now and again. Having had the experience of parting with my library twice—leaving half with my ex-boyfriend, and the rest languishing in boxes in a neglected playroom—I knew I could survive another Inquisition.

I held my books, one by one, wondering if I was likely to read them again. I was ruthless. If it hadn't made a first great impression, out it went. Mandatory readings during my PhD that I hadn't been thrilled with were also out. Literary theory, now that I had reverted to reading as a layperson, was destined to secondhand bookstores. How-to manuals and travel guides couldn't compete with the Internet.

I got rid of more than three-quarters of my library and fitted the rest in my seven-by-seven-foot walk-in closet, which now, after applying the same method to everything I own, holds my clothes, shoes, hats, jewelry, files, photo albums, family mementos, and a couple of hundred books.

I can't say I don't miss some of my old friends. I've found myself looking for one and feeling a pang of regret when I realize it isn't there. But, for the most part, I'm at peace with the loss.

Their absence reminds me of my book-loving boyfriend, whom I cherished so for years. I thought we would always be so thick, but he slowly slipped away, like a beloved boat sailing into the horizon. If I close my eyes, the vinyl scent of brand-new benches and the salty aroma of the sea fill up my nostrils. I admire again the portholes and the shiny cherry cabinets. I taste the grilled fresh trout, the leaves of firm white flesh bookmarked with parsley, lemon, and onion. But when I open them again, I catch only the sight of a tiny white triangle bobbing on the waves.

Although my old books can still haunt me, I'm busy getting acquainted with the new ones. The piles accumulating below my desk, on top of my nightstand, and on the coffee table do not lie. Even if I substitute the steadies with the new infatuations, we are destined to love each other forever, my books and I. ■

ASTRONOMICAL INVESTIGATIONS
Daniel Uncapher

AN INTRODUCTION

My mother was an astronomer, but that doesn't mean I'm any good at astronomy. She was also a swinger, and I can hardly talk Andy into having sex with me. Yet that's why I took an interest in metaphysical astronomy just the same.

My work as an astronomer was far-reaching and diverse, but the central area of my research from the very beginning, the beating heart at the core of my intellectual process, was something called *orbit theory*, or the movement of bodies around bodies, which is what, in the self-defining way of things, brought me to Colorado, where I met Andy, whose mother was an astrologist.

The main thing to understand about orbit theory is something called the *three-body* problem, which involves trying to calculate the positions of three different bodies in gravitational motion at any given point in space or time. According to the status quo this is basically impossible, unlike the *two-body* problem, which is apparently just two trivially easy *one-body* problems. Naturally, this characterization seemed intuitively and immediately incorrect to me, and my research has proven me correct in my misgivings; the so-called two-body problem may in fact be two one-body problems, but the one-body problem is decidedly *nontrivial*.

The ensuing work covers a lot of ground that may prove challenging for the layperson. I can't simplify things any further than I already have and refuse to insult the intelligence of myself, my reader, or my own findings by attempting to do so, or to qualify myself at all. Good science takes time, and metaphysical science can take practically forever.

DRINKING COFFEE LATE AT NIGHT

I hadn't been in Boulder long before I met Andy at the Good News. I'd come to Colorado to study under my esteemed colleague Ethan Neil, or at least to pick his brain for a few hours over something called *coupled oscillations*, but I got cold feet as soon as I arrived in the foreign city and ended up passing most of my time at the night café consulting Zoltar, the mechanical fortune-teller.

Zoltar was acting up when Andy approached me. It wasn't the first time, but now it felt personal. After mumbling something about the payoffs of labor through his inaudible 2W speaker, he had the nerve to eat my fortune card, too, which was basically the whole point of the thing, a written contract, the good news itself put into permanent print. I hate to say it now, but I was so upset at being cheated out of my fortune that I hit the machine more than once with my carpals, and I might have even kicked it, too. Andy walked up with her coffee and basically advised me not to do what I was doing.

"Just try another dollar or something," she said.

"I don't have another dollar," I said.

"How unfortunate," she said, and I'm not ashamed to admit that I laughed quite a bit at her joke, because in the depths of furiously brilliant scientific pursuit a human being must still be capable of bursting out laughing now and then, or forever just be sad in silence.

She took a dollar from her purse and fed the machine. We knelt together next to the crackling speaker to listen, making out only bits and pieces; "struggle now, work will pay off later," or maybe it was "today will be full of good decisions," or "look out for a good man in a bad hat." It was impossible to tell.

Finally it coughed up a card, which Andy snatched up and read: "You have a lot on your mind right now, but maybe what you've needed the whole time is right next to you. A dog is a good friend, but it can't pay for dinner. Relax, and remember that as long as there is rain, there can be flowers."

"Wow," I said. "That first line is pretty prescient."

"It's garbage," said Andy. "It doesn't sound like anything, just generic phrases, machine logic."

"You're right, actually." I examined Zoltar with a new and profound disappointment. "It's a shame really. I bet I could make a better Zoltar. I'm certain I could produce better audio, and print a better ticket, too, let alone write one. But the puppetry is actually pretty good, and if I know one thing about marionettes, it's that I'm not a gifted marionette maker. I wonder where he's from?"

"Oh," said Andy, examining her card. "He's from Boulder City, too. That's weird."

"Are you from Boulder City?"

And so on until early morning.

A WORKING KNOWLEDGE OF ORBIT THEORY

The closest point between a satellite and the body it orbits is called the *perigee*, which is also where the satellite moves fastest and is therefore not very useful for data relay or surface surveillance.

A satellite's farthest point in orbit is called the *apogee*, and in a highly elliptical orbit, the satellite will, after veering so hard and so fast around Earth in its brief moment of perigee, spend a relative eternity spinning sluggishly in the cold white noise of space—or as they call it in the satellite business, "long dwell time over desired area," so-called *excellent coverage*. That is the basis of apogee, and satellite scientists agree: they love it.

Sometimes two bodies meet in the cold dark of space and enter a mutual orbit, satellites of satellites, around a gravitational center of mass called the *barycenter*. Calculating the miraculous barycenter is the heart and soul of the two-body problem, which is allegedly just two trivially easy one-body problems. I obviously disagree with this; I've found these "trivial equations" for myself, substituted Andy and I for x and y and so on, and found the whole thing literally incalculable.

There is another kind of orbit theory out there, something flashy and conspicuous that I can't quite get a handle on but I believe to be of basic fundamental importance to my own research: the so-called *real time closed orbit correction system*, as explored in the seminal and titular paper from the 1989 Particle Accelerator Conference (a particle accelerator, of course, being that which speeds things up *for collision*). The jargon here is as impenetrable as it is enriching—"The feedback forces the coefficients of a few harmonics near the betatron tune to vanish and significantly improves the global orbit stability"—and I have only yet begun to unravel it.

But orbit theory has a lighter side, too. It isn't all dark mystery and metaphor. In fact orbit theory has so many sides, so many delightful applications, that it can be dizzying at first. A good spacefaring satellite should consider its own unique orbit depending on mission interests, time frame, technology, etc., and it's up to the delight and creativity of the orbit theorist to dream up how these satellites will spend their lives. A Molniya satellite, for example, has a *highly* elliptical orbit that takes a mere twelve hours to circle Earth, which is pretty crazy if you think about it. According to the extremely qualified Steve Dutch of Green Bay, Wisconsin, the Molniya's "great eccentricity" allows for ever *longer* periods of contact at apogee. It's a classic spy satellite, and basically everyone uses them.

And don't ever forget the famous flyby assist, or gravitational slingshot, the ultimate application of so-called *unbounded orbits*, which

I learned about from the beloved mathematician Ethan Neil of CU Boulder, who also taught me many of the terms I now pass on to you like *calculus of variations, coupled oscillations,* and, most foreboding of all, *rigid body motion*; or, in simple English, the total human experience.

ASTROLOGICAL INTRUSIONS:
AN UNWELCOME CONSIDERATION

It was Andy's idea to take her out on a so-called date and when I felt the time was right, around a half hour to closing, I took her to my Dairy Queen. I was in a hurry to get back to my work (which I felt was rounding in on a satisfactory conclusion) and in no mood for small talk, so when Andy took it upon herself to ask me when my birthday was, I had no idea what to make of it. "October," I finally said.

"October what?"

"October 18," I said, touched and alarmed by the question.

I went on about how October comes, like, nine months after Valentine's Day or something, which is why there are so many October birthdays, even though I knew perfectly well that my mother's birthday was what came, like, exactly nine months before October 18 but didn't want to set a precedent of talking about conception during dinner.

Only later would I realize why she'd ask such a strange question, and it wasn't because of pure romantic interest in me after all, but a matter of scientific curiosity: I found her on Tinder, where her profile read *Pisces*, and I realized that I'd just been analyzed by a living astrologist.

I immediately searched the internet for *pisces libra compatibility horoscope* and couldn't believe the kind of nonsense I was up against; the nature of my work underwent a complete and radical transformation.

"Conversation may become a source of frustration," read one site, "which may be initially surprising, as you are both flexible and considerate communicators . . ."

As if! Bad start. I scrolled on.

"You live more in your head, while your Pisces lives more in their heart. While this sounds like a trivial difference, your objective and analytical style will create difficulties in compromising with your emotional and intuitive Pisces, who often has opinions that don't stand up well to objective analysis."

The rhetorical flourish of referring to the hypothetical Pisces as *my* Pisces had an endearing effect on me, but it didn't last long. In the section for Pisces: "Your Libra is diplomatic and concerned with fairness, while you're caring and flexible. Conversation may become a source of frustration, which may be initially surprising, as amongst other things you're both flexible and considerate communicators."

Suddenly I felt betrayed. An uncanny repetition in the phrase *flexible and considerate communicators*. What a lazy writer! My entire faith in the system started to fall apart as soon as it had begun to erect itself. In fact, I, in my capacity as a Libra, became incredibly skeptical of horoscopes in general and proceeded to read as many as I could find, in order to better understand just how destructive they could be.

FREAKY DANCERS

Two bodies in two separate orbits are brought into relation by some freak alignment of an otherwise totally hostile set of circumstances of time and space for one brief moment, not quite touching but flirting with one another's unique gravitational pull nonetheless, just enough to warble and alter their respective orbits such that any and all future orbits must be totally recalculated; and if the effect is strong enough to change their orbital courses so significantly that they are mathematically destined to eventually come *back* into contact, then they will do so with even greater force, colliding at even sharper inclines until they sure enough are totally stuck together, two bodies all tangled up and confused until a natural point of orbit forms between them, which means the spontaneous generation of another mysterious barycenter around which they move in what can only be described as a dance as they fly through the otherwise totally inhospitable certitude of deep space, pushed and pulled by infinite gravitational bodies but none enough in part or in whole to tear the new couple from their intimate footwork, which is becomingly increasingly complicated.

SEEKING A SECOND AND THIRD OPINION

When I confronted Andy over my discovery that she was an astrologer, she had the gall to play dumb. I told her that I'd looked the matter up on the internet and admittedly our relationship didn't look so great on paper but those websites could be written by anyone and it wasn't fair to hold a not-so-thrilling horoscope diagnosis, or I should say misdiagnosis, against an otherwise healthy if somewhat imbalanced relationship between two consenting adults.

"Which ones did you read? You can't say that they're written by anyone and then not concede that *anyone* can include incredibly talented lifelong astrologists who are more qualified than any given random skeptic to go on the internet," she said.

"I'll show you," I said, and I pulled up my computer.

7 Reasons a Libra and a Pisces Make the Ultimate Power Couple.

"Never mind," I said, scanning the page. "This one's about a Libra woman and a Pisces man."

I moved on to the next link and read: "A Libra man shies away from any kind of conflict and disharmony. He has a deep appreciation for life's luxuries, especially fine art. He enjoys material possessions and his appreciation for beauty doesn't stop there. He'll flirt with a pretty woman even if he's happily married. It isn't that he's disloyal, to him it's harmless fun. Libra men love to entertain and are accomplished hosts. He's a romantic and knows how to charm the opposite sex."

Andy was all grins, but I felt personally scandalized. "There, see? This is off-the-charts nonsense. Verifiably untrue. Specifically engineered to breed disharmonious thoughts at the highest level. Boundless inanity with no regard whatsoever for the world *as is the case*. At this point it's practically libelous. I'm ashamed to even know this kind of material exists."

Andy scrolled on and kept reading. "They enjoy the occasions to support others and to indulge with sweets from time to time."

So we took the auspicious words at face value and walked downtown to get donuts, and ate less than one half of one of them between the both of us. I don't know why Andy wasn't eating, but I know for my part that I had just started to develop a yeast infection again, and all I could think of whenever I ate was of feeding the yeast.

A REVELATION REGARDING THE INCALCULABILITY OF REAL TIME CLOSED ORBIT CORRECTION SYSTEMS

I don't know how I missed it for so long, always so keen to consider myself an almost pathologically astute observer of my surroundings, but there it was, right in front of me the whole time: "'Real Time Closed Orbit Correction System,' presented *20 Mar 1989*."

March 20—a *Pisces*! No wonder the paper didn't stand up so well to objective analysis.

I called Andy right away to report my findings but she didn't answer. Of course Andy is not necessarily an ally to hard science either, and she has already lied to me once. The problem is that Andy *knows* the horoscopes I'm suffering from are nonsense and is just pretending to be dumb to the whole affair to control me; she has her own source, some undoubtedly esoteric and incredibly wise forum of psychic interlocutors on the deep dark web far from the reach of the technocapitalists and shadow governments, potentially subscriber based and for-profit but potentially totally pro bono, where actual astrological knowledge is accurately recorded by far more talented minds than mine, a source that I'll never find and never access and even if I did I wouldn't ever know that it was *the* source, *Andy's* knowledge, and even *then* I wouldn't know if Andy had decided to even take it seriously that day at all, or if she had her own information, perhaps she only used the true source as counterintelligence gathering and actually did the opposite of whatever it said; whatever the case, I could never know in about a hundred different ways, so the best I can do is pretend it doesn't exist, and believe that Andy is as dumb and naïve as she's pretending to be, and no greater forces are at play, and that I am agent in my own life of my own accord after all.

Not that I'm surprised by these developments. The exceedingly influential physicist Carlo Bocchetta, in his perpetually far-reaching wisdom, warned me of this almost directly in one of his more insightful PowerPoints: "Uncertainties in model, errors in the response measurement, inappropriately placed correctors or BPMs in betatron phase can lead to *singular* or *ill conditioned* matrices. Leading to large corrector settings and *bad convergence of the correction procedure.*" Emphasis mine.

As for my work with orbits, it would've taken an act of Congress to make any meaningful progress under such contradictory conditions. In fact I became a little bit confused. Say there *were* a so-called third body after all, whatever that means. Another body trying to get into orbit. Would it be possible to calculate the orbit of a third body without both original bodies noticing what was happening, or could the third body hide out, like a little Molniya secretly whipping around the far side of the far side of a body, the apogee of someone's secret apogee?

I swept the entire contents of my desk onto the floor with one mopey stroke of my arm and declared the third-body problem once again to be nonsense, and decided I wasn't going to waste any more time trying to calculate nonsense.

RELATIONSHIP STATUS: CONTINUOUSLY AT WORK

On the relationship between astronomy and astrology I don't think much really needs to be said. The metaphysician Ennis Duff has a remarkably instructive take on it: "Stars and planets are but manifestation [sic] of matter in space and always obey the law of gravitation, and Astrology is the science which records their influence on human and terrestrial affairs. *Cohesion, adhesion, gravitation* and *chemical combination* are universal forces which are *continuously at work . . .*"

Emphasis mine. According to Duff, the birth of a baby is an incredibly momentous experience because all the angular formations of planetary rays are varying every second, but that's true whether you're a baby or not, so here I believe Duff has missed the full picture. Indeed, the angular formations of planetary rays vary practically every second, and their influence is in turn varying. So basically everything is crazy virtually all of the time.

THE GALILEO GAMBIT

If my research here puts me at the fringe of some spooky so-called scientific consensus bogeyman then I can only say that I can finally really understand how Galileo must've felt, and I wear the scarlet letter of institutional dissent more proudly than my opponents could have ever anticipated. There are those that would try to mask me, silence me, criticize me, those that would try to write me off as scientifically illiterate. But these are people who wipe the coagulated shit from their rectums every morning, who projectile vomit when a large foreign object has gotten stuck in their intestines, who can watch, like, three straight hours of superhero shows every night, eating popcorn, and go to bed more or less satisfied. I'm a madman for all that myself, certainly, but I take no part in it now, not now that I'm so close to a breakthrough, and you won't see me currying favor from those that still do.

ONLY OBJECTS AS FAR AS YOU LOOK, WITHOUT END (THE BODIES-IN-SPACE EDITION)

"Is there a smallest particle that can be identified? The largest universe? Many physicists doubt either of those extreme possibilities. Instead, there might be only objects as far as you look, without end," I read to Andy.

When Andy is listening very closely she snarls, the left side of her face contorting in the most hateful possible way.

"I've been seeing sun signs everywhere," she said. "I feel like I'm going blind. They fill up my vision. Everything's a blur."

"Maybe you're just going blind. Maybe you'll never see me again."

"They're like sun spots but they don't go away, they don't occupy any physical space at all."

"You'll be fine," I said. "It's just a super sunny day."

"You're right, it's beautiful out. What're we doing inside?"

"It's like summer out there," I said. "It's absolutely terrible. Totally unsettling."

"What? Oh," she said, snarling. "Global warming."

She went for a walk anyway and I took the opportunity to immerse myself in the next leg of my project. But when she didn't come home I started to get worried, and as the sun came up I found myself online again, this time downloading CU Boulder's Honor Code, an immaculately crafted document that holds every student *personally responsible* for knowing *and* adhering to the totality of the so-called integrity policy, violations of which include, but are not limited to, cheating, plagiarism, aid of academic dishonesty (that is, accessory to the crime), fabrication (emphasis here), lying (also emphasis), bribery (de-emphasized), and threatening behavior. "All incidents of academic misconduct shall be reported to the Honor Code Council."

I made a few minor changes to the text in Photoshop and submitted it for review to my own hastily assembled Honor Code Council of which Andy and I were to be the chief and founding members, which meant pinning the revised Honor Code to the corkboard in the kitchen and waiting for Andy to sign her name, as I had so carefully signed mine.

A CONCLUSION

Andy said that apparently we only remember our experiences for real one time, and after that we're just remembering memories, and the original experience is forever lost. And memories are wildly suspect, which basically any memory scientist worth her salt knows.

For example, I *remember* going to CU Boulder and asking for Ethan Neil, and I remember meeting him in the lobby of this ugly building and asking him as politely as I could about coupled oscillations and the fundamental insolvability of the one-problem body, I mean the one-body problem, I said, getting frustrated and nervous. When he asked me about the nature of my work, I remember becoming defensive and demanding in turn to see *his* credentials, and in fact perhaps I remember threatening him quite directly, which is so extraordinarily unlike me and totally regrettable in virtually any circumstance *except the one I found myself in*, like a really good-hearted, by-the-book beat cop on a really important if somewhat under-the-table mission having *no choice in that circumstance* but to commandeer a civilian's car, and perhaps not even intending on really paying them back for it, because anyway how could she? So I remember being forcibly removed from whatever spit-shine wannabe-university the charlatan Ethan Neil works at and then being gently questioned by some armed hooligans in full uniform until dumb old nagging Andy came to take me home, but I wanted to go to Dairy Queen first, so first we went to Dairy Queen, where I remember getting into a confrontation with the cashier over a mix-up between the cherry dip and the chocolate dip, and then I wanted to go home again, where Andy (at long last) left me alone with my work; but that isn't to say that any of this actually *happened*, especially now that I've remembered it twice and thus absolved myself of any commitment to any sort of experiential fidelity, so I guess you'll have to find Andy if you want to get a better idea of the truth, or just go straight to the source and consult the stars. ■

FAREWELL TO YUANER DEPARTING FOR ANXI
Wang Wei
(Tang)

送元二使安西

（唐）王维

渭城朝雨浥轻尘，
客舍青青柳色新。
劝君更尽一杯酒，
西出阳关无故人。

Morning rain washes the dust from Weicheng.
The willows and the guesthouse are now the
    same vivid green.
Have another cup of wine,
You'll find no friends on the other side of
    the border.

—Translation by
Gary Young and Yanwen Xu

ON THE DOUBLE NINE FESTIVAL, I THINK ABOUT MY BROTHERS

Wang Wei
(Tang)

九月九日忆山东兄弟

（唐）王维

独在异乡为异客，
每逢佳节倍思亲。
遥知兄弟登高处，
遍插茱萸少一人。

Far from home, alone in a foreign town,
A festival arrives, and I miss my family more
    than ever.
I know that everyone will have climbed
    the hill outside our village
And put their hair up with a sprig of
    dogwood, but one of us is missing.

—Translation by
Gary Young and Yanwen Xu

FISHERMEN ON THE RIVER
Fan Zhongyan
(Song)

江上渔者
(宋) 范仲淹

江上往来人，
但爱鲈鱼美。
君看一叶舟，
出没风波里。

Travellers on the river
Love the taste of perch.
The fisherman's boat, small as a leaf,
Fights the wind and waves.

—Translation by
Gary Young and Yanwen Xu

THE LOST MAN
Corey Davidson

This is a conversation I recently had with a man who was sitting on the bench at the bus stop near my work. He was a tall individual, at least six feet, late forties, with an extraordinary black walrus mustache that didn't match his gray hair. The mustache was made even more extraordinary by its scarcity in this era of full beards and clean-shaven faces but little in-between. Such is today's mustache ignorance I had to look up the kind of mustache it was. I found its definition on the American Mustache Institute website and was quite surprised to discover there is an American Mustache Institute.

A leather satchel lay on his lap and a large, hard-shell suit case sat on the ground beside his feet. He was dressed as I imagine every middle-aged male film extra dresses in every scene of a bus stop or subway station in NYC or Chicago, which is to say he wore a light brown overcoat, dark suit jacket, white shirt, tie, and dress slacks. He even had a newspaper tucked under one arm. The only nonconformity were his shoes, which were worn out sneakers instead of Brogues or Oxfords.

But this isn't New York City or Chicago. It's a small city of fifty thousand souls, hours by car from New York, a day from Chicago. And I use this bus stop every day, and I sit on the green bench every day, and I'd never seen this gentleman before, so I knew he wasn't from around *these here parts.*

When I introduced myself, as I'm wont to do, since I'm a gregarious type, not paranoid at all, he admitted he indeed wasn't from around these here parts, and I could tell right away he was every bit as gregarious as me—and definitely paranoid.

"You're observant," he told me. "It's an important trait. I'm very observant. I observed you're observant, you see."

"I don't work for the CIA or the FBI or anything," I said. "I'm a desk jockey. I work one of those jobs that robots will replace soon, right after they take over fast food. Maybe before. I'm surprised to hear that I'm observant. What's so important about being observant anyhow? You know, for a regular guy."

"You're kidding me," he said. He seemed genuinely surprised.

"I'm not kidding you," I asserted.

"It's a survival trait."

"You're kidding me," I said.

"I'm not kidding you."

"Where are we?" I asked. "Is this the African savanna? *When* are we, the Pleistocene?"

"Sure, we are. In a manner of speaking."

"I would have thought we're on the corner of Broad and Oak, in any manner of speaking," I said.

"It's the same thing," he asserted. "It's a place crawling with animals."

"Crawling with animals?" I was incredulous. "Do you mean like saber toothed tigers and giant sloths."

"Crawling with animals," he repeated.

"I see some pigeons," I said. "That woman over there is walking her dog." It was a Shih Tzu. As a kid, I always made sure to pronounce it as 'shit zoo.' Actually, I still do.

"If those are the only animals you see then you're not as observant as I gave you credit for."

"So, you mean people, of course." I didn't want to lose my status as an observant man so quickly, even if dubbed so by a perfect stranger.

"Of course," he said.

"That's not terribly nice. Where I'm from, calling someone an animal is derogatory," I said.

"It's terribly true though," he insisted. "We're all just animals. You and me, the woman walking her dog, the lady who's feeding those pigeons now. Animals. Mammals."

"Yes. Yes," I said. "I understand we're all animals in the zoological sense. But we're awfully civilized animals. How many other kinds of animals could you crowd around a street corner like this without any kind of incident, without chaos?"

"Oh, sure most of us are civilized. Most of us are true human-beings. Or more accurately, we're wonderful at putting up civilized appearances. We've come to understand that we can satiate most of our simple urges while bobbing and weaving around the law, by crawling under or over the law. But those who can't get their rocks off from the simple things in life are dangerous—and far more dangerous than any 'lower' animal, and that's because we're the most cunning animal of them all. Awfully cunning."

"Are we really that cunning?" I asked. "I mean, just the other day a guy blew his wife and his wife's lover away in the kitchen of their house. They caught him the next morning in a hotel downstate. Easy as pie."

"Crimes of passion are easy to solve," he suggested. "Even the least observant police investigator can solve those."

"So, you're sticking to your guns. People are cunning," I said.

"Sure."

Then he told me something I didn't know.

"Almost fifty percent of murders go unsolved," he said.

"Is that so?"

"Absolutely," he said. "If it were just crazy incompetent types or scorned spouses who murdered wouldn't the stat be much lower than that? In this age of advanced forensic science, security cameras above every door, and people carrying out endless surveillance on their portable surveillance devices—carrying out surveillance on their innocent dinner plates even—crimes still go undetected, murders still go unsolved. I'm an observant man, and in the last twenty-four hours I've noticed that this town has layers of law enforcement; this town is a veritable parfait of law enforcement: city police downtown, campus police around the college, a county sheriff's department, state troopers on the highways, mall cops, and even a small branch office for the Federal Bureau of Investigations… despite this police presence, which is the same in every city everywhere I go, forty-eight percent of murderers get away with the deed. That's damn cunning."

"So that's why you are so observant," I said.

"That's why I'm so observant, and that's why I keep moving."

"What do you mean you keep moving?" I asked.

"I mean just this: I don't stay anywhere for more than a few days, a week at most. I keep moving. It's more difficult to hit a moving target. If I keep moving I'm less likely to be murdered."

"Now wait," I said. "Do you mean I'm more likely to be murdered because I live in one place, work in one place, and sit on this bench every day at five-fifteen waiting for the same bus to pick me up?"

"Yes."

"Now wait," I said. "Do you mean I'm more likely to be murdered because I buy my groceries at the same grocery store every weekend—usually at the same time—and because I get my coffee at the same place and buy a paper from the same man at the same bodega every weekday?"

"Yes."

"But that's absurd," I said. "Isn't it? I mean, wouldn't we all be dead by now? Wouldn't all of us who follow the same daily pattern have knives in our backs by now, bullets in our brains by now?"

"Well how many people do you see doing exactly what you do every day?"

"I couldn't say."

"Maybe you should think of changing things up a bit."

"And you change things up every two days."

"Definitely," he said. "It's like what they tell you in Cub Scouts."

"What do they tell you in Cub Scouts?" I asked.

"They always tell you the same thing in the scouts, which is this: if you're lost in the woods, stay in one place because it's harder to find someone who keeps moving around. That's what I do. I stay lost, in a manner of speaking."

"But how can you move around all the time?" I asked. "How can you afford that?"

"I sleep at the Y and hostels and as a last resort, fleabag motels. During the day all sorts of places will let you hang around for hours if you're reading the paper. It's as if nobody on earth could be dangerous if they're reading the newspaper. Like no terrorist has ever solved a cross word puzzle."

"My goodness," I said. "But how do you eat?"

"I eat cheaply and well. The rule is no meat. Meat is expensive. Raw fruits and veggies cost a few bucks a day. The only bread I eat is whole grain. My colon is clean as a whistle. You could slide through my large intestine like a water park ride without feeling the need to take a shower afterwards like you do with a water park ride. Sure, I always feel a little hungry. That's the rule though: always feel a little hungry."

"But life without cheeseburgers? No thanks."

"Life without cheeseburgers, barbecue ribs, steak and so on."

He seemed a little wistful reciting that list.

"But you need *some* money," I said. "Nothing is free."

"I'm transient, but I'm not a bum. I work on the go."

"Are you a pharmaceutical salesman or something?" I asked.

"I'm a science fiction writer. I write about the robots who will take over your job someday. This case down here holds my word processor."

"Ah, what? You mean a laptop?"

"I mean a word processor. Specifically, a Smith Corona X5200. You don't think I would write my stories on a hackable device, did you? Have you been listening?"

"And you can make a living doing that?"

"I only need a few hundred bucks a month to keep going. The magazines pay between seven and twelve cents per word. If I can sell one story a month I'm alright."

"No kidding," I said.

"No kidding."

"But wait a minute," I said. "I just thought of something."

"What is that?"

"If you're constantly moving around. If you're in a new place practically every day. Doesn't that increase the chance you'll be murdered? I mean, you're jacking up the number of people who you're meeting. Wouldn't it be safer if you found some tiny little hamlet somewhere or better yet just a shed in the woods to write your science fiction stories?"

"That would be worse," he said.

"How would that be worse?"

"Because then I would get to know the people around me and eventually my family would find me. My family is stubborn like that. They're like a bunch of magnets that want to click together no matter what is between them. A pair of ingested magnets will do a number on you by the way. Once I stayed in the same town for a week and lo and behold there was my brother knocking on the door of the fleabag motel I was staying in."

"Your family is a big drag then," I said.

"Not at all; my family are nothing but wonderful people. The best people I've ever met. In all my travels I've never met any people as wonderful as mom and dad and sis and my brother. I even like my brother-in-law. And that's why I have to keep away from them."

"I guess I don't follow. What's so bad about getting to know people around you? And if your family is so great why would you want to avoid them?"

"Are you kidding me?" he said.

"I'm not kidding you."

Then he told me something I hadn't known.

"Did you know that eighty percent of murder victims knew their killer? Did you know that sixteen percent of murders are committed by family members?"

"Wow," I said. "I did not know that." I meant it. Wow.

"Let me tell you, the better someone knows you, the more likely they'll want to kill you."

"Do you really think someone in your family would kill you?"

"Not at all. But you never know. Maybe I'm protecting them from me."

I was going to protest that surely the more someone knew me the *less* they'd want to kill me, or that there was no way he would kill anyone, but I've always been a lousy judge of character.

"One last thing before you go," I said. "Why talk to me at all? It sounds like you're pretty worried about getting murdered."

"It's a calculated risk," he said. "Few people are murdered in broad daylight on small town street corners who aren't dealing drugs by someone who is essentially a stranger. If I didn't occasionally share little human moments like this, I'd be nothing more than an animal."

"Sir," I said. "You're a human being."

"And a human going." His bus had pulled up. "Are you on this one?"

"No, I'm north bound," I said.

"Well, it was nice talking with you."

"The same," I said. "Very educational."

He climbed aboard, rolling his big suitcase behind him. With a pneumatic hiss the bus released its air breaks and left the curb. I watched it dwindle away until it made a turn and disappeared.

And there I sat. Unmoving. Grounded to that spot. Everything around me moved more than I was. I felt like a single atom frozen to absolute zero. Compared to me, the trees practically danced. Their leaves fluttered, their branches swayed. Overhead, clouds drifted against the deepening blue. They congealed, stretched apart and broke like taffy. The pigeons murmured as they strutted around. Their jettisoned feathers somersaulted in the breeze. I turned around to look at my building, convinced it was probably sinking a millimeter or so per year.

I knew everyone who worked in that eight-story building. I knew the janitor who emptied my waste paper basket and the guy who delivered the bottled water. I knew my administrative assistant, and I knew the woman on the top floor who ran the place. I had attended her son's high school graduation party. She's from Nevada.

I thought about getting up and walking to the next stop down the line. I didn't like how the woman across the street was taking so long with her shit zoo and peeking at me every now and then. ∎

THE NIGHTMARES OF JENNIFER AIKEN, AGE TWENTY-NINE
Rebecca Turkewitz

I. JUDGMENT

You duck into a church doorway to get out of the rain. You should have accepted Ann-Marie's offer of a ride home, but you'd thought the storm would hold off until the afternoon. Besides, you didn't want to seem needy. You and Ann-Marie have only been seeing each other for a few weeks, and you're someone who can always find your own way home. Your hair sticks in dark clumps to your neck and chest and your feet slosh in your shoes. A gust of wind blows a sheet of rain into the archway and you try the church door. It swings open and you stumble inside. When the door clicks shut, the noise from the storm fades to a low hum. Since you're still wearing last night's low-cut dress, you're glad that you haven't walked in on a service. There doesn't seem to be anyone else inside. You take off your wet heels and go sit in one of the pews.

You haven't been to a church service since you graduated from high school, over a decade ago. Even when you visit your parents, who are regular churchgoers, you sleep late on Sundays. Your mother has finally stopped nagging you about this. She finds plenty to nag you about anyway: how little you call her, whom you choose to date, the state of your apartment, the second glass of wine you have at dinner, the clothes you wear.

You wring out your soaking hair and wind it into a long a coil. The church is cool and damp, like a basement. Above the altar, the statue of Christ is especially gruesome. His expression seems to reflect malice instead of divinity. You wonder what denomination the church is and consider praying, since you're there. But the thought of praying after all these years makes you laugh out loud. Immediately you wish you hadn't. The noise echoes off the angles of the vaulted ceiling and comes back to you as the sound of a child giggling. You shiver. Churches have always given you the creeps.

Abruptly you rise and take three long strides toward the door, but you're halted by a man's urgent whispering. When you stop moving, the noise stops with you. You scan the dark room and feel the blood pulsing in your head. Then, distinctly, you hear the voice rasping again, above you. You glance up at the choir balcony and see the silhouette of a branch scratching against one of the stained glass windows. You let out your held breath.

You start towards the door again but realize you've forgotten to grab your shoes. You run back to the pews and drop to your knees to search under the seats. Out of the corner of your eye you see a woman materialize in the shadows. You jerk up and crack the back of your head against the bottom of the bench. A high-pitched buzz fills your skull and your vision blurs. When the pain subsides enough, you scramble to your feet and discover that you've freaked yourself out over a statue of the Virgin Mary.

"You're not so scary," you say to the statue. "But fuck my shoes. I'm getting the hell out of here." When you reconsider what you've said and where you've said it, you whisper, "I'm so sorry." Then you feel impossibly silly—apologizing to a statue. A gust of wind throws rain against the windows. Wet leaves slap dully against the glass. But when the wind dies, a softer, closer rustling sound remains. Then, a noise like a person cooing to a newborn.

"Hello?" you call. The rustling continues, and through the balcony balustrade you see something white moving. "Who's up there?" A low pained call escapes from behind the railing. You turn and sprint for the exit but slip in a spot of wetness, scraping your knee hard. You try to get up too quickly and your ankle gives out. You crawl forward on your hands and knees, but you can't help looking behind you. You watch, a cold panic spreading through your chest, as a white figure writhes and flops against the railing and then slips through an opening in the bars. You see wings flapping and hear a horrible high screech as a small squat creature half-flies, half-falls to the floor. You scream, and your scream cuts through the quiet like a freight train, extending long after you've closed your mouth. The demon, writhing on the floor, resembles a hunched bird.

It is a bird. A large white owl with one wing unnaturally bent hobbles near the organist's bench. You climb carefully to your feet and test your ankle, which is tender but not sprained. "It's okay, little guy," you say, approaching it. "Poor baby. How'd you get in here?"

The owl leans back and fixes its black eyes on your face.

"Stay away from me, you whore," the owl says, and then it lifts its head and lets loose a laugh that sounds like metal being ground to dust.

II. PROXIMITY

When you notice movement outside the sliding glass doors of your first-floor apartment, you mute the television. You watch the dark yard for a full minute but you don't see anything unusual. Whatever was moving is still. This is what happens when you stay home alone on a Friday night. Your mind starts to play tricks on you. When you consider how nice it would be to have someone to curl up next to on the couch, you almost regret breaking it off with Ann-Marie for what you've decided will definitely be the final time. She was starting to feel like your shadow instead of your girlfriend. In your last fight, she'd tearfully informed you that you'd eventually leave her because all bisexual women leave their girlfriends for men. At least you haven't proved her right. You didn't leave her for anyone else; you left her because she was desperate and a little pathetic, and every woman deserves better than pathetic. Although, the fact remains that you're home alone on a Friday night watching *Gilmore Girls* in your pajamas. So maybe you're a little pathetic yourself. You check your phone. Chrissie, who should know you might need a little cheering up on a night like this one, hasn't texted you back yet.

A few minutes later you see something moving by the bushes again and this time it's unmistakable. Something is pacing back and forth in the yard, and that something moves a whole lot like a person. You slowly pull out your phone and get as far as dialing 9-1-1. But what would you tell the police if you called? There's something that you can't quite see moving outside your apartment complex? On screen, Lauren Graham shouts and you startle. You turn the volume down and tiptoe to the door. You check the lock, which is firmly in place, and then shield your eyes and put your forehead against the glass. You don't see anyone, but the hedges are overgrown and the sky is moonless. There are plenty of places to hide. When you walk back to the couch, you keep your eyes pinned to the window. You consider closing the blinds but somehow that seems worse. You can't stand the idea of someone lurking out there, unseen.

You try to focus on the show. You consider calling Ann-Marie. But you don't want her in your life, you just want her on your couch for one night, and you know that isn't fair. She'd be over in ten minutes with one word from you, and it's tempting.

You glance one more time at the window and shriek. A person, a dark figure that looks like a person, is marching straight towards the door. As the figure draws closer, you see that they're holding a knife. 'It's locked, it's locked, it's locked,' you think over and over as you fumble with your phone. You force yourself to jump off the couch and flip the lamp on. The light makes the person's features sharpen, and you can see the deep holes beneath their eyes, the muscles in their jaw tightening. Even in your panic, you know this isn't right. The light shouldn't illuminate these features.

You see your own face—your mussed hair and your wide eyes—reflected as crisply and as clearly as your attacker's. You spin around just in time to see Ann-Marie raise the knife to your neck.

III. PERFECTION

You're walking down a suburban street that you don't recognize and your eyes won't adjust to the brightness of the day. The expansive lawns on either side of you are well trimmed and Easter green. The houses' large bay windows reflect the sunlight, and when you try to peer in through the glass you have to squint and look away from the glare. Every now and then you catch a flicker of movement behind the windowpanes, but nothing outside is moving, except for you. You're not sure what you're heading towards but you know you have to keep walking. Ahead, the road ends in a cul-de-sac and a huge brick house looms at the end of the street.

As you draw nearer to the house, you notice one rough patch in the otherwise immaculate lawn. The weeds don't belong here, in this flawless, sunlit place. They've gone unnoticed by the residents of the house, but you've spotted them. You realize now that this unkempt patch of grass is the reason that you've come here. This is what you've been walking towards all along. You feel a kinship with this impeccable property. It is not so different from the house that you used to imagine you'd one day live in, with a family of your own. You step onto the house's lawn. You wind the long, fine plant tendrils around your hand until you have a hard grip on them. You pull.

At first nothing happens, except that the blades of grass dig into your balled-up fist and your muscles flex and strain. You yank again. Nothing. You clench your jaw, take several deep breaths, and tug as hard as you can, and this time you can sense the dirt shifting and the earth turning soft under the strange weeds. Something gives, and a large irregular sphere, like an oversized turnip, emerges from the ground. The shape spins, dangling from the many plant strands that are wound around your fingers. You reach out with your free hand to grab hold of it. When the sphere steadies, you can see that you're holding the small, shriveled head of a woman. The lips are frozen in a soundless scream and the eyes are wide open with clumps of dirt still stuck to the corneas. Maggots pour out of the dead woman's mouth. You try frantically to free your hand from the tangles of the corpse's green hair, but it is as if the strands are winding themselves around your fingers and tightening their grip on your wrist, as if they are the only part of the woman left alive.

IV. ANCIENT

For work, you have to travel to Richmond, Indiana. After your meetings you decide to explore the town, since you have the rest of the day off and it's only a two-hour drive back to Columbus. You visited Richmond once before, when you were a little girl. Your mother was visiting a childhood friend and she brought you along. Your mother's friend showed you an album of faded photographs of her and your mother as schoolgirls. Looking at the pictures was like looking into a mirror. You cried for a full hour at the revelation that time might one day do to you what it had done to your mother. Later that same day, after you'd calmed down, you visited a small park next to a rose garden. On the windowsill in your parents' kitchen, there's a Polaroid of you posing on the stone rim of a lovely fountain. The caption on the picture reads, *Jen, age six.*

The picture is in your pocket, suddenly. You take it out and study your mother's precise, self-assured handwriting. You miss her.

At a diner in the center of town you drink burnt coffee and ask the waitress for directions to the fountain. You show her the Polaroid. The waitress's hair is dyed copper red and she has a small stud in her chin. She calls you ma'am. She says she can point you to the rose garden, but she doesn't know of any fountain. An old man sitting at the counter lowers his newspaper. His skin is leathery and ill fitting, too loose for his bones. He introduces himself as Charlie.

"I know the fountain you're talking about," he says, his voice low enough that you have to lean forward to hear him. "The foundation crumbled fifteen years ago. But the water's still running."

The waitress rolls her eyes.

"I'm not fooling around," Charlie says. "The fountain was fed from an underground spring that's still running, and it's still as clear as glass. If you follow the walking path on the west side of the rose garden, you'll see the *Madonna of the Trail* statue. What's left of the fountain is a few hundred feet back from there."

You thank Charlie, pay the bill, and then you're at the rose garden. If you find the spring, maybe you'll take a picture of the remains of the fountain so you can send it to your mother. Maybe you'll take a selfie of yourself sitting on the pile of rubble, so Mom can put it next to the picture of you as a girl. *Jen, age twenty-nine.*

You find the walking path easily. The trees are just starting to lose their leaves and the air has a chilly edge to it. Soon the path becomes overgrown, and your fingers begin to sting from the cold. Just when you've decided that Old Man Charlie was only playing a trick on an out-of-towner, you spot the statue. You leave the path and the grass gets in under your pant cuffs and scratches at your ankles.

There's an old woman kneeling at the bank of the spring. When the woman hears you, she turns her face up and pulls her hands quickly back, tucking something behind her. The woman has the same leathery skin as Charlie. Her face is puckered so all her features seem to be slipping towards her nose. When she opens her mouth, a gray moth flutters out.

"I didn't mean to startle you," the old woman says. "Not many people come out here anymore."

"I'm sorry." You feel your face flush. "I'm not from here."

"How'd you find the spring?" the woman asks.

"I was here once, as a little girl. I wanted to see it again. I don't know why."

"You're still just a girl."

You laugh. "I'm not as young as I look."

The woman tries to climb to her feet, but her legs quiver beneath her. You rush to grab her arm and help her up. The woman is holding a jar full of water so clean that it catches the sunlight and glows.

"Is the water good to drink?"

"*Never* drink this water."

"Why not?"

The woman thinks for a moment, and you can see that she's trying to puzzle something out. "Sit with me," the woman says finally. "I'll tell you."

You sit on the one remaining ledge of the fountain, careful to leave space between her and you. Up close, you feel a guilty disgust for the woman's decrepit features and the baby-powder smell her body gives off.

The woman asks you if you believe in magic. You don't, really, but she is peering at you so earnestly that you shrug and tell her that maybe you could be convinced. And then she launches into her tale. She explains that the water from the spring comes from deep within the earth and has special properties. Anyone who drinks from it will extend their life for decades longer than they would normally live. She says that she is well over a hundred years old. She tells you that the fountain, once celebrated, has since been destroyed and forgotten by most of the people in town.

"An actual fountain of youth?" you ask to humor her.

"Not youth, no. More like longevity. That's why it was destroyed. Because once you drink from it, you grow old too quickly. And then you stay old for one hundred years. Your teeth will fall out, your hair will grow wispy and gray, and your bones will turn as brittle as ice. But you won't have the mercy of death, at least not for a long, long time." The woman shakes her head. "It's no way to live. It's cruel, what time does to all of us. When everyone you love is wasting away and dying, and your own body betrays you."

"I'm sorry," you say, trying to think of an excuse to leave. "That must be so hard."

"But I've sealed my fate. I have to keep drinking it, to at least keep some strength up. But you must not *dare* drink it. Promise me."

You promise her. "But I'm late now. I have to go. I have to get back."

"Of course you do. Because when you're young you have people waiting for you. When you're young, time matters. You have things that fill your day. That's good. Be glad for that now."

"It was nice meeting you," you say. "I hope things get better. I'm sure they will."

"Yes. I'm out of sorts today, but you're right. Things aren't so bad." The woman's voice breaks. She's close to crying.

"Goodbye. I'm sorry I can't stay." Your underarms are sweating. You stride quickly towards the path, and when you look back you see the old woman drinking hungrily from the jar, her throat expanding and contracting with each swallow. The woman drinks until there is no more water and then raises a boney hand to wave goodbye.

On the way back to town, you jump at every small crackling in the trees. You quicken your step and check behind you. You half expect that any minute the woman will appear, sprinting with unnatural speed, clawing at you with her skeletal hands. Was she delusional or just recounting a local myth? Perhaps she was purposefully messing with you. Or she just wanted someone to talk to. A lonely, sad woman reached out to you, and you fled as soon as you could. You try to reassure yourself that she must have children and grandchildren waiting for her. She'll bring them freshly squeezed lemonade that she made with the cold spring water and they'll laugh over how Grandma spooked a city girl.

When you arrive at the rose garden, you find someone tending to the flowers. You're so relieved to find a person who looks like she's from this world that you say hello. You remark on how strange it is that the flowers still grow in October.

"Rumor has it that there's something in the groundwater in this part of town," the woman says.

Suddenly, you're telling her all about your encounter with the old woman and her fountain.

"That's quite a story she told you. She's just messing with you, I'm sure."

"Of course I don't believe any of it. But to see the way the woman drank that water down, in three big gulps, it made me queasy."

The woman's face clouds over. She drops the spade she's been using. "She drank from it? You're sure?"

"Yes," you say, backing towards your car. You wonder if everyone in this small town is a little unhinged. "So what?"

"We have to get back there. I have to call someone." The woman yanks off her gardening gloves.

You waver, fighting the impulse to flee. "I don't understand."

"That spring is toxic. It's full of arsenic."

Your head begins to throb. You close your eyes and see the old woman drinking hungrily. You see her watery eyes watching you walk away. You see the small, wilted hand raised in one last salute.

V. REASON

It starts with the sound of footsteps pacing outside the bedroom door in your new apartment, even though you live alone. You're sleeping there for the first time. When you get the nerve to jump out of bed and throw the door open, there's nothing in the hall. About half an hour later, the footsteps start again. And then there's giggling.

You turn on the light, grab your cell, and walk into the hallway. You creep into the kitchen, ready to call the police if necessary. In the middle of the tile floor you find a ratty teddy bear. When you stoop to pick up the toy, it disintegrates and seeps into the ground like sand. You're a reasonable person. You believe in evolution and science and logic. You mostly do not believe in ghosts. But how else can you explain this? You think of calling Chrissie or your mother, but you know you'll sound ridiculous. You're just overtired and frightened by the unfamiliar apartment, and the teddy bear was just a trick that your mind is playing on you. You're not in danger. Ghosts don't exist. The apartment isn't haunted.

You open the cupboard and pull out a glass. Before you can fill it with water, you notice a small ivory-colored bead in the bottom of it. You tip the glass over and catch the stone, and find that it's a small tooth. It looks like a baby tooth that someone might leave for the tooth fairy. You throw it into the sink and wipe your palm on your shirt. You take a step back and feel a sharp pain in the heel of your bare foot. When you lift your leg up, you find another tooth lying on the floor. You rush back into your bedroom. You pull back the covers of your bed and discover three more teeth standing out against the navy-blue sheets.

On the far side of your bedroom, a shadow morphs into a human form. When you examine it more closely, the shadow expands and seeps into an amorphous splotch, blending in with the patterns of light that your lamp throws against the wall. You hear giggling—a little girl's giggling—coming from the closet, and you know you have to get out of the apartment.

You grab your purse and race outside in your bare feet. You pull out of the parking lot so fast that the undercarriage of your car scrapes the curb ramp. You don't believe in ghosts because you're rational, but a rational person considers new evidence. And there is a lot of evidence supporting the idea that your new apartment is pretty damn haunted. You call Chrissie when you're already halfway to her place.

Sitting on Chrissie's couch with a cup of tea in your hands, you can't stop shaking. You want Chrissie to take you seriously. You're trying to seem calm. You're going to need to find a new apartment. In the mean time, you might have to stay with Chrissie and her husband for a while. You explain about the footsteps, the teddy bear, and the teeth. You start shaking when you talk about the shadows and the giggling. Chrissie gives you the look that she usually reserves for when you talk about dating— about the new girlfriend who will be perfect, as soon as she stops talking quite so much about her ex.

"Sweetie," Chrissie says, putting a warm hand on your knee. "It sounds like you're driving yourself crazy. You've totally spooked yourself. It's all in your mind."

"You didn't hear the noises. You didn't see that shadow. They were real."

"You've been so stressed lately. Moving is tough. I know you haven't been sleeping. You need to relax."

"What about the teeth? How do you explain the teeth?"

"I don't know. They're probably just pebbles or something. What did you do with them?"

"What do you think I did with them? I threw them out!"

"Listen, Jen. You're welcome to stay here until you calm down, but this is all in your mind, okay?"

You notice something stirring in the corner of Chrissie's living room. You look past Chrissie and see the blurry figure of a small girl. The girl smiles, and her mouth is a cave of pink. She has no teeth. You pull backwards and spill your tea, which causes a quick stab of pain on your stomach. Chrissie looks behind her to see what you've reacted to.

"What? What's happening?" Her voice is filled with concern.

"You don't . . ." You stop. Chrissie doesn't see the girl. Chrissie wouldn't hear the footsteps. No one else would see the teeth. "It's nothing," you say. "I think you're right. I think it's all in my mind."

VI. DOUBT

You start awake in your own dark bedroom. You can't quite remember the nightmare you were just having, but the imprint of its terror still flashes with every beat of your heart. At first, you're afraid to move and afraid to examine the shadowy expanse of your room. But after several tense moments, the fear begins to become muted. You still taste the sourness of adrenaline on the back of your tongue, but you also feel a rush of relief. Whatever threat was looming over you in sleep is gone. You're facing the wall, and you roll over to take in your bedroom. All is as it should be. Your desk sits unassumingly, cluttered with assorted objects that you've unpacked but haven't yet found a place for. Your jeans are draped across a chair. The clock reads 5:47 a.m. It's almost daybreak. You can lie back and wait for the light.

Although you're sure nothing's wrong, your muscles still pulse with tension and you can't bring yourself to close your eyes. You listen to a low, steady humming—white noise from the refrigerator or the telephone wires outside. You're still adjusting to the sounds of the new apartment. You pull the blanket tighter around you, even though you're sweating.

You wipe the sweat away from your temples and then reach for the wetness at the nape of your neck. What you touch is not the thin consistency of sweat. It is thick and viscous, like saliva or slime. You jerk your hand away and examine the strange gelatinous liquid. When you pull your fingers apart, the slime clings to itself and stretches, the way drool would. You frantically search the dark corners of your room, but, as far as you can see, you are alone. ∎

PEONIES
Marjorie Skelly

This evening, the gift of May slips me back in time when,
for one fragrant moment, I believe, daughter, that I am

once again like you, twenty-one, falling in love at first sight
with the young man walking through our front door.

May moon not yet ripened, Pinot Grigio catching candlelight,
he asks me if I need help carrying wine glasses

to the porch. And so, I slip generously
into a former night, as if into an expensive gown.

Yet, even in my borrowed youth,
I see you, daughter, talking with him

in the forever here and now.
Later, alone, the night older, I remain young

in the silence of midnight and budding trees
when I bend gracefully to smell the peonies,

then touch them with my fingertips
in their finest magenta hour,

their carnal, unchaperoned rising,
filled with the deception of eternal blooming.

THE EROTICS OF MEMORY: JEREMY IRONS' VOICE
Doug Dibbern

I've been thinking about Jeremy Irons' voice for a long time now. More than any other actor I know, his speaking style manifests an enticingly illicit sexuality. Even children who've heard him only as Scar in *The Lion King* catch on quite easily to how attractive he can make naughtiness seem. Think of Orson Welles and his resonant chamber of a voice, the aural equivalent of a catacomb or of the vault of a gothic cathedral; it's impressive, but hardly sensual. I remember, though, how Irons draws sentences out, twisting them like streams winding perilously near the edge of a cliff, at every moment tempting his listener with the potentials of a waterfall. His timbre is both reserved and ostentatious; its risqué flirtation hints at an inarticulable, subterranean voluptuousness, but also at incitements and intrigues. And it's this very mixture of indecency and restraint that is the source of its allure.

His voice has sunk itself in my memory, resurfacing now and then, disappearing for an age or two, but always suspended somewhere in the borderland between the conscious and unconscious, always echoing, always there. Most movie fans, I'm sure, don't spend much time thinking about the sultriness of Jeremy Irons' voice; even for those few who've found themselves succumbing to its charms, I suspect it hovers only on the peripheries of their attention. Yet its roguish perversity keeps coming back. It's become central to me—perhaps because its tendency to evince and explore latent desires, I've come to believe, parallels the very essence of the cinema as well as the very foundations of the self. And since we infuse our interpretations as much with our selves as we do with the object under examination, my memory tends to detect in his voice—or wants to detect—a pleasant hint of homoerotic longing striving for liberation.

When I imagined writing about his voice, I thought the topic would allow me to expound upon an undervalued aspect of the art of film, but even more, I'd come to suspect, the idea of the voice would enable me to explore other, more personal concerns. I tend to be more cerebral than emotional, and I was raised by parents from the Scandinavian, Lutheran Midwest, so over the years I've absorbed the unthinking Christian sentiment that the intellect and the spirit are the fundamental aspects of the self and that the body is just their inconsequential vehicle. But the voice has an unusual relationship with the physical and thus the sexual: the body is its source and yet it floats away from the human form that gave it birth to live in the air as the primary manifestation of human thought, on the one hand the very obverse of desiring carnality, while on the other hand, the physical projection of the body itself.

The voice, then, can serve as a refuge for those intellectuals and aesthetes who nevertheless yearn for some form of somatic bliss. By studying the voice, one can embrace the sensual while continuing to perpetuate the illusion that one has disavowed crude corporeality. And yet, the voice has physical qualities of intimacy that the body alone can only rarely put into play. Because it begins with sound waves travelling through physical space, the voice actually touches people, caresses them, enters their eardrums, generating bodily sensations in others across vast distances. And since its primary function is to communicate between people, to create bonds, it's no coincidence that words of love don't just precede but in fact can help animate the physical act of intimacy itself.

When I think about Jeremy Irons' voice, I'm mostly thinking about *Brideshead Revisited*, the British production from 1981 that many people, including myself, consider to be the greatest miniseries ever made. I first watched it when it originally aired on PBS, and it was, as far as I can remember, the first time I'd seen gay characters on screen. I was ten and I saw it with my mother, just at that age when I'd begun to take notice of my interest in other boys. For a movie made in 1981, the filmmakers made the romance between the two male leads surprisingly obvious, and yet at the same time—not surprising, in retrospect—they also knew that they could make the novel's gayness explicit only in the most indirect ways. They couldn't show two men kissing, so instead they hinted at sexuality through mannerisms, costumes, and accoutrements: the dandy Anthony Blanche wears eyeliner, casts appalled sidelong glances, and holds his cocktail glasses with an upturned pinky, while the aristocratic Sebastian Flyte carries around an oversized teddy bear and adorns himself with silk cravats and sweaters thrown loosely around his neck, so exquisitely dressed that even in his most drunken state, his undone neckties hang across his shoulders with a louche elegance. And Jeremy Irons' character, Charles Ryder, observes both of these more flamboyant young men from a reserved but jealously appreciative distance. This type of coding made the protagonists' gayness obvious to a knowing audience but plausibly deniable to the population at large. It was this strategy of misdirection that was precisely why the filmmakers chose to express so much through the instrument of Jeremy Irons' speech.

The film's most remarkable formal feature is its reliance on Evelyn Waugh's prose—especially since it's long been filmmaking dogma that narration is somehow uncinematic. It often feels, in fact, that we hear Waugh's language as much as we do the characters' dialogue. Since they adopted this unusual stylistic tactic partly because they could not make visible the story's homoerotic center, Waugh's lush prose becomes the bearer of the film's queer sensibility. Irons recalls, for instance, going for the first time to meet Sebastian Flyte, the dissipated son of the Marquess of Marchmain, in sentences whose style itself speaks more than the words alone: "I went there uncertainly, for it was foreign ground and there was a tiny, priggish warning voice in my ear, which, in the tones of Collins, told me it was seemly to hold back. But I was in search of love in those days and went full of curiosity and the faint, unrecognized apprehension that here at last I should find that low door in the wall others I knew had found before me, which opened on an enclosed and enchanted garden, which was somewhere, not overlooked by any window, in the heart of that gray city." Later, we see the two young men lounging together at the base of a tree, their legs touching, after they've shared the basket of strawberries and the bottle of Sauternes that Sebastian had deployed to seduce Charles, smoking cigarettes as if in postcoital reverie. Here, the director cuts to a close-up of Irons' face as he gazes down tenderly at his new friend. "We ate the strawberries and drank the wine," he says, then hints at the erotic sensations that the image could never reveal, "and as Sebastian promised, they were delicious together. The fumes of the sweet, golden wine seemed to lift us a finger's breadth above the turf and hold us suspended."

But because I'd experienced Jeremy Irons' voice only through a film— an aestheticized object one step removed from the physical world—my understanding of its reserved lusciousness has been bound up not so much with its actual qualities as it has with my memory's reconstruction of it. Waugh's language, too, evoked a sense of premature nostalgia, helping to nurture this tension between the physical trace of Irons' narration and the more subjective workings of my mind. So when I watched *Brideshead Revisited* again recently, I found that Jeremy Irons' voice is not as I remembered it. Revisiting—and this time studying—the miniseries made me recognize once again how memory, with its continual revisions of itself, imposes meaning upon the work of art that originally inspired it as much as the artwork is able to infuse its meaning into our recollections of it.

On my last viewing, in fact, Jeremy Irons' voice was as chaste as his image. I catalogued his voice-overs, copied them down word by word, timed them to calculate his words per minute, and listened to hear if he does in fact bend his phrases, if he does idiosyncratically accentuate a syllable here or there. And I came away disappointed. If anything, I discovered that the genius of his voice lies in the fact that he doesn't do much of anything at all. He just reads aloud the words on the page. True, whenever he speaks from the novel's present—the tail end of World War II—when Waugh's language most eloquently takes on the poetic quality of nostalgic reminiscence, he does draw out his sentences much slower than normal speech: "Oxford in those days was still a city of aquatint. When the chestnut was in flower and the bells rang out high and clear over her gables and cupolas, she exhaled the soft airs of centuries of youth. It was this cloistral hush that gave our laughter its resonance and carried it still joyously over the intervening clamor." But then, whenever the narration returns to its normal mode—inhabiting the past as if recounting the present—Waugh's prose becomes more informational and Irons takes on a more pedestrian cadence.

On closer inspection, I could see that my memories were the product not just of his voice, but of the full range of cinematic aesthetics. The sensual elements I'd attributed to Irons' speech derive more from the formal decisions that the director, cinematographer, and composer made than they do from the actor himself. The movie, in fact, introduces and surrounds his voice-overs with a recurring set of cinematic motifs. Almost every moment of narration is underscored with a quiet chamber orchestra; it's Geoffrey Burgon's score, in fact, that creates the resonant, luxuriating tenderness I'd associated with the power of speech. Often, before we hear his voice, Irons turns on-screen, and as if anticipating the onset of language, a silence blooms on the audio track for a brief moment before a French horn, a flute, or an oboe comes in to herald the sonic space for his narration to breathe. These arching, plaintive whole notes—not so much a melody as they are the impression of a theme—are often undergirded by a rhythmic surging of strings, which, now and then, break free to outline a swirl of notes of their own. And the director, Charles Sturridge, pairs these indolent refrains with montage sequences that accentuate the wealth and lyrical splendor of their milieu—overhead shots of the campus of Oxford University, sun-dappled branches of trees, picture postcard views of the Marchmain estate—as if the clothes or the architecture itself could speak more ardently of the two men's affection than could their words alone. Jeremy Irons' voice, then, is never just a voice, but always an agglomeration of the senses, always an organized deployment of a multifaceted cinematic expressivity.

It's not unexpected, then, that I'd misremembered his voice. One of film's essential goals, after all, is to exploit its host of perceptual tools so seamlessly that the audience won't be aware of them—so that the means of production and indeed the style itself become invisible, as it were. And because the cinema has this essential task of deploying its formal features precisely in order to conceal them, it makes sense that the repressed aspects of any film might become the guiding principles of that movie—and thus of my memory of it as well. My mind had pulled the voice out from the miniseries' multisensory experience because its disembodied qualities resonated within me. And the aesthetics of memory function in much the same way. The fact that memory discards some bits of evidence while holding on dearly to others—as if memory had a mind of its own—parallels the role that repression plays in shaping the formal features of cinema itself.

The last time I revisited the movie—my third or fourth viewing—I noticed that it's not just the voice that I had misremembered; in fact, I had forgotten once again almost the entire second half of the series. Unlike the luscious Oxford years, the last seven hours of the miniseries, devoted to Charles Ryder's life after school, are dominated by an increasingly brooding tone, cramped interiors in a darker palette, and a self-denying heterosexuality inculcated by Catholic theology. Charles' life as an adult takes a few unexpected—and generally depressing—turns: he enters into an unhappy marriage, but then eventually begins to fall in love with another woman—oddly, with Julia Flyte, the younger sister of Sebastian, his earlier gay love. But as the film progresses, Julia's increasing devotion to Catholicism—which the film presents as enigmatically alluring despite its irrational repudiation of joy—makes their plans to get married impossible. In the final sequences, as the atheistic Lord Marchmain returns home to die, the Flyte family gathers around, desperately trying to inspire him to make some penitent gesture of faith on his deathbed in order to save his soul. When Ryder quietly disparages their behavior as the most banal superstition, he drives the final stake into his impending marriage with Julia. And yet, one of the most remarkable qualities of the movie is its unexpectedly complex relationship with its own conclusion: it's not entirely clear in the final analysis to what extent Charles, Waugh, or the film itself admires or rejects the intrinsic repression of the Catholic faith—or, conversely, to what extent they embrace or spurn the liberating joy made possible by the film's queer efflorescence.

I had repressed most of the plot, then, because my own experience of the film had been shaped by the analogous and interconnected forces of memory, cinematic aesthetics, and the miniseries itself, which had all been conditioned by this tension between repression and the freedom of expression. The entire movie is structured, after all, as a flashback in which Jeremy Irons' delicious voice-overs about his youth emanate from the present of war-ravaged Britain in 1944, so that the film, at its core, is an account of Charles Ryder poring over the memories that have fashioned his current apathy, and thus an explication of how our past inevitably shapes—and plagues—our current condition.

So my memory of Jeremy Irons' voice is not exactly a static entity floating through the orbits of my consciousness, but is, in fact, an ongoing operation, one of the defining procedures of mental life, whose purpose is to cope with the flux of experience—in this case, by participating in the movie's meaning-making. And this, too, is arguably one of art's major tasks: to determine and defend one's own values in order to construct a cohesive sense of self. At the same time, memories are not just the signifier of repression's anchor in the mental realm, but are, in fact, an inseparable component, the visible or audible link to their conjoined, camouflaged twin. So it's only because the cornerstone of repression is so firmly set within me that I still sense Jeremy Irons' voice—not always as a sound, sometimes as just the conceptual echo of that luscious timbre—reverberating, making itself known from that source that is unknowable, the desires that roil, presumably, beneath the surface, both flamboyant and concealed, effusive and reticent, the driving force of art and of my recollections and of my identity as well. ∎

LEAVING YOKOHAMA
Shawn Fawson

On the banks, a fisherman stands
wrapped against cold.
                              Reeds incline
like mourners, and the sky's a distant kiss.

A cluster of kids sinks nets
and hoists the fish up. Fresh
from the salt. Open and close, open
and close. What enters the mouth?
A mute story, mute song.

On the ship's deck, my mouth
swallows down the cold air. Back
and forth, and back and forth.

Are you going home? An American girl asks.

I say *yes, no,*
yes and no like the fish.

Never mind coming from or going to.

I knew what I saw:
the trees on water were dissolving
into pieces without sailing away.

HANDS
Shawn Fawson

The day my father survived the reactor's acid
exploding across his face and body,
a farmer's wife walked me from my school
back to her farmhouse in Futaba. She talked
with her hands, tutoring me in the language
of the living. Oxen came to the sound
of her fingers stirring grain in the pail.
We cleaned up warm milk from a mare
who was standing over her filly, choking
because there was too much. Each night
my hair smelled of fish from the unbraiding
motion of her hands. I remember asking—
How long will I be here? I didn't understand
the answer in Japanese. But, I learned what
waiting was worth when on the train platform,
minute by minute, she either tapped her watch
or held my face before the train arrived. I know
waiting is a life, which could have been a true life.

10W-40
Larry Watson

"Uh, that's a wig, you know," she says.

She's lying on her stomach on his bed, and she raises her head and looks over her shoulder at him. Her blouse is off, tangled somewhere in the sheets, and she's wearing a black bra and jeans. The bra is unclasped but still looped on her shoulders. "You were sort of getting up under there," she says.

It's true. That was definitely the territory he'd been working, having been told in his teenage years that kissing and caressing a woman's neck is the way to get her to unlock her legs. He didn't believe it then and he doesn't believe it now, but since he doesn't really have anything else to go on, he's kept the practice in his repertoire, insofar as he has a repertoire. But in truth, he'd really rather travel the other way, down the narrow trail of her vertebrae. She has a beautiful back, not a blemish, not a mole, just a perfect taper from shoulder to waist before the flare of her hips. The groove of her spine is a darker shadow in the darkened room.

Since the moment has already stalled, he says, "What did you say?"

"A wig," she says. "I'm wearing a wig. I thought you knew."

"How would I know?"

"Huh. I suppose I should be flattered."

He's been trying for weeks to get her up to his apartment. They'd met, if that was the term, at Butler's, on a night when it was so crowded people were lined up three deep at the bar, and they'd both been part of the scrum at the neglected end of the bar. "We guessed wrong," she said to him. "It looked like the smart choice for a while," he replied. He raised a hand to wave to a friend who was about to place a drink order, and just at the moment, the crowd surged and her head was pushed into his armpit. She laughed and then sniffed the air thoughtfully. "Slightly oaky," she said. "Subtle notes of tannin and currants. Old Spice?" "Right Guard," he said. "With an undertone of Lifebuoy?" "Irish Spring," he said.

By the time they got to the bar, they'd introduced themselves and discovered that they'd both moved to that part of the city recently. "So this will be our bar?" he said. "Our usual meeting place?"

She smiled again. "Could be. You never know."

A crowd pushed them together again a week or two later. He was at a party on a late winter night so warm and mild that many of the partygoers went out onto the balcony. He was wedged into a corner by the sliding door, and when she came out, he said, "We meet again."

"Are you here with the bride or the groom?" she said.

"The dog."

"He pointed me in your direction," she said and laughed. She had a wonderful wide-open laugh.

"I slipped him a couple bucks."

"Bones," she said. "The line is 'I slipped him a couple bones.'"

They talked about their host, who was soon moving to Minneapolis to work for a museum, and about his friends who were ruthlessly jockeying to take over his lease. About the unseasonably warm weather, which, in true Midwestern fashion, no one trusted. And about baseball. They were both White Sox fans in Cubs territory. When another group pushed its way through the door, she was pressed against him. He kissed her and she kissed back.

And now she's on his bed. But play has been suspended. "You don't want to know why?" she asks him.

"Why what?"

"You are slow, aren't you? The wig. You don't want to know why the wig?"

"Only if you want to tell me."

"It's not cancer. If that's what you're worried about."

"Who says I'm worried?"

"Arrggh. You're turning into a lot of work, you know that?"

"Okay," he says. "I'm happy it's not cancer. But it's, you know, your wig. Your wig, your reason. I just assume—"

She flips over on the bed, a sudden motion that seems spontaneous, yet she manages to keep her breasts covered. And though she's facing him now—and he has access to her lips, her breasts, to say nothing of the button and zipper of her jeans—this position is somehow less promising.

"I cut it off," she says. "My hair. And then I shaved my head."

He's been with women who have done stranger things to their bodies with metal, makeup, ink, or dye. For that matter, she has one of those tiny coils of wire through the wing of one nostril. "With an electric razor or a blade?"

"Is that *really* what you want to know?"

On the floor next to his running shoes and her boots are the whiskey glasses from which they'd both been drinking. There's a little whiskey left in both, watery from the melting ice and neglected from when their necking seemed as though it would surely lead to fucking. He picks up one of the glasses now and drinks. The apartment is his, yet it feels as though he should be ready to leave.

"Why'd you choose it? The red."

She's propped up on an elbow now and turned toward him. "I'm not sure." She laughs. "To get your attention?"

"Mine?"

"It worked, didn't it?"

"Something did. I mean," he says, "the red looks good. If you're not a natural redhead, you sure could be. Good choice. *Great* choice." He's aware that he's trying to salvage something of the evening. Sex, he supposes, yet that possibility feels less and less likely, though she's lying right here.

"I didn't exactly choose it," she says. "This is actually a loaner. The wig master said the lead wore it last year in *Wit*. And she shaved her head in that so . . . Kind of makes sense."

Now he remembers. She works in costumes or makeup or something at the Colby Theater. "'Wig master,'" he says. "That kills me. What an occupation." "'What do you do?' 'I'm a wig master.'"

"It's not full time."

"No?"

"He's actually a barber."

"Well, he made a good choice. With the red, I mean."

She brings a hand up to the side of her head. "Do you want to see? I can take it off."

"Whatever you're comfortable with."

She props herself up on her elbows and smiles. Her breasts remain covered but barely, and she doesn't seem to care one way or another. "You don't really want me to. I can tell."

"It's your call. Really."

She lies down flat again and tilts her head back in order to see out the window they're next to, though she won't be able to see anything except a featureless night sky. The street is five stories below, but the street lights and the neon from the stores, restaurants, and bars on the block make it impossible to see so much as a single star.

"I shaved it," she says, "because my boyfriend put oil in my hair."

"Whoa! *Oil?* Like—"

"—hair oil? No. And not like 'anointed my head with oil.'" She laughs, and he knows she's used that line before.

"He put oil in your hair. On purpose?"

"Yep. He put oil in my hair. On purpose."

"Because . . . ?"

She laughs again. "Because he was pissed off at me!"

"So this was—"

"—motor oil. Like 10W-40 or something."

"Jesus."

"I was lying on the sofa at the time. Ruined the fucking sofa, as you can well imagine."

He's afraid now, though he's not exactly sure of what. Of her? Because she's someone who can make someone so angry he'd pour motor oil on her? No, that's not it. Because she once had a boyfriend so passionate he poured motor oil on her head, and he knows he can't measure up to that?

"I tried washing it. Over and over. With different shampoos. I even washed it with a bar of soap. Finally I just said fuck it and cut it all off. But it still felt oily. That's when I shaved my head. With a Gillette razor, to answer your question. Believe me, I have new respect for those guys who shave their heads. I had these little nicks and cuts all over. And then when it started growing back it still felt kind of, I don't know, slimy. So I shaved it again. I know that makes me sound like a total fucking nut job."

"Can I ask? Your boyfriend—"

"—gone. But not forgotten."

"He had *motor oil*? In the house?"

She props herself up again, this time on one elbow. She reaches out and strokes his arm lightly with one finger. "Adam's one of those guys who believes in changing his own oil. 'Why should I pay someone to do what I can do myself,' he'd say. You know the type."

He did indeed. He could not change his own oil. "Adam . . ."

"Who we're talking about?"

"Yeah, but . . ."

She stops touching his arm. "Because I drank the last Coke. Isn't that what you were going to ask? What I did to piss him off? I drank the last Coke."

"Jesus."

She shrugs. "Adam liked his Cokes."

"Is this Adam still around? I have to say, he sort of scares me."

"He's harmless," she says unconvincingly. "Except where I'm concerned."

Now she lies down on her back again. She closes her eyes. She's tired. They're both tired.

After a moment, she opens her eyes again. "Hey," she says, "I thought we were going to get something going here. Was I wrong?"

Could he ask to see her back again? Would that seem strange at this point, maybe even a little perverse? What if he offered to rub her back? Worse?

Instead he says, "I've never had sex with a bald woman."

"You still haven't." ∎

CENTERPIECE
Ben Masaoka

I t was the beginning of the day and they faced each other in the kitchen. She sitting, he standing. He removed his work cap for something to do. He held the bill in one hand and softly thumped the cap into the palm of the other.

Ruby stubbed her cigarette into the abalone shell she used as an ashtray and studied his passive face intently. She was a large, aging Caucasian woman with hard, angry features, and they had been married now for many years.

"You never answered me last night. About the two piranha fish."

He allowed himself a sigh.

"Well?" she asked.

Kenzo pursed his lips together. He had a habit of doing this, sucking on the insides of his lips when frustrated. But seeing that Ruby was watching him, he stopped. He felt for the pack of Marlboros in his shirt pocket and shook one out.

"Gee, I don't know," he said. "They need a big tank. There's no place to put it."

Ruby sniffed, "I thought that's what you'd say."

"I don't know, maybe we could sell the typewriter and the roll top, make room."

"I need the typewriter and roll top."

"The sewing machine? Just a thought," he shrugged. "Something has to move."

They lived in a small two-bedroom place on a corner lot in Culver City. The yard was neat and well cared for, as might be expected from a gardener. But the interior of the house was disorderly. The spare bedroom and most of the living room had been taken up by junk. There were bundles of newspapers, boxes of green stamps, a pile of drapes, old clothing, stacks of *National Geographic*, broken floor lamps, a bicycle, a dusty sewing machine with spools of colored thread, and the latest acquisition, an IBM Selectric electric typewriter bought new when they came out last year. It had been greatly used for a week or two, the silver golf-ball-type head clacking all day and night, then forgotten about. It sat on a small rolltop desk almost buried by shoeboxes filled with old receipts.

The only semblance of order in the room was a card table beneath a window where Kenzo kept a spiral notebook and pamphlets from a plant nursery, and where he sat in the evenings to smoke and drink and look out the window.

"I've already thought of that," Ruby said, exhaling a plume of smoke and stubbing out her cigarette. With her fingers she wiped her nose and looked around for a tissue. Not seeing any, she put her hand in the pocket of her housecoat. Pointing with her chin, she said, "Those boxes of green stamps. I'll paste them into booklets and redeem 'em. That will make a little room. If you retie our *National Geographics*, they are stout magazines, it would be as good as a table. We could set the aquarium on top." She looked up at him, her blue eyes flecked with gray. "It *could* be a centerpiece."

"Okay," he said. His cigarette dangled from his lips and he pushed away from the counter to signal that he was leaving. "Let's think about it."

"I've thought about it. I want the fish."

"I have to go to work," he said.

"Fine," she said. "Then go to work."

* * *

He pulled the tarp off his old pickup truck, uncovering the tools of his trade: gas and push mowers, shovels and rakes, clippers and spades, a coiled watering hose, several neatly folded canvas tarps to which he added the one that had covered the truck bed. In the cab he turned the key and the old truck rattled and smoked.

"The Mexicans are going to steal your tools, you know," Ruby liked to say. When she ran out of things to complain about, she would bring up the Mexicans and the Negroes that lived in the housing project some blocks away. But he didn't keep his tools in the garage because there wasn't room. Along with more useless junk, there was the faded blue-and-white Oldsmobile they drove to Tijuana on their honeymoon. That was fifteen years ago. It had been old even then and didn't run anymore, yet Ruby wanted to keep it for the memories, she said.

The Oldsmobile brought back memories for him as well. Good memories, they used to be, but now painful to recall. Driving on the freeway that sunny day in 1945 through San Diego with Ruby, just married, her arm hanging out the window, pretending it was an airplane wing dipping up and down, the long sleeve of her shirt flapping in the wind, and her singing along with the radio. She did have a sweet voice and liked to say she thought someday she could be on the air just like the

Andrews Sisters. When they waited in line at the border, the song "Rum and Coca-Cola" played, and Ruby changed the first line to "If you ever go down *Tijuana*" and they laughed so hard the serious border guard almost turned them away. And later that night, dancing together at a bar, pressed in on all sides by Mexican couples, Ruby had said, swaying and leaning on his shoulder, "Being around these different kinds of people makes me feel so close with you, Kenzo."

"Yes, wife," he said, the word so new in his mouth.

"Being here makes me feel that, even though you and me, we're different too, but we are . . . oh, I don't know how to say it. The same people, cuz now we're married. Right, husband?"

* * *

Kenzo's mood rose as he pulled onto the interstate and got off near Westwood, the first of his stops that would end, as the day went on, in lower Beverly Hills. It was a good route, many times better than the one he had worked before. This route had wealthy Caucasians who paid on time. They lived in lovely houses with beautiful blue swimming pools and elegant patios for entertaining. Kenzo had inherited it just a few months ago from his friend, Tatsuki, whom he had served with in France during the war.

It had been Tatsuki who had convinced Kenzo to start his own business.

"I don't know anything about gardening," Kenzo had said.

"It doesn't matter! *Hakujin* don't know that."

At times, in the beginning, Kenzo had been terrified. When customers wanted advice about their yards, he simply did not know what to say. Out of pure fear he mumbled and fell to rubbing his jaw in silence. Amazingly, it was the perfect thing to do. He learned that if he said nothing, they would eventually tell him exactly what should be done.

"I want an Oriental look, sort of a tea garden kind of deal, some bamboo, a couple of those midget trees, some natural-looking boulders, you know what I mean."

"Oh, yes," Kenzo would nod, "how about here, and here, and over there," randomly pointing at the first empty spots he saw between the bushes.

"Yes! Beautiful!"

Later, standing with the owner looking at the dead plants, Kenzo could say, "I was afraid of this, you know. Wrong climate. But I thought,

'Hey, what the heck? If it's what you want, let's give it a go!'" This was usually met with a handshake and a clap on the back.

Most of the time he didn't see anybody, and that's what he liked. Kenzo wasn't a silent man by nature, but when customers complimented him on his English, he cringed inside. He knew they meant well, and he tried not to let it bother him. He told himself it didn't matter. It was a small, insignificant quirk of *hakujin* people trying to be friendly.

* * *

Ruby watched Kenzo leave that morning, hating the way he looked wearing his dirty dark-gray khakis with his matching dirty dark work shirt. Even his cap, for Christ's sake, matched the rest of the outfit. The cap was the worst of all. Frayed along the bill and greasy from his hair. If he left it anywhere she would yell for him to come and get the damn thing. She wasn't going to touch it, so old and worn and the inside rim all filthy from dirt and sweat. It had an odor, too. He liked to say that his people didn't stink, but that was a lie. He had one change of work clothes and wore them all week, and by the time the weekend rolled around, shove it under anybody's nose and they would say it stunk. Shove it under his sister's nose and she would have to admit it, too. There were many things about him she couldn't stand, such as when this morning he sucked on the insides of his lips. It repulsed her. With his black hair and slanty eyes, and his wooden-colored skin, it made him look even more like a little brown monkey than he already did.

When he was gone she thought, "Finally. Now I have the whole day to make plans."

She lit a cigarette and drank another cup of coffee. She leaned an elbow upon the kitchen table. It was tiring, this life, and everything about it. Ash dropped onto the sleeve of her pink housecoat and she brushed it away and rubbed what was left into the fabric. Pretty soon she'd get up and throw some water on her face.

But first she had to gather her plans and spread them out before her so she could see what was what. Her plans were vague. The ocean was about three miles away and sometimes fog rolled in so thick that if she told anyone about it back home in French Lick, Indiana, how thick it was, they wouldn't believe her. Fog that thick, it was dangerous to go outside. She could stretch out her arm and not see her hand at the end of it. The figure of a person might suddenly materialize, and then, just as quickly, disappear in one or two steps. Her plans had the same quality. They came upon her fully formed, out of nowhere, and struck a chord within her that rang with so much sense. Gratitude, that's what she felt. And hope. But when she needed to see the details, or even what the plan was actually about, it was like grasping at a shape in the fog that disappeared as soon as she raised her hand to touch it.

That is how her plans appeared this morning, and a familiar, lonely resignation curled around her legs and threatened to overtake her. But she drew up straighter in the chair and reminded herself of what she knew to be true. That to accomplish big plans she must first accomplish little ones. Wasn't that how she'd spent her life, in a series of small victories? First, getting the hell out of French Lick, where her mother worked at the TG&Y and her father at the sorghum refinery, where he came home every night from work smelling sickly sweet. The back-biting neighbors were on her for years, calling her jail bait when she was young and a runaround when she was older. She made it out of that small town of small-minded people, all the way to Chicago. That was a victory, no one else she knew had done that. It's where she met Kenzo, just back from the war, exotic looking and handsome in his uniform, and a war hero, she heard people say. She liked that he was different, he was everything that people from her hometown were not. It was a whirlwind, that's what it was. Two weeks later they were in Los Angeles, staying with Kenzo's sister and her husband, and their little baby boy. They had plans already for another. It was exciting at first, and then so hard. Kenzo's large, extended family. These Japanese people, they were different, that was for sure, and she couldn't stand their food. So much fish, even raw fish! And rice and seaweed and some kind of paste that looked like baby poop. She wanted to scream, "Can't I just have a steak and some damn potatoes?" They were nice to her, they were, and the women had fortitude, as tough as any Indiana gals. But the men had all been in the war together, part of a special military unit made up of only Jap Americans. Like a secret society, and the women too, being wives of those secret society men. Oh God, she felt like an outsider. But then came her next victory. She was pregnant. And everything changed. The women became truly friendly, some of their blood in her now, she figured. And that was all right, she liked it. With these people, blood was everything. It made their differences vanish into thin, clean air. She snapped her fingers when she realized this and lost her shyness and began singing around the house, and they all said she had a sweet voice. The relatives put money together and soon they had enough for a down payment on a home. That was the last good thing to ever happen.

They found the little two-bedroom house and she decorated the baby room, and the women visited, and one night they barbecued steak in her honor. She cried in gratitude, it was silly, steak and potatoes making her feel that way, and they all laughed, but it felt like the laughter of kinfolk. It was later that night when Kenzo forced himself upon her. They hadn't had relations since she'd found out she was pregnant. When she was young her mother warned her not to let the husband do that. Because germs could get in that way and infect and kill the baby. And that's what happened. It was in the fourth month of her pregnancy and that's exactly what happened. The doctor said it could have been for many reasons, but she knew exactly why it was. Kenzo had been drunk, drinking all night, and later in bed begged because it had been so long, and she kept saying no, no, and offered other ways of pleasing him, but he kept on and she couldn't stop him anymore and gave up and laid there praying while he grunted and moaned. The doctor said it could have been anything, but the doctor was one of them, a secret society man. Still, Kenzo accepted the blame and he swore he would make amends, but how was that ever going to be possible? It was all a long time ago.

And this is what she knew to be true. To accomplish big plans she must first accomplish little ones. She had to have patience. She had to take it step by step and in this way gain small but important victories. Going to the liquor store was always a good place to start.

It was a short walk through the neighborhood and she didn't feel the need to do more than wrap a scarf around her hair, find her purse, and walk out the door.

Outside, the sun was in full force and the lawns were phosphorous green. She could feel heat rising from the white sidewalk. A car drove lazily by, a shiny metal-flaked blue Chevy Impala, the body a mere two inches above the hot black asphalt of the street. The rear window had Gothic lettering, *Low Men Limited*, it read. Ruby sniffed and followed it with her eyes until it turned onto the arterial and sped away.

The liquor store was a tiny building with dirty stucco walls and neon beer signs in windows behind iron grills. There was a small wooden bench off the street, placed against the wall on the side of the building. Ruby sat there to catch her breath and smoke a cigarette. The building shaded her. She prided herself on her delicate white skin and didn't want sunlight ruining it. She liked to sit and watch the traffic on the arterial go by.

There were yellow school buses filled with kids, their faces crammed against the windows. One of them saw her and waved. Ruby waved back. Cars zoomed by, cars of many colors, the flashing of chrome in the sunlight made her wish she had thought to wear her dark glasses, ones just like Jackie Kennedy had. As she smoked, she gazed beyond the traffic to the white concrete L on the hillside of Loyola University. There, above the

Hughes Aircraft buildings, the thirty-foot-tall letter still fascinated her, and the midday tolling of the bell that sometimes she could faintly hear all the way from her house. She liked to imagine her initials written large upon the hill in place of the L. Ruby dropped her cigarette onto the sidewalk, crushed it with her slippered foot, and kicked it out to the street. Then she stood and walked around to the front and pushed open the door. A bell hanging from a clip on the doorframe jangled and she stepped into the cool, dark room where a radio played what she called cucaracha music. There, a man awaited her from behind a wooden counter. Behind him was a wall of shelves lined with bottles. When he saw who it was, he didn't need to speak. He took a pint of Gordon's vodka from a shelf and put it in a paper sack with a pack of Salems and matches. Then he reached under the counter and brought out a ledger, found the page, and jotted down some numbers. He flipped it around and pushed the ledger towards her, tapping his finger on a place on the page. Ruby made her initials and gathered up the bag and left. The bell on the door jangled twice again as she opened and closed it behind herself.

She blinked against the sudden light. Shading her eyes, she turned the corner and saw a couple of Negro girls sitting on the bench. They had taken her place in the few minutes she had been gone. Those two girls with long skinny legs cast out in front of themselves were blocking up half the sidewalk. They were talking and giggling. Ruby paused to let them know they should move their legs so that pedestrians might safely pass. When they saw her waiting, they fell silent. They withdrew their legs one by one, bringing their knees up and crossing their arms over the tops, eyeing each other and smiling as they did so. Ruby held her face straight ahead as she began to pass by, but then, inexplicably, even to herself, she stopped and turned to face them. "Shouldn't you girls be in school?" she asked.

When they didn't answer, she gave them a stern gaze and walked on. In a moment she heard them burst out in laughter.

* * *

She woke from her nap in the late afternoon. Her housecoat was on the floor and she pulled it around herself and went into the bathroom. She sat on the toilet and urinated, wiped, pulled her undies up, and bent over the sink and splashed water on her face. She glanced at herself in the mirror and left the bathroom and followed the path through all the junk and into the kitchen. Her cigarettes were on the table and so was the pint of vodka, empty now. She sat down and lit a cigarette and thought about how she might finish her day. She had so many projects! Maybe she would try to learn how to sew, again. There had been lessons she began but did not complete. They might give her a refund or let her finish out the course. She considered the electric typewriter. Maybe she would start writing her life story again. She knew it would be interesting to an editor, maybe *Life* magazine? The story of an American who became a colored person in her own country. This time she would begin with her parents, not her grandparents. That was so long ago, and besides, she was only a little girl when they passed. She smoked and thought about her options.

She remembered the piranhas.

There was an article she had found in *National Geographic* with the most amazing photographs. She didn't understand how these fish could make her feel so emotional. Why was that? They were powerful when they worked together. They could strip an adult tapir down to its skeleton in a matter of minutes, the article said. They attacked in a group, driven by duty and love she imagined. That was the way of all creatures on earth. Death to outsiders. It made her feel something but she couldn't say what. She wished she had someone to discuss this with, or sewing, or the story of her life, but there wasn't anyone she talked with except Kenzo's relatives, and it was only polite talk because they didn't like her.

There was an exotic fish store in Crenshaw. It had been three weeks ago when she spoke with them on the telephone. She'd almost forgotten. The fish were expensive, coming special all the way from the Amazon River, but the store would cut her a deal on the aquarium. They were due to arrive tomorrow.

She thought about how she told Kenzo to use the *National Geographic*s for a table, but she had never meant to put those expensive fish on stacks of magazines. Ha! They were supposed to be a clever people, but she was way ahead of this one. She already figured he would not agree to redeeming those green stamps. He believed the stamps belonged to his sister. Without that, without the extra space from getting rid of them, there was only one spot in the room. His ridiculous office. "Let's take a look-see," she thought.

She picked up the empty vodka bottle, squinted at it, then dipped it in her mouth. Pushing herself up, she maneuvered between piles and stacks of junk until she stood before the card table that Kenzo liked to sit at in the evenings. In her mind, she swept off the spiral notebook and little pamphlets of shrubs and plants and visualized the glass-sided tank in their place. Small blue rocks filled the bottom, plastic underwater plants undulated. There was a treasure chest, and a figurine of a man in a diving suit, and two disk-shaped silvery fish, with luminous orange eyes and daggers for teeth, that hovered and flicked and turned in unison.

* * *

Late that afternoon when the sky began to pale, Kenzo pulled into the driveway and parked, rinsed off his tools, and threw a tarp over them. He went inside the house and saw there were a couple of Swanson frozen chicken pies heating in the oven. He took a shower and when he came out he stood in the kitchen doorway and watched as Ruby took the pies out and flipped them upside down on paper plates and lifted off the aluminum bottoms. She smeared a dab of butter on each one and took them to the table with two plastic forks. Kenzo sat down with cans of beer for him and her.

They ate and drank in silence. Kenzo got up and brought back two more beers from the fridge. They had a rule about not smoking during dinnertime, but they never followed it. They smoked and shoved their cigarette butts down into the empty cans and picked the cans up and jiggled them around so there wouldn't be any smoke rising out.

Kenzo gathered up the paper plates and forks and stuffed them into the trash can under the sink. He turned on the small TV that was on the kitchen counter by the toaster and sat down after getting another couple of beers. He slid one over to Ruby and waited for the picture to come on. They watched some reruns of *The Lawrence Welk Show*. He had to get up a couple of times to adjust the rabbit ears. Then he took the fifth of Seagram's Seven from the cupboard, a couple of glasses, dropped ice cubes into them, and poured whiskey over the ice. He found an open can of Coke in the fridge and splashed some in one glass and gave it to Ruby, and put the Coke back without using any himself. He liked to taste his whiskey. He picked up his pack of cigarettes and looked at Ruby. She was wearing glasses and he couldn't see her eyes because of the TV light glaze.

"I'm going to my office," he said and went to sit at his table in the living room.

He cracked the window to let smoke drift out and opened the notebook. He ran his finger down a line of dates and the names of his clients. Names like "Douglas," "Peterson," and "Hudson." He made check marks and some notes. He shuffled through a few pamphlets. It took about twenty minutes and he closed the notebook, his work done for the evening.

Then he remembered he had to pick up some bougainvillea plantings for the Morgans and flipped through a nursery pamphlet to see what he could get, when suddenly Ruby was there beside him. She wavered a bit on her feet and put her hand on the backing of his chair to steady herself. Her pink housecoat fell open. All she wore beneath it was an old, frayed bra and baggy panties, both the same grayish shade of white. Her flabby stomach unmarked from child bearing. With her free hand she clutched at her housecoat and pulled it closed.

"The fish are arriving tomorrow. We need to go and get them. It's just over in Crenshaw."

Ruby stared down at him, her mouth open, breathing. She squinted her eyes as if trying to see him better. She stood above him like a drunken bird of prey.

"I thought we were going to talk more," he said.

"I didn't tell you. I sent them a check three weeks ago. They cashed it."

"Let's go to the kitchen," Kenzo said, putting his hands on the chair and pushing himself up. "Let's figure this out." He didn't want to argue by the open window.

"Let's figure it out, here," Ruby said. "Because here is where the fish are going to have to be." She nodded at Kenzo, letting go of her housecoat and stabbing her finger at the card table.

"No, this is my office."

"It's the only place."

"What about the *National Geographic*s? You said . . ."

"We'd have to redeem the green stamps to make room." She swayed a little with a look of triumph.

Kenzo glanced down at the table. He touched his nursery pamphlets and gazed out the window. It was a quiet night, and then a car went slowly by, music suddenly there and then gone.

"Your sister says I stole them."

"Let's talk tomorrow."

"She says I stole them when she was in the hospital, when I took care of her kids. All your relatives believe her. But that was a lot of work for me. Where was your brother-in-law?"

"At the hospital with her. They made him a cot."

"I'm going to sit down," she said.

She looked around to see what was close behind. There was a stack of bundled newspapers she had gathered for the local paper drive five years ago. Ruby tried to sit on it. She teetered for a moment then rolled off and fell to the floor.

Kenzo stood and offered his hands. "Let me take you to bed. Okay? Let's talk about the fish tomorrow. It's Saturday. We can talk about it tomorrow, can't we?"

From the floor she lifted her arms to him. "Help me," she cried.

He grasped both her hands and pulled her upwards, bracing himself and struggling until she was once again standing on her feet. She leaned on him, her arms crossed behind his neck, breathing heavily.

He heard her say, "I am lost, Kenzo."

He walked her sideways towards the bedroom, rocking her from foot to foot as he might a chest of drawers. "Lost? You are not lost, you are in our house and I'm going to put you in your bed. You are not lost."

"Where are my people, Kenzo?"

He stopped and brushed her hair away from her eyes and looked into them. They stared at each other, unmoving, frozen in the step of a dance. "I'm right here, Ruby. I'm right here."

"I'm your people, too, Kenzo," she sobbed.

* * *

By the afternoon of the next day, the aquarium with two piranhas occupied the space of what used to be Kenzo's office. It was a large, heavy tank, and Kenzo spent the morning fortifying the card table with two-by-fours. Other than that, it was a perfect fit. Blue gravel filled the bottom of the tank, plastic seaweed undulated with the currents, and a deep-sea diver figurine exhaled bubbles above an open treasure chest. The fish were smaller than Kenzo had imagined, but they were formidable looking, with large eyes and sharp, jutting teeth.

"Aren't they beautiful?" Ruby asked.

Kenzo had to admit they were impressive.

"It's our centerpiece," Ruby said.

In the end, she always got what she wanted. But Kenzo was relieved, as he was every time, to please her even temporarily. There had been so many things. He expected to come home in a few weeks and find the fish belly up. He hoped this time he'd be wrong.

She disappeared into the kitchen. Kenzo heard the refrigerator door open and close. Ruby returned with a small plastic bag full of water. In it was a fat goldfish. It reminded Kenzo of a prize his nephews had won at the neighborhood fair.

"Don't worry," Ruby said. "They discount if we buy in bulk."

She removed the lid from the tank and placed it to the side. She untied the plastic bag and dumped the goldfish into the tank. It didn't take a second until the water was tinged with pink and a shred of golden flesh, floating, unraveled like thread. And that too, in the very next moment, was snapped up. ■

APHASIA
Karen McPherson

Ghosts of syllables sluice in; I'm
grasping for purchase, one word
at a time. Listening fingers slipping, slipping

on a rounded edge, I'm aching for the clarity
of birdsong: trebles, blooms. Even just
to let it all drain out, be left blessedly

untroubled by seepages. But I'm struggling
to come to terms with dissolving accretions, willing
to abandon morsels, deft, incisive,

the well-punctuated phrase too painfully
labored over. Why still so enamored of the line
break? What is so precious about a proper name?

More to the point: What century is this? The heavy
furniture exhales the vapors of curtained conversations
I can't quite hear, echoes of families

I once lived on the outskirts of. In that childhood
a grandmother knew how to coddle eggs; wit
was universally admired; books were mappable

places, vast territories visited and claimed
and named and owned. Now in this current century,
the table is set for a meal

I haven't planned. Floral centerpiece, napkins intricately
folded into birds, but the knives are all dull
and I can't remember which side the fork goes on.

LAZARUS
Natalia Nebel

In the fall of 2014 I had an emergency operation to remove a malignant brain tumor that had begun to cause bleeding in my head. I went into the operation with complete serenity because I'd spent that summer accepting my impending death; I'd come to peace with my life and said goodbye to the world before any doctor's knowledge of my cancer, and actually before any external proof of it. In our culture we're extremely, perhaps necessarily attached to external proof, and all I had was an internal truth that came to me on a May morning while drinking coffee:

"I'm going to die of a brain tumor at the end of this summer."

This was expressed in a rational, matter-of-fact way, as in a weather forecast, and yet, I recoiled from this truth, pushed this knowledge away, asking myself why I'd think such a thing. I hadn't had headaches or seizures, and brain tumors are extremely rare, numbering twelve cases per one hundred thousand people. And as for knowing the exact date of my death . . . that made no sense at all.

I've come to learn that the tumor I had is called the silent tumor because of where it grows. Its symptom markers are different from those of other brain tumors. From May onwards I began to experience those different symptoms. I slowed down. Dramatically. A dedicated walker, I didn't stop walking my three or so miles a day, but what had been effortless required more and more work. Was it my imagination or had I developed a sad-turtle's pace? Not my imagination. One day, an old person overtook me and passed me by, then another did the same. I slowed down at the gym too, and the routine two and a half miles I liked to do on the elliptical machine shrank down to two hard-won miles; I'd lost half a mile into thin air.

I began sleeping ten and eleven hours every night, waking up exhausted, feeling as though I hadn't slept. My willpower always kicked in, and after forcing myself to get out of bed, I'd walk to the shower, turn on the water, step under the water's stream. Getting out of bed became the most difficult moment of my day.

I also became clumsy, and I sometimes wondered if I had MS, again ignoring the message that had come to me about a brain tumor. I promised myself that I'd ask a doctor to check me for MS if things got worse.

Despite my new clumsiness, I continued to drive, although it became harder and harder for me to back my Honda Civic into my garage or park on the street. I didn't have to do either very often, however, because I began going out less and less. I missed my friends, but didn't call them, and went out only when they suggested it. These outings became harder and harder as well. For example, meeting friends at a restaurant in early August, I parked blocks and blocks away from where we were to meet. And, for reasons surely related to my tumor, I was no longer able to drink alcohol. I told people that I was on antibiotics and unable to drink because of that. How else could I explain my sudden abstention if I couldn't explain it to myself?

I also began gaining weight, and between May and September I gained fifteen pounds. Everything in my body was slowing down, including my metabolism. I attributed it to perimenopause, the simple fact that I would turn fifty-two at the end of the year. In any case, church became much more important to me than the gym. A lapsed Catholic like most of my Catholic friends, I began going to a church called Immaculate Conception, having been taken there by a friend in early June. He didn't return, but I did, every Sunday. I'd get there twenty minutes before the twelve-thirty mass and sit in the little garden they'd created in a corner of their parking lot. In the center of this garden was a large bronze relief of Christ, his outstretched arms holding children dressed in nineteenth-century clothing. "Let the little children come to me, and do not hinder them, for the kingdom of heaven belongs to such as these," were the words carved into the bronze.

The fact that Christ protecting children had been chosen for that spot moved me greatly, because Christ's suffering had been the justification I'd always given myself for the needless suffering I'd experienced growing up in a home that knew more about cruelty than kindness. Christ's love for children as embodied in the lines carved into the relief were among my favorite lines in the New Testament; I felt seen and loved through those words. And so, that summer of 2014 when I was slowly dying, the only place I wanted to be was there, in the middle of tall grasses and purple lilies, where I found peace in my little sanctuary for the soul. The bench I began to consider mine was always empty—who in their right mind finds sanctuary in a parking-lot garden? I always sat where the sun's rays slanted down to form a perfect Earth-to-sky pathway, a temporal-to-eternal stream of an unseeable, absolutely pure light. The garden teemed with life despite its small size; I marveled at translucent dragonflies flecked with gold and fluttering butterflies; I loved the elusive birds that flew around me, and I saw with clarity that all life-forms are miraculous, perfect in themselves and also complete within large and small ecosystems.

We live in the center of a miracle and are not consistently grateful enough for what we've been given because we live in a secular world we can rarely escape, a world that drives us forward with increasingly inhuman exigencies that drive out the sacred; I understood all this, along with the profound damage that it does us.

At 12:28 p.m. I then entered the humble basement church. Because it was summertime, it was always almost empty, and this made it a silent, holy refuge for solitary, oddball people like me. And then, the Jesuit priests who gave Mass in rotation were good: they spoke of doubt as though it was natural, not sinful; they came down into the aisle to share their sermons rather than remain behind the altar; they shook hands with everyone individually in that universal sign of peace; their sermons were always compassionate, showing awareness of the difficulties in our day-to-day world. The familiar structure of the Mass was a comfort to me as well, and I found that ancient prayers I'd learned as a child were still a part of me. But most of all, I went there to take Communion and receive grace. The holy wafer that dissolved in my mouth reinforced the god-love I felt in the garden, took me into a higher spiritual realm where I felt blessed and everything around me became infused with higher meaning. Once back in my pew I'd kneel, feel harmony and love from a realm I'd always believed in but never before experienced. I came to accept my life, and my death, through that love.

Funny that, while I'd never loved the world more, I also accepted my upcoming death, felt grateful for it. I'd been through very much in the prior ten years: a cross-country move back to Chicago from New York City that triggered a depression that led me to a therapist I went to twice a week for five years and then once a week thereafter; my marriage becoming an emotional desert and then the discovery of my husband's unfaithfulness; a phone call from my therapist only a few days after this shock where she told me she had cancer and wouldn't be able to see me for months during her treatment; my parents' strange unwillingness to give my husband up, which I experienced as an emotional betrayal by them; my husband's loss of his job in 2008 and the financial difficulties that followed from that; my mother's death in 2010; my husband's terrible suicide in 2011; the discovery shortly after his death that he'd moved in with a Chinese prostitute only months after he'd left our home; a painful lawsuit over his life insurance involving this prostitute, which dragged on for two and a half years because she wouldn't settle; my father going back on his word that he'd pay my lawyer's fees, leaving me in even more financial difficulty; and then, when the judge ruled in my favor, not the euphoria I'd expected to feel, but only an almost negligible relaxation, a relief from stress rather than joy and putting into action all that I'd planned to do with the money. This lack of euphoria was eventually explained: I won the lawsuit in July of 2014 just six weeks before my emergency operation.

And so, I'm not ashamed to write that I felt grateful for my impending death, because my incessant suffering, a suffering that had begun in childhood, showed no sign of ever letting up, seemed only to increase. And now, it was as though I was finally being released, released in the most gentle way possible, to become part of an eternal, life-giving love that I'd had the great good fortune to live within before dying. I was on the threshold and I wasn't afraid. Perhaps it had been my suffering for so long that had allowed for this gift. "*I see my light come shining / from the west unto to the east. / Any day now, any day now / I shall be released.*" Each Sunday when I returned to the garden and then church I was more tired, closer to my end in the material world. Getting there in the first place was becoming more and more difficult. And yet, revelations continued: one morning in the garden, my eyes closed, warmed by the sun, I understood why the Egyptians had turned this sun into their god, Ra. Another Sunday, I understood Plato's philosophy of an ideal world that the earth is a copy of. His dislike of art because it was an imitation of truth finally made sense. Coming out of the cave into light, I saw illusions for what they were, and for the first time in my life, I surrendered my ego, which, in the Buddhist sense, had impeded me from living fully. More precisely, you could say that in losing myself, I found unending strength and serenity.

There are many things I don't remember about that summer, but I do remember deciding to terminate therapy because I was done with life. There was no longer a point in going. I remember my therapist's surprise when I told her I was done with therapy, when I thanked her for all she'd given me, for her patience with me, for having never given up on me. I believe she parented me in just the way I'd needed as a child, made it possible for me to trust the world and those I loved as much as I ever could. She advised against stopping, asked that we give it a few more sessions to explore. I agreed. Two or three more sessions couldn't hurt. She then proposed that I go on antidepressants because, as she told me later, I was displaying very little affect. I refused. I knew I wasn't depressed.

My therapist was the only person I tried to say good-bye to.

Sometimes I became irritated with my friends and family for not calling me, for losing our last chance of spending time together; and then I'd remind myself that they didn't know I was dying. It wasn't their fault. Even the roommate I had at the time, Jason, who was staying in my spare room rent-free for that summer—my favor to him—didn't pick up on my deterioration, my dying.

My summer, my beautiful summer when I experienced all the wonder that can be lived on this earth. Blessed, ready to go, and then, called back.

I was called back to life from the threshold of death on September second, the day after Labor Day, the official end-of-summer date in the US.

In my kitchen the May morning of that year, I'd gotten the date of my death exactly right. How can that be possible?

Brilliant people have explained the workings of the body, the world, the universe, but who can explain its beauty, its poetry, its life-giving soul, its electric power that transforms over and over into the material for a short while before then slipping back into the ethereal?

On Labor Day weekend, Sunday, I drove out of Chicago to visit my friend Laura, who'd recently moved out of the city. Before leaving my house, I looked at the directions I'd written, couldn't understand them. Not being able to decipher what I'd written gave me a moment of pure terror. What was wrong with me? And yet, I didn't hesitate to get in my car and drive out of Chicago. I believed I'd get there, and in fact, enough of my brain was functioning for me to make it, although I got lost on a rural highway at the end and had to call Laura. I'd missed her turnoff by only half a mile. I made a U-turn and then found Laura's private road because she had left her house to meet me.

Laura is one of the few people I can always be myself around, perhaps because we accept each other completely and because our intelligence works in similar ways. My multitalented friend! A former litigator, then corporate lawyer, a mother, an excellent poet and playwright, she has always understood me on the fly. And she cared for me so generously that day! She'd bought a special wine for us to drink with a delicious lunch she'd made. If only I'd still had a sense of taste. We watched a movie together, talked, went for a walk in the countryside that surrounded her cottage. I found it almost impossible to walk, this mild effort exhausted me immediately, but even so, I didn't feel the terror I'd felt when looking at the directions I couldn't read.

Laura lives within a wetlands area, and at one point we passed a pond that makes up part of her landscape. Laura called out to me: "Look!" We stopped walking. She pointed to a large tree filled with still, white egrets. It seemed as though they were watching us, paying special attention to us. I'd become deeply connected to the natural world through the tiny church garden, and this seemed like a continuation of that link; I received it as a gentle good-bye. I'll never forget the quiet, solemn gazes of those birds. Another blessing.

Later that day, Laura asked me why my left shoulder was twitching. "Is it?" I couldn't feel or even sense it. I looked, but the movement had stopped. Months later, a doctor told me that I'd been having a seizure. I then understood that I'd had my first seizure two days before my trip to Laura's when my hand jerked away from me as I was bringing a coffee mug up to my mouth. I'd stained my shirt, attributed it to clumsiness, become irritated with myself.

I slept at Laura's place, and the following day, Monday, America's official end-of-summer date, we went into her new town, Antioch, walked a charming street, explored a vintage clothing and household items store. Tiredness forced me to sit down. I wasn't my usual self. And yet, I thought, after all I've been through these years, why should I be surprised by intense fatigue?

When I left Laura that late afternoon, I wasn't afraid of driving. I remember getting on the expressway, barely aware of the cars and strip malls on either side of me, everything receding, real but not real, and I too, fading out and away from what many religions call the illusory world.

It must have been instinct that led me home in the same way that it had gotten me around Chicago all summer; certain pieces of knowledge were wired deep within or throughout my brain in unbreakable threads, the last things to go. I don't remember getting home or falling asleep that night. The next day, Tuesday, I had a therapy appointment. I dressed, ate, got my car keys out, then didn't think I could make it. I called my therapist, told her something was wrong with me, I didn't know what. I was confused, and I felt a dim fear. Because my therapist thought I was suicidal, she asked that I go to see her anyway.

If I hadn't had therapy scheduled that day, I would have stayed inside, fallen asleep, and, according to the doctors, not woken up. My brain tumor had grown so large that it was causing not only seizures, but bleeding.

Jason happened to be home and, when he saw me leaving with my car keys, he expressed shock that I was going to Skokie. "Are you sure that's a good idea?"

"I'll be all right. I've driven that road at least three thousand times."

Any fear I'd had was gone, I had something I had to do, a challenge and a chance to show my therapist how much I trusted her. Jason thought I'd been drinking even though I've never been a daytime drinker; he felt guilty for months afterwards because he hadn't stopped me from getting into the car. If he'd stopped me, however, I don't think I'd still be alive.

I drove at the fifty-five-miles-an-hour speed limit on the expressway, unusual for me, and I concentrated on keeping my car in my lane. I had the feeling my car was occasionally swaying to the left and then the right. In retrospect, I'd entered the last stage of my dying, which was to see everything as though it was happening not to *me*, but to *someone else*. Perhaps it was because of this that I began finding many things quietly funny.

I don't remember getting to my therapist's office. I have a visual flash of talking to her and of her saying something serious. Later she told me that she thought I'd had a small stroke and had asked me to call a friend for the name of a doctor that I could see the following day. She'd called a psychiatrist friend of hers while I was there, described my symptoms, and he said that they didn't sound too serious, believed I could wait sixteen hours before getting a CT scan. I called Laura—don't remember talking to her—and because Laura thought I sounded incoherent, she didn't want me to wait a day to see a doctor and asked to speak to my therapist, who called an ambulance for me.

I don't remember getting into the ambulance, but I remember the paramedics, who inspired much apprehension, no confidence. Late twenties, blonde and blue-eyed, one had a beard and both of them had beer bodies. I knew that they had no idea what was wrong with me, and that they should have asked me questions that might have pointed them in the right direction, but that they weren't going to. When they got lost trying to find the entrance to Skokie Hospital's ER, they fought. "Go right here!" "No." "It's in that direction, I'm telling you." "And I'm telling you no!" Their haplessness struck me as borderline hilarious. That my life was in the hands of these two didn't frighten me. Laura met us at the hospital; I don't remember that either. She told me later that I'd introduced her to the paramedics saying, "These two young gentlemen were kind enough to bring me here."

I spent at least three hours in Skokie Hospital's ER and have only visual, unconnected flashes of that time. My therapist had a cancellation from a patient of hers who never cancels and drove to the ER to be with me. This allowed her, along with Laura, to fight for my life.

I wasn't in a position to advocate for myself. Feeling myself unravel produced in me only detached amusement; I was nonchalant and, to the external world, conscious, while in reality fading in and out of consciousness.

The paramedics presented the ER with two possible diagnoses: either I was dehydrated (they'd taken my pacing for pointless wandering) or I was a psych case. Because of this, I was immediately assigned to a recently minted social worker. My therapist tells me she went to this social worker's office with me, trying to convey that she'd known me for ten years and that I'd never had a psychotic break in that time. In addition, she actually worked as a consultant with hospitals. I don't remember the questions I was asked, but I apparently drove this young woman to excuse herself from my case: "I'm in over my head, I don't know what's going on."

At some point after that I must have been taken back to my ER cubicle, where Laura tells me that nurses asked me several times for a urine sample. My response to that request was always, "I'm sorry, but I really can't go to the bathroom right now."

Finally, I was given a large glass of water to drink, and then a nurse said—encouragingly or admonishingly? I'll never know—"After you drink all that you'll be able to go."

Apparently when I went to the bathroom and once again wasn't able to produce a sample, the nurse blanched and ran to find the ER doctor. My gallbladder was empty; I believe all my organs were shutting down. The doctor must have become concerned, because he agreed to give me a CT scan, something that my therapist and Laura had been arguing for from the minute they'd stepped foot into that hospital.

I have a memory of being on my back and of something closing over my head and face. Again, my emotions were muted, and I didn't feel scared as much as annoyed by the great tediousness of it all. I'd waited almost three hours for something that should have been done right away. They'd wasted my time, and the time I had to waste was so little that it could be measured in hours and minutes. But I also felt an infinite patience that prevented me from getting angry, and a consistent distance that turned the situation into a comedy.

I remember being with my therapist and Laura in my curtain-protected cubicle waiting for the results. Because I'd spent that summer accepting my death and saying good-bye to the world, I wasn't afraid, and I actually felt compassion for the man who ran into my cubicle while putting on a white doctor's jacket over a pink button-down shirt. I'll never forget the expression of regret and shame on his face. I can't say what he looked like with any confidence, but I took away the impression of a man in his early forties who had curly, receding brown hair. His cheeks were certainly flushed. Out of breath, he must have run from the lab room where he'd read the slides and sprinted to where I was.

From his chair—I was sitting on the bed and still in my clothes, and I had a feeling of looking down on him—he told me that I had a large anaplastic oligodendroglioma that was causing bleeding, that they'd called an ambulance to take me to Evanston Hospital, where I'd be operated on as soon as possible.

Later on, Laura told me that the doctors at Evanston Hospital said that someone with a tumor as large as mine shouldn't have been able to walk or talk. I did both. It wasn't apparent that I was in a semiconscious state, that I was responding to stimuli but not registering anything in my memory, except for the most dramatic moments, which I take to be the paramedics' argument over directions, and the ER doctor rushing into my cubicle with bad news, along with three other moments I'll describe now.

One is very brief. Having been told I'd soon be operated on, I texted Jason to let him know I wouldn't be home. I didn't want him to become concerned by my absence that evening. Here is the text I sent, once again finding humor where others didn't see it: *I won't be home tonight: getting my head cut open.*

Much later, Jason told me that he was at a bar when he read my text and that his shock registered immediately on his face; he thought I was about to be killed. The friend he was with asked what had happened, had someone died?

Two is longer: My MRI at Evanston Hospital. They must have told me to remain perfectly still, simple protocol, but I didn't retain those directions, and I remember "waking up" to a metallic voice within the MRI machine telling me that I was moving too much. I'd been completely unaware of any movement, but the technician's voice, in waking me, helped me focus on keeping still. The loud, clattering noises that came in dozens of variations and without any foreseeable pattern were unbearable. I fought my desperate need to get out. I remember being afraid that people would be angry with me for moving so much, but instead the three women who helped me out of the machine—were there really three?—were very kind.

The last and third moment I remember is one in which I'm standing in the middle of a large group of medical staff, which I list here in what I believe to be hospital hierarchy: surgeons, doctors, interns, nurses, technicians. This hierarchy was expressed by the color of their jackets, the quality of their watches and jewelry. They must have asked me many questions, but I remember only an intern who said, "A history of depression and anxiety, yes." More than his voice, I remember his apologetic glance, his understanding kindness. I'd told them about all my griefs and pains? And then, still in that room that might have been ICU, a moment of complete silence similar to the silence near the egret-full tree; in this case, the soul of everyone in the room became visible to me.

Words that I've always loved so much, language set in moving meter and rhyme schemes that take years to become fluent in, language in your most expressive rawness, coming from the heart and describing all that's worst and best within us, passing through anger and fear to end in pure joy, help me put the most important moment of my life into a paragraph that will communicate in a way that's compelling and profound. Don't let me be pompous, don't let me sound like a Holy Roller, don't let me be trite. Let me arrange my sentences in a way that won't make me seem crazy. I was called a psych case once when I wasn't. At least for this short while, make me eloquent.

Human beings in white, dark-blue, and light-blue jackets, some holding clipboards, all looking at me with huge, caring eyes, I saw each person's soul extend upwards from their body, transparent, unwavering, an exact copy of the physical selves, or rather, the physical was an exact copy of the ethereal, and the ethereal held me up, formed a ring around me, transmitting a love so powerful that I knew that I'd live. All residual fear left me, and I gave myself over to faith.

The world is beautiful, every living creature in it is precious, we are miracles spun along through space and simultaneously fixed within each moment, and this is our great tragedy and gift.

Laura tells me that when I lay down on a stretcher so that I could be wheeled away for the night—it was one o'clock in the morning and they'd operate a few hours from then—my last words to her were, "Please don't worry about me because I'm fine with either way this surgery goes."

And I don't remember saying that, but I know it's true.

On the first day of fall in 2014, I almost died, just as my inner voice had prophesied I'd die. For reasons I don't know, I was pulled back from the brink, brought back to life. Given warnings I didn't take, I was nevertheless treated with compassion and even given the greatest gift possible; that is, to know what it's like to be reborn into this beautiful, heartbreaking world. ■

RUMORS OF EMPTY SPACES
Beverly Burch

Holes in the sky now, gaps in the ozone.
      And down the street a sinkhole caved in
as if purely exhausted. Kids ready to leap in.
          I had to use that adrenalined word: *Danger!*

When I use a spade to open
      my plot of earth, I remedy it with tea roses and maidenhair.

O holy frightening holes. Their meaning wholly
      what I was raised on. Holes in his hands and feet.
Cruelty and confusion.

      A hole here and there to be expected:
mind the gap, fill 'er up please. But absence, piercing vacancy.
      In the kitchen I arrange plums, peaches in a bowl,
each fruit holding its own pit.

Pocket of air, cleft in the rock.
      O round sequence of mystery, circular relic, sacred cenote.
I want to fill you up, little chink in the heart.

SINKHOLE
Toni Graham

Slater sat planted in the green leather armchair, watching the mole channel. That and drinking Anchor Steam in his white terry robe were his primary away-from-work activities since his wife took a hike.

It was a curious thing, really, the mole-channel phenomenon. The cable channel was one that featured true-crime stories around the clock, each more vicious and compelling than the last. He spent hours watching reenactments of people being stabbed in the eye by ice picks, run over by trucks, sexually assaulted and then set on fire with kerosene, skewered in the groin with katanas. Nothing could be gained from watching these programs, other than the slight distraction and moderate numbness provoked by immersion in horror.

But what held Slater's attention more than the savagery of the crimes depicted was the mole factor. Actors and actresses reenacted the crimes, playing both the felons and the victims. Slater envisioned all these striving actors going to auditions over and over again, eager to bag a slot on a crime show rather than still another margarine commercial, or—much worse—myriad shifts as a server at Chili's in West Hollywood or Hooters of Burbank. Surely, the producers and casting agents had a nonillion wannabe actors prostrating themselves at their office doors. So why did this true-crime channel utilize only actors and actresses with unsightly moles on their faces and necks? Aside from their moles, the actors were all exceedingly attractive. Now, in high-def, a man with a small mole on his neck choked out a woman with a dark dot on one of her breasts. Enough of this; he switched off the set and finished his Anchor in the dark.

* * *

Dog love was the only love that was constant; Slater had discovered that long ago. Who knew that human love that had endured for more than thirty years could disappear like a bad smell doused with Febreze? Beth was not coming back. She had taken their springer spaniel, Solomon, with her when she moved out. Slater did not want another springer; Solomon's hair had too easily clogged up the Roomba vacuum—thank god she had not taken that, too. But being alone with beer and TV, or scrutinizing student projects in the evenings after he came home from campus, left him feeling hollow. He had even found himself trying to lure the neighbor's grey tabby into the yard, just so he could pet something. He logged on to his laptop and searched *AKC-registered dogs, Hope Springs, Oklahoma, area*. Some beagle pups were offered for sale in Guthrie. A short-haired dog, just what he needed. Before he called the number posted with the ad, he Googled beagles.

The Beagle: *The Beagle was originally bred solely for the hurt,* began the entry. He could hardly believe what he saw. To think that he would search randomly for a purebred dog and that beagles would be for sale not all that far from Hope Springs, and that the beagle was bred to aid the hurt, perhaps as the Saint Bernard was bred for rescue work. Maybe beagles served as therapy dogs for injured people. Well, that's me—I'm the hurt, he thought. But when he read the rest of the blurb, he realized he had misconstrued what the entry actually said. It was not bred "for the hurt," but "for the hunt."

He scrounged in the magazine basket and pulled out yesterday's *Hope Springs Clarion*, checked to see if there were any beagles for sale in Hope Springs itself. No go, nothing but a pit bull and a cockapoo. But on the same page as the classifieds was a box ad for a business called Li'l Stinkers. Though he read the *Clarion* nearly daily, he had never before seen this advertisement. "Let us take care of that extra work and undesirable mess!" exhorted the ad. Beneath the words "Satisfaction guaranteed" was a bulleted list: Dog walking, affordable pricing, waste services. Waste services! Good Lord, you could hire someone to clean up dog shit? I'm in, he decided, and called the breeder in Guthrie to arrange to see the puppies for sale.

* * *

An old Hollywood movie had been reprised on TV one summer when Slater was a kid, a black-and-white cornball called *The Mystery Squadron*. What he most vividly recalled was the villain: the Black Ace. The good guys in the movie—perhaps the Army Corps of Engineers?—were building a dam in New Mexico, but an evil squad of flyers known as the Mystery Squadron, led by the dashingly sinister Black Ace, kept attempting to destroy the bridge. Maybe there had always been something a bit off-kilter about the Slater family psychology—Slater's sister, when watching Disney's *Snow White*, had seemed mesmerized by the evil queen, uninterested in the bland heroine. After they returned from the theater matinee, Slater's sister had gone to work with scissors, cardboard, and a length of black cloth from his mother's rag bag and had begun constructing a tall collar of the sort the evil queen wore. "Mirror, mirror, on the wall," he heard his sister whisper in an incantatory tone.

When Slater saw the Black Ace on the TV screen, he felt a stirring in his chest. The bridge-engineer guys were steadfast, admirable doers of good, but the Black Ace was the one with panache. Taking a cue from his sister, Slater had borrowed his mother's shower cap and a pair of his father's Ray-Bans and fashioned a quasi flying helmet of a bygone style, the sort that resembled old-fashioned leather football helmets. Still, the derring-do of the Black Ace did not mean that the young Slater had not felt the bejesus scared out of him when he viewed scenes with the Ace at the helm of his plane, a menacing glower twisting his mouth, diving treacherously toward the dam.

One weekend later that same summer, Slater and three guy pals from the block went exploring an undeveloped ravine behind their housing tract. Finding a secret cave was like manna from heaven. Yes, it was small, uncomfortably seating four, but a cave nonetheless. Slater wore his makeshift flying helmet, the Ray-Bans rendering the cave even darker than it actually was. After his pupils adjusted to the dark, he saw it: a leathery, goblinish face emerging in bas-relief from the wall of the cave. If that were not terrifying enough, the thing wore a jaunty green hat with a feather in the band. Inexplicably, Slater found himself shouting, "The Black Ace!" and hauling ass out of the cave. The others ran behind him as they all hoofed it on shank's mare back to the block where they lived, yelling, "Help!" and calling for their parents.

When Slater and his pals ran to their parents after the sighting in the cave, shouting, "The Black Ace! We saw the Black Ace!" he had been surprised by how quickly the fathers all sprang to action. What ensued resembled a scene from a George Romero film: the entire male population of the neighborhood took up shovels, sledgehammers, and pickaxes and began running grimly toward the area where the cave was located. Were it nighttime, they might have hefted torches, or at least Maglites. These days, many of them would undoubtedly have guns. When the dads reached the cave, stooped and peered in, they saw nothing.

It was right there, Slater insisted, pointing, but the dads glanced away from him and from the cave. One father said, "It must have been a gopher," and started the walk home, followed nearly immediately by the rest of the dads. Many years passed before Slater understood the parents' initial reaction: the words "the black ace" to them suggested that there was a person of color lurking down in the ravine, someone who could not have been living in the neighborhood at that time, when there was still de facto segregation. No Jim Crow in New York; rather, the realtors, banks, and property owners had a pact: We lend to, buy from, and sell to whites only.

Gophers don't wear hats, Slater argued, not considering until years later that there had been no hat, had been no visage. The Black Ace had been a figment, the first of many airy nothings he had conjured through the years, duping himself by way of his own imagination. There were times, more of them recently, when Slater felt his entire life may have been such a construct, his actual self a phantom.

* * *

The plane landed midday in Dallas after the short flight from Oklahoma City. Slater was to give a talk at UT Dallas that evening, invited by the professor who taught the Modern Architecture course; Slater had met the guy at an AIA convention a couple of years ago and they had stayed in touch. The odd thing was that though Slater had been in the DFW airport many times, as well as Love Field, somehow he had never walked out of either of those airports, but had only transferred to other flights. He had been living in Oklahoma for eight years since accepting the professorship in Hope Springs, but somehow had never set foot on Texas soil, except when segueing from one flight to the next. He still recalled the first time he set foot in the DFW airport and stopped in one of the bars in the terminal for a beer. The place had been packed with loud-voiced, red-faced males wearing cowboy hats, as if he had stumbled into a fetish bar in the Castro.

As he plucked his carry-on bag from the overhead bin, Slater weighed his options. Should he take a taxi straight to his hotel and catch a nap before his evening lecture, or should he grab a bite to eat here in the terminal, first, or did he have enough time to see a bit of Dallas proper before lunch or checking into the Hyatt? He went out the door to the ground transportation area and climbed into the first available taxi. On impulse, he asked the cabbie, "How far is it from the Hyatt Regency to Dealey Plaza?"

"Not even a mile," the cabbie said in accented English that could be anything—Iranian? Pakistani? "Where you headed?" The driver looked into the rearview mirror at Slater, waiting.

Slater told him: Dealey, then hotel. The taxi smelled oddly of something like tomato soup, and Slater sniffed the air as discreetly as possible. He wondered if the cabbie might have body odor but stifled the thought, worrying the notion might suggest some repressed racism on his own part. The sky beyond the taxi was sunny and a clear, vivid blue, just as the day had been on 9/11 in NYC, and for that matter, in Dallas on that day in '63.

Slater was no different from anyone else; he had seen photos and films of Dealey Plaza ever since he was nine years old and Kennedy had his head blown apart there, and more recently he had seen the entire Zapruder film myriad times. But, being now in Dallas, a forceful desire to be on-site had overtaken him. If he were instead lecturing at the Austin campus, he knew he would want to see the tower from which Charles Whitman had gunned down more than forty people, killing more than a dozen of them. While in downtown Dallas for perhaps the only time, he felt compelled to set eyes on Dealey Plaza. He knew the Zapruder film could not carry the gravitas of being in Dallas and looking directly at the building that had housed the Texas School Book Depository.

Sure, it was the most common cliché in American culture—one that bored or amused Slater's students, born so long after the fact: Everyone remembered exactly where they were that Friday when Kennedy was blown away in Dallas, when Jackie's pink suit was splattered with blood and brain matter. Everyone. In Slater's case, it was 1:30 p.m. New York time when Oswald took his shot, and Slater was sitting in a little desk at PS 61 watching Mrs. Levine chalk long-division problems onto the blackboard, when the classroom door flew open and the male teacher from the classroom next door strode into the room with an unhinged look on his face. Without prelude, the man said to Mrs. Levine—to everyone in the room—"Kennedy's a dead duck."

That pronouncement had come back to Slater decades later, when he encountered his father lying in bed pale and deceased. After the paramedics and the cops, as well as his father's body, had left the premises, Slater telephoned his sister, not really knowing how he would tell her. And, as if via time's own arrow, the words shot from Slater's mouth: "Poppy's a dead duck."

"There it is!" he said, his gaze landing on what he recognized as the sixth-floor window from which Oswald had shot his way into history.

"County offices, now," the driver said. "You wanna go sixth-floor museum?"

Slater declined, saying he did not have enough time. But then he saw the grassy knoll; it was still there. He was astonished that the mound had remained grassy, and that it had not been built upon or in some other manner obliterated.

The driver pulled over to a space directly across from the knoll, and Slater opened the window and raised his iPhone. He had expected there would be a monument or marker denoting the location of the assassination, but Dallas seemed to be trying to keep a low profile on this particular historical site. But someone was always out to make a buck, and there he was: a man holding a crudely hand-lettered cardboard sign—Grassy Knoll! An arrow drawn on the sign pointed in the direction of the mound. Slater could not determine what the man was selling. Some sort of tour, maybe?

Just as he raised his phone to capture the site, a couple stepped into frame. The man smiled broadly, giddy as a goose, and his female companion held her hand to his head, thumb and forefinger forming a gun. The pretend shooter looked directly at the taxi where Slater sat and crooked her finger, pretending to shoot her clearly unsuspecting boyfriend in the head. Slater's camera caught the precise moment the girl mouthed, "Bang."

I feel ya, buddy, Slater thought. The last time he had seen Beth, when she picked up her furniture in a Ryder truck, her transformation had been no less mystifying than Patty Hearst's transition from a Hillsborough coed to a machine-gun-toting revolutionary. Beth had driven the rental truck herself, wearing a pair of overalls—overalls!—and a porkpie hat. At first, he had not recognized her at all—had assumed she was a man, or maybe a nice, husky lesbian truck driver.

Things seemed to have shifted for Slater; these days, things slipped in and out of their true shapes. When he was a kid, he had always thought people had two faces: one, the first time you looked at them, and the second when you looked at them closely and studied their features. In school, he had spent a great deal of time staring at the teacher and at other kids, watching the first face transform into the second face, and back again, like a blinking neon sign switching from "Bar" to a martini glass, and returning to "Bar," flashing back and forth. A moment ago, the grassy knoll looked like a shocking bit of history recalled; right now, it looked like a piece of lawn, the backdrop for a mock shooting, a cheap tableau.

* * *

The weekend after he returned from Dallas, as Slater was reading the lunch menu at his usual table in Siesta Sancho's, a couple entered the restaurant. The male was a dwarf—little person, Slater mentally corrected himself—who held the door for his female companion, a woman of normal stature. Slater placed the menu facedown on the table and swept his gaze around the restaurant. He was the only person who would be eating alone. He could not keep the thought from coming to him: Even mini-men have mates. He was only newly single and had no concept of how to meet women, his courting days decades behind him. He had checked out one of those online dating services, but had been crestfallen by the profusion of what seemed to be shopworn divorcees or morbidly obese women. If he were more candid, he did not desire a woman his own age, but he was fully aware he was no longer attractive to women younger than he. An older guy with a bald spot like a yarmulke, hair on his back, and the large ears of older folks, he was not exactly desirable. Still, it galled him to note everywhere he went that he was nearly always the only person who was by himself. Not only did little people dine with tall women, but when shopping in Walmart he had seen toothless men shopping with nice-looking women sporting shining blonde hair and gleaming teeth; he often saw grizzled guys about town, bald, limping and wearing faded, stretched-out T-shirts, arm in arm with comely female companions. The universe seemed to have a grudge against Slater. There was an ominous possibility that the last time he would ever have sex was the final time he and Beth had cranked out a ho-hum marital lay, Slater not realizing Beth was soon to be out the door. The waitress approached his table, chirping, "Would you like some iced tea?"

Do I look like an Oklahoma iced-tea swiller to you? was what he felt like saying, but instead he said, "I never drink iced tea before five. I'll have a Dos Equis." The girl gave him a puzzled look. Slater added, "And a Sombrero Burger with queso, please." The server flashed her management-mandated smile and moseyed off.

But, out of nowhere, Slater felt an unfamiliar and disagreeable sensation at waist level. An itching, tingling feeling raked at his midsection. He gave in to the impulse to scratch furiously at his waistline. Shit, the itching immediately morphed into pain. He sat morosely, watching the dwarf order dinner for his lady and himself, having donned a pair of harlequin-frame eyeglasses in order to read the menu.

Suddenly Slater understood: The unpleasant sensation at his waistline must have something to do with the liposuction he had secretly submitted to last year in Santa Monica. He was being punished for one of his deadly sins, vanity.

* * *

Slater and his beagle pup, Darwin, were lying on the bed, watching *Karma's a B*tch!* on the mole channel and sharing a beer. The dog's share amounted to licking a sip from Slater's fingertips when offered. He kept

Darwin's sips to a minimum, not wishing to resemble the sort of animal abusers who got their dogs and cats drunk, or stoned on cannabis. Now Slater knew the real reason for his unhappiness. It was not just that his wife had left him for no good reason; not because he was slouching toward his demise; not because the university where he taught was in Oklahoma; not because he was tired of whining or pushy grad students and sick to death of his colleagues in the department; not even because he was balding and paunchy and bore not a scintilla of resemblance to the man he had been in his youth. No: His gloom could be attributed to the fact that he did not have type 2 diabetes rather than painful sores. His doctor had diagnosed his shingles just this afternoon, reminding Slater he had declined the immunization recommended to him a couple of years before.

Nearly all the television commercials today hawked "medications." Every couple of minutes, someone pitched prescription meds one should "ask your doctor about." Remedies were offered for any ailment you could think of: acid reflux, overactive bladder, atrial fibrillation, weight gain, hair loss, itchy genitalia—you name it, some pharmaceutical company could make it go away. But for the most positive presentation of diseased people in treatment, one had to examine the ads for type 2 diabetes meds. In these advertisements, portly people frolicked and cavorted in euphoric groups. They tap-danced; they participated in water sports of all stripes: waterskiing, boating, swimming. They picnicked; they bowled; they held coffee klatches, grinning in diners. During all these activities, they not only smiled furiously, but laughed continuously, one long Möbius strip of hilarity.

Seems he would be better off being one of these manic tubbies than being the guy who got stuck with shingles. People in shingles commercials did not romp, rollick, and gambol. No, the shingles ads showed a scowling Terry Bradshaw, sharing with viewers the hell he had gone through with shingles. "It was like being blindsided by a linebacker—*boom:* I didn't see it coming. You don't want to be tackled by shingles," Bradshaw advised. He grimaced as he described the condition: "Blisters—red, *ugly* stuff. Lots of 'em."

Well, that was what Slater had around his midsection, primarily on his right side, like a wrestler's belt that had been cut in half. When Slater was a kid, his mother had often offered didactic truisms to her offspring. One of these ditties, aimed at Slater when he was about fourteen, was, "Never sell your individuality for a mess of pottage." He had asked what pottage was, but his mother had not responded. He had to again wonder if messing with Mother Nature was what had brought him to his current state of blistered misery. If he had simply accepted the spare tire that had formed around his middle, rather than having liposuction, maybe he would not have this painful belt of shame. Probably he had been sucked in by advertisements focusing on abs and six-packs and had lost his individuality. Hell, he did not even obtain a mess of pottage, only a less flabby midsection and now, in the very same area of his torso, throbbing, oozing shingles. Sometimes, Mom had gone holy on him when cautioning him about vanity. When he was about sixteen and asked to have his nose bobbed, she had said piously, "The book of Kohelet said, 'Consider the work of God: for who can make straight that which He hath made crooked?'"

After another commercial, an ad for an erectile-dysfunction medication, featuring middle-aged men riding Harleys or driving vintage convertibles or listening to blues music as they lay in hammocks with long-haired, young-looking women, he switched the channel to CNN news. A stunned, bedraggled-looking man spoke into a reporter's microphone, pointing to some houses behind them. "Everything was gone," the man said. "My brother's bed was gone, my brother's dresser, my brother's TV. My brother was gone."

Slater did not know what the reference was to, but the order of the guy's list was perhaps askew—seemed to him "my brother was gone" ought to precede the absence of the bed, dresser, and TV. He thought of that teen girl who was kidnapped by a family friend after he murdered her parents. When she was interviewed a few days after being released, some reporter said, "Tell us, what have you *lost* because of this man?" She responded without hesitation, "My phone, my iPod, some money. And my family."

"The ground just swallowed him up," the reporter stated in a grim tone. The camera fixed on a shot of a massive sinkhole, rimmed by rubble and with a perimeter of wide yellow tape reading Police Line Do Not Cross. My God—it seemed that in Florida a sleeping man's bedroom had been sucked down by a sinkhole and taken into nothingness. The unfortunate soul was slumbering in his own bed when out of nowhere a sinkhole had opened under his house and pulled him into a vortex, furniture and all. The man's brother, from the living room, heard the man in bed scream, but when he ran to the bedroom, all he could see was a huge hole in the floor, with the corner of a mattress sticking out. His brother was lost, whirled away like Dorothy in the tornado, but he wasn't going to end up in Oz.

Slater began to imagine himself coming to such an end. He looked around the bedroom, envisioning everything being sucked away. The mahogany bureau Beth had bought in a junk store and refinished; the antique steamer trunk where extra blankets were stored; their stationary bicycle, dusty from lack of use; the bedside table with the bottle of Anchor Steam and an old issue of *Architectural Record*. Even the quilt on the bed, made by his Grandma Slater. All of it, along with Slater and Darwin, whooshed into nothingness, eddied into the netherworld, ceasing to exist. Beth, it seemed, had already been swirled into that gulf, an event as unforeseen by Slater as the sinkhole by the poor devil who had disappeared from his bedroom.

The doomed man had been only thirty-seven years old, the prime of life. Certainly when the fellow slipped into bed that night, he had no earthly idea that he would soon lose his corporeal being, would be whirlpooled into darkness forever. Now that Slater was pushing sixty, he had begun to realize that he could drop dead any moment, that any day in his life could be his last. He hoped it would not be today, a day when he was tired and bitter, his midsection burning with the pain of shingles, alone save for a beagle—a companion he had bought and paid for. No one knew when their number would be pulled—knowledge of the end was as elusive as a yeti. He agreed with something by Kamel Daoud he had read: "No one is granted a final day, only an accidental interruption of life."

* * *

Slater was walking Darwin, who stubbornly pulled on the leash. They were only a few classes into their obedience-training sessions, so there was hope the pup might shape up soon. But suddenly Darwin began baying—Slater had been unaware before purchasing the puppy that, rather than barking, beagles bayed like bloodhounds. But now the reason for the dog's straining against the leash and baying became clear. In front of a church, snaked down the block and around the corner, stood a line of people with animals, the first in line being a schnauzer with an older man, both wearing orange sweaters. There were dogs of all sizes and breeds on leash with their owners; cats snugged in wicker baskets; children holding fishbowls with goldfish in them; a bespectacled lad with a turtle in a cardboard box. In gilt on the church's façade were a crucifix and the words "Saint Boniface."

"Heel, Darwin!" Slater could come to no sensible conclusion about the reason for all the animals lined up in front of a church. Wasn't Saint Boniface Catholic or Episcopal or something? In Hope Springs, anything other than a Baptist church—or worse—was rare in any case. When he and Beth had gone to temple during the High Holy Days, they'd had to drive to Tulsa to do so. He guessed he had never given much thought to whether there were any Catholic churches in town. On Sundays after church, the fundamentalist churchgoers flooded into the town's restaurants for lunch, guzzling gallons of the iced tea they favored. Many of Slater's undergraduates held part-time jobs as waitstaff, and they complained to him that they dreaded Sundays, because the churchies left no tips. Yeah, what would Jesus do? Maybe tithing was the only coughing up of do-re-mi they were willing to do.

Darwin was sniffing the rectum of an Irish setter accompanied by an equally red-haired woman. "What's up with all the animals?" Slater asked the redhead.

She turned to him, first glancing down at Darwin and smiling, and said, "It's the Blessing of the Pets. They do it every October."

What the—? Slater said only, "Oh," and turned to walk off, but the redhead said, "What's your dog's name?"

"Darwin," he said. "You know, the *Beagle,* Charles Darwin's ship." He saw that she was younger than he, but wondered if she could possibly be flirting with him.

"I got my name in a peripheral way like that," she said. "I'm Irish, and my parents named me Joyce, after James Joyce." She pointed to her dog. "She's named Molly, upholding the tradition."

Slater had never read Joyce, but he nodded as if he understood. He felt himself suddenly smiling like an aging matinee idol and made a concerted effort to look attentive, rather than lecherous.

"I don't think I've seen you at Saint Boni's before," Joyce said, stooping to pet Darwin, affording Slater a glimpse of cleavage.

"I'm Jewish," he said, taking a step backward and tugging at Darwin's leash. Jesus—she wasn't going to have a go at trying to proselytize him, was she? Or ask for his religious credentials—a holy card, or whatever. "I'm not particularly observant," he added.

"No worries," she said. "The blessing of the pets is entirely ecumenical—there are even some women in hijabs a bit further back in line. Here," she said, gesturing to where she and her setter stood. "You can bring Darwin in with Molly and me."

Slater began to say, I don't think Darwin needs blessing, whatever that is, but Joyce's face was so artless, her smile so welcoming, and Darwin was showing every sign of having a crush on her dog, Molly. The sun turned both Joyce's and Molly's hair to a burnished copper and Slater felt something shift inside him. "I'm Dave," he said, "David Slater." He held his hand out to shake hers, and the contact sent a thrum of electricity through his hand, as if Joyce palmed a joke handshake buzzer.

"*Enchantée*," she said in a mock tony voice and laughed. He was somehow letting this happen: Darwin was about to be blessed, solely because something was going on with Slater's loins. He and Darwin and Joyce and Molly were crossing the threshold of the church together. Seemed he was willing to follow "the scent of a woman" even into a Catholic church. Maybe he was no different from the beagle: "bred for the hunt."

Two priests in long white dresses like the one the pope wore stood in front of an altar, both holding bowls of what he assumed was water, dipping into the receptacles like dowagers at a dinner party dunking into finger bowls, and then touching the foreheads of the pets. He wondered how they would handle the goldfish situation. One of the frocked men chanted, *Lord, grant that these animals may serve our needs and that Your bounty in the resources of this life may move us to seek more confidently the goal of eternal life. We ask this through Christ our Lord.*

It seemed to Slater that everyone in the chapel, with the exception of himself, responded in unison, "Amen." He stared at the crimson carpet on the floor, clenching every muscle in his body and pretending he were anywhere else. He had to hope there really was no afterlife. If his father could see him inside Saint Boniface for a "blessing," Isaac would straightaway rocket from his grave at Mount Hebron and throttle him with his cold, dead hands.

What his father never knew was that Slater had ventured beyond the temple on multiple occasions, though never with serious intent. He had been to Mass with a former girlfriend—embarrassing her when he refused to kneel; had attended the baptism of the infant son of his Methodist former roommate; had even been to some Holy Roller sort of service once with a friend in school when the guy was writing a paper for his world religions course. But the foray into the world of gentiles' worshipping that had surprised and pleased him occurred when he was in San Francisco visiting a musician friend, who took him to a church in which the congregation worshipped John Coltrane. The service had begun with the deep resonance of a gong, and the musicians commenced playing the opening of *A Love Supreme*. The service might have been more like a jam session than a religious convocation, but nonetheless the dignity of the music had invoked an unanticipated feeling of reverence in Slater. The pastor, himself, had played a fierce tenor, and the libretto was handled by a female choir with nearly ethereal pitch. Slater could not remember any other instance when he had felt drawn into, rather than repelled by, what could be called worship. He had, for a moment, sensed transcendence.

If attending a Saint Coltrane church had not been odd enough, here he was with a strange woman and both their dogs, in line to be blessed by a priest. What he remembered about his unfortunate experience at a Catholic Mass was how quiet the church had been. When he had gone to temple as a child, congregants had chatted among themselves in a conversational tone before the prayers began. Before Mass, however, his girlfriend had shushed him sharply when he spoke to her in church. When he looked around the chapel, he saw that people either had their heads bowed with eyes closed, or leaned close to a companion, whispering. Now in Saint Boniface, there was no hushed silence. Parakeets gabbled, dogs barked repeatedly, children laughed, adults called out, "Down, Thor!" and "Sit, Zoe!" Cages and boxes rattled and rasped.

Joyce and Molly stood directly ahead of him in line, so he watched what Joyce did, so he could get on board. She told the priest Molly's name, and the priest sprinkled water on the setter, saying a few words Slater could not quite hear. Presently, he and Darwin were standing in front of the clergyman and Slater said, "Darwin," hoping the priest would not assume he was baiting him. The priest did not flinch, but responded, "Darwin, may you be blessed in the name of the Father, and of the Son, and of the Holy Spirit. May you and your caretaker enjoy life together and find joy with the God who created you." Slater certainly was not going to say amen, and he repressed the impulse to say thank you, simply nodded and moved on, followed directly by a squawking macaw in a brass cage. He felt a heat in his throat he could not explain to himself; probably it was only that pets had always carried an emotional charge for Slater.

As they had filed back outside into the sunlight, the Irish setter yanked sharply on its leash, and Joyce steadied herself by putting one hand on Slater's shoulder. He noticed she had a piercing near her left eyebrow, a tiny gemstone, absinthe green. The stone glittered in the sunlight, winking like a signal light, beckoning.

When he had visited the Saint John Coltrane church, the service had taken place on a special day: Coltrane's birthday was being celebrated. Along with the regular clergyman, who played a really fine sax, was a guest celebrant, a very tall, slender man with extremely dark skin, calling to mind a black El Greco. He wore a long dress like the priest in St. Boniface, but it was bright red, startling against his skin. On his head was a red skullcap, giving the man the appearance of a cardinal in a Fellini film. The cardinal guy seemed to have been serving as a euphonic adjunct to the pastor, chanting sacred musical prayer as a cantor would do in a synagogue. The red-gowned cantor's song in a deep baritone had been curiously uplifting.

As he and Darwin walked along with Joyce and her dog, maybe he was dizzy from incense or muddled by an allergy to parrot feathers. But he had the sudden notion: What if the man who was sucked into the sinkhole in Florida could be drawn along as if through a wormhole and end up in the same place as John Coltrane? Maybe Poppy would be there, too, and Mom, along with their long-dead family Airedale, Scrapper. Possibly everyone did not have to go to hell in a handbasket, or to molder in their graves at Mount Hebron or elsewhere, rotting into nothing—from nothing, to nothing, as he had always believed.

While the Coltrane pastor played a heart-twisting rendition of "Abide with Me," the red cantor sang along: *Shine through the gloom and point me to the skies.* He raised his very long arms toward the high ceiling, the horns wailing, his elegant elongated fingers pointing upward, singing, "Reach, reach to the Highest! Reach up."

Thinking of Coltrane seemed to have given Slater an earworm; he could hear his favorite Saint John in his head as if over a public-address system: Coltrane's cover of Miles Davis's "So What." *Duh, duht* played in his head, *duh, duht.* His midsection stung like a viper's bite, but the music and the red hair of Joyce and her setter were like a salve. He sang along internally with the earworm: *Yes, they both left the stage, / clean out of sight . . . So what?* ■

MEDITATION BESIDE
STEPHENS LAKE
Andrew Mulvania
for B.S.

We were sitting on a slightly uncomfortable metal bench
beside the semi-urban pastoral beauty of Stephens Lake
in Columbia, Missouri, talking about our lives, hopes, dreams—
how impossible and unworkable it all seemed—
what with your new, high-pressure tech job in St. Louis
and the long, exhausting commute; the continued need
for me to remain rooted to this spot
because of my 9 ½ year old son and old pull
of family commitments;
your equal and opposite pull—
Newton's Fourth, Unrecorded Law of Doomed and
        Seemingly Hopeless Relationships?—
toward travel and Ecuador in five months,
Barcelona always looming somewhere out there in the future,
and then…who knew where;
and me, like Dmitri Dmitrich Gurov in Chekhov's "The Lady with
        the Little Dog,"
when he finally realizes how much he loves Anna—
"this life, still so warm and beautiful," the shoulders on which he lays
        his hands
which *"were warm and trembled"*—and feels compassion for her
only now, after all the other women,
and only now that his hair was turning gray (as he suddenly notices
in the mirror of the sordid hotel room), clutching his head
and saying, "How? How?"—how could it possibly work out
between them?

Meanwhile, someone was dying, possibly, or might soon
in the Flight For Life helicopter
making its way toward the helipad on the roof of Boone Hospital
where my sister and brother-in-law had taken me first
when they thought I was suicidal and "going crazy," again
(both of which I was); just in front of us,

two men were swimming laps
in the area of the lake so designated for such activity,
just as I used to do so often in the pool at W&J
during the noon-hour free swim
back in that old life when I was a tenured professor
and not the sad adjunct I've become,
adrift in the wilderness of the chronically underpaid
and trying desperately to retool and reassemble
the pieces of my life
for another push, a freshly-mounted campaign
only now in middle age, now that *"his head was beginning to turn gray";*
children were playing in the "Spraygrounds" across the lake
that smelled faintly (and pleasantly, I thought, as we passed)
of chlorine in the evening air; a group
of sorority girls were doing team-building exercises
or having a bonding experience together
in the grass beside the walking path; joggers jogging;
lovers holding hands as they strolled, no space or separation
between them; husbands and wives long-together
and "out-of-shape"; a Muslim family having a picnic
on the grass; a girl, or "lady," walking her "not-so-little" dog
(" 'How? How?' he asked, clutching his head. 'How?'"):
Would it work out, or would I be sitting on this same bench, someday,
alone, thinking back to "How it was when I had you"?

A POOR TRADE
Richard Huffman

The wind was cold and came off the sea and up through the valley to her place where she waited for the dog. It had been over a week, and she decided he might be gone for good this time. He was always reckless and she knew it might get him into a mess someday. She blocked the waning sun with the palm of her hand over her brow and looked down the worn trail he always used. "Damned fool dog," she said, her heart too aggrieved to let on it was so.

After a time she walked back into the darkening cabin and lit a kerosene lamp. There was a sound then from outside, but there were always sounds there in the foothills where she lived alone but for the dog. She went outside—a vague hope quickly tamped down when there was nothing but cowbirds at the scarecrow. The straw under his hat a nesting material. "Shoo! Go on. Leave him alone." She waved her arms and watched the dull-colored birds fly off.

The scarecrow and the dog were her only companions but for a straggler once in a while that she treated as well as she could. It was usually a hunter. The visitors seemed to think she should be gratified that they had taken time to stop in and be friendly to an old woman with sallow skin caving against bone and a faint gray moustache sprouted beneath a beaky nose.

"Keep an eye out for the dog," she always admonished, even if Dusty was there, in the cabin on his rug.

"I wouldn't mistake a dog for a deer," one said, affronted anyone might think he would.

"Didn't say you would. Someone that might though—I got that thirty-aught hanging on those pegs over there. Got a good scope. Hit a pie plate at a hundred yards."

The hunter had scoffed at that and stood and said she had better watch who she was threatening.

Friendliness was a trait God had left wanting in her. She was not of a philosophy and found conversation a tight-knotted rope difficult to loosen. "Not a threat," she said.

It was usually a "well then . . ." from the visitor and a quick departure. She was relieved and sad when she was alone again. "Nothing I can do about it," she would say to the dog and scratch his ears and let him lay his big tawny head in her lap while she read something from the Bible, telling the dog, "What a load of hogwash." Even so—being an unbeliever—she was taken by the stories.

* * *

It was two weeks and a day after he went missing that the dog was brought in. The boy seemed too young to be out hunting on his own, but there he was, shamefaced, with the dog slung across his shoulders, its legs draped over his camouflaged chest, held together in one of the boy's hands. His rifle in the other hand, held loosely at his side.

"Someone down below said they thought it might be yours," he said when he laid the dog down. His voice struggled over the words. He seemed about to cry. "I thought it was a mountain lion," he said, choking out his explanation.

She squatted by the dog and ran her hand over his hair and saw the place where it had been shot, matted in dry blood. "Mountain lion has a yard-long tale and is twice the size," she said through clenched teeth.

"I am sorry," he said. "I am so sorry. I'll get you another dog," He cleared his throat. "I mean—I know it won't be the same. Whatever you want. I need to make this up to you."

"You think that'll clear you of it, getting me some other dog?" She didn't know how the words coming out did so, attended over as they were by an inner fear that gnawed at her bones. It was all she could do to keep from being sick. She sucked down the bile that was in her throat and turned to a different way of seeing things to keep from being sick. *An eye for an eye*, she thought. It eased her some, thinking that way. A conclusion to this that would level a rift in her world the boy had caused.

"Over there in that shed," she said, tipping her head toward it. "There's a shovel just inside the door and an old blanket on the floor he used sometimes." She glanced up at him to make sure he understood.

He looked away from her, ashamed. "Okay," he said, weakly agreeing.

"Just leave your rifle there. Nobody'll bother it. You'll have all you can handle with the shovel."

He nodded and walked to the shed and came back with the shovel and the blanket and stood mutely.

She stood up and took the blanket and knelt by the dog and laid the blanket down. She gently pulled the dog onto the blanket. He was heavy, nearly eighty pounds. She wrapped the blanket over him and stood and told the boy to pick up the dog and follow her to a place for burial. She took the shovel.

She led him back toward the shed and told him to wait a minute and went in for his rifle. "Still loaded?" she asked, back outside.

"Yes, but I thought . . ."

"It's all right," she said. "You go ahead of me. This path takes us into the woods a ways. There's a spot there under a tree."

The boy looked at her, the shame gone. "Why do you need my rifle?"

"Caution. Might actually be a big cat around."

The boy hesitated. "I think I oughta go on back."

"And not bury Dusty?"

"No. I mean, yes. I should. It's just . . ." He shifted the weight of the blanketed dog he carried in his arms.

"This won't take long. Go on now. This needs to be done." She held the rifle lightly against her stomach, the barrel cradled in the crook of her arm.

They had a small hill to climb just inside the woods and then across a marshy area to get to the tree she had in mind. It was an oak that came from some ancient time, its gnarled, heavy limbs spread in every direction, some but a few feet off the ground, seemingly too heavy to not give way to gravity. There were woodpecker holes as precise in girdling the branches as any engineer could conspire.

It was cool under the oak. A flittery breeze ruffled her shirtsleeves. Her hair, dry as dust, wisped stiffly about her head and resettled, in part, where it had started. There was an unkempt wildness to her, standing there, as she was, with his loaded rifle, that frightened the boy.

"Here's good," she said and toed a rough rectangle in the loamy ground. "Stay away from the trunk and if you hit a feeder root we'll dig another place."

The boy laid the dog on the ground. He had his own dog and felt the misery he had brought down. It made him think about giving up hunting. It was in his family's blood and he had been at it a good two years now. It was a wound to himself that he had done this. It was something he could not tell his father or uncles, and he hoped the people down below, who had told him where she lived, did not know any of his kin. Known word of what he had done would lie as dark as soot.

His thought of his misdeed and the consequences mingled with his worries over what she was going to do. He thought about grabbing the rifle but it would be a struggle, seeing how tightly she held it against her belly. He thought of asking what she intended but worried the mere saying would suggest something she may not have in mind.

"Right here then?" he said, his throat dry.

She nodded and stepped back.

He sunk the shovel in. It was soft and easy digging and he hit but a few small roots. He began to sweat and thought about taking off his vest. What would she think of that? There was a mood he wasn't sure he wanted to change. The balance in which way this could go was delicate. Every few shovels full he glanced over at her. Her eyes always met his. Why didn't she go over to the dog, he wondered? It seemed to him like she should be sorrier and tearful. Instead, she was remote and cold in her observation of his efforts.

"Getting hot," he said.

She nodded, almost imperceptibly.

"Think I'll take off my vest."

She didn't say anything.

"That okay with you?" he asked.

"Up to you."

"This'll be a good spot," he said. "Maybe we could say a prayer when its time."

"Up to you," she repeated. "If you need it, go ahead."

"Just as respect for your loss. I told you how sorry I am."

"Yep."

"I mean," he said clearing his throat, "prayer for your dog."

She shifted the rifle in her arms.

He dug a few more chunks out of the earth, straightened and wiped his forearm across his brow. His hands were shaking. He shook his head.

"It was purely an accident," he said. "There was a mountain cat down below, in the valley, getting bold, and folks were afraid for their kids. Cats been known to take babies." He watched to see what she might think of this. "Missus Pomeroy—you know Missus Pomeroy?—she was fearful of something happening. Her husband was off on business and they live right at the edge of the woods where folks had seen this cat. She asked me to keep an eye out for it and shoot it if I saw it. Said it was a big one, according to its tracks. It made me a little cautious.

"Afterwards, when I was off by myself, I heard something rustling in the brush behind me. I turned and let off a shot, thinking it was going for me."

He waited for her reaction. When there was none he went on. "I mean . . . I guess I was a little scared. I'd hate to be eaten by a cat." He tried to make a joke of himself and forced a laugh that came out a raspy cough.

She glared at the boy, her eyes moist with age and sorrows. She thought of the book of Nahum and said, "*The lord is slow to anger, and great in power, and will not at all acquit the wicked.*" The words came slowly and impassively off her lips in brittle avowal of truth.

The boy opened his mouth to speak and could not and found his own lips in a tremor and shook his head. "I . . . I don't know what that means. I'm not like that. I go to the high school there—Lincoln Valley. I'm on the baseball team. Those folks down below—they know I'm up here." He looked to his right into the trees and then the other way as if one of those might appear; a fellow student or one who had told him where she lived. He dropped the shovel and wiped his hands against his denims. His knees felt week. His voice shaky. "I need to get going. My mother's expecting me for dinner. You mind giving me back my rifle?"

When she didn't say anything he stepped to the side. He stopped when she lowered the rifle and swiveled the barrel forward, the stock lying against her hip. Was it meant as a warning or a repositioning for her old, tired arms?

"*There is no healing of thy bruise; thy wound is grievous,*" she said.

She must be crazy. "My father . . . he wouldn't . . . ," he began and could not piece together what it was he wanted to say. Something to make her understand.

"Your father," she said flatly. He might as well have said any name or thing. She had grown herself up without a father, brother, uncles. Husband being as foreign to her as some distant country. The world of men a language she laid in little effort to decipher.

"What is it you want?" he asked. "I . . . I don't have any money."

"You only got one thing I want," she said.

There was no rain that day. No sudden downpour to mark the day. No thunder or lightning or omens from the gods. It was just another sky-blue day in a string of sky-blue days with a few white clouds and birds flitting from tree to tree and her two-room cabin where she had lived these many years that ran into each other as each day does until a year is used up and then another and finally a life.

The day after, she took up the rifle from the corner where she had put it and took it apart and cleaned the bore and oiled the stock. She reassembled it and lifted it onto wall hooks above her own and sat back in her wood-worn rocker. Her head nodded rhythmically as she rocked. Her eyelids grew heavy and her rocking slowed and her chin drooped onto her chest until she fell into a sleep filled with dreams of Dusty and the boy—bringing her the dog, alive, happy to see her, and the boy laughing when he saw how the dog loved her and was happy himself that he could bring such light into the day for someone he didn't know.

When she woke up it was dark. Rain pattered against the roof. She groaned with the effort of getting herself out of the rocker. She saw his rifle there, above hers, and wondered briefly how it had come to be there. "Oh," she said, remembering. It was a poor trade. ■

LAST SUPPER

D.M. Aderibigbe

You are sitting in our memory
cross-legged, your left elbow
on the table, right hand

cutting into the mountain
of fufu I made for the night.

Just a punch of the mountain
in your mouth,
I repeat,

just a punch,
you push the table.

The table, a city
in the aftermath of an earthquake.
You rise, you walk in the ruins

of my happiness
toward the door.

I hold onto your arm.
Olowo ori mi, I hold
onto your arm,

as one who's afraid of falling
holds onto a tree.

Look, release me, I'm tired
of you, olorun ngbo. You say.
Because love is no longer a god,

when left to one person to worship,
I let go of your arm.

MAL-FUNCTION-ING
Seth DuWayne Slater

My uncle was schizophrenic, a volcanic eruption of haircuts for Locks of Love, shattered rear windows of lit-up police cruisers (busted with size-fifteen boots), s'mores marshmallowed together on cold Oregon beaches under tarry night skies, countless cigarettes inhaled self-deprecatingly (the only way he knew to self-medicate besides booze and weed and speed: numb the "malfunctioning" brain spitting out "malfunctioning" thoughts ripening into "malfunctioning" emotion that ultimately culminated into a "malfunctioned" life). My mother says when she first met him he was a regular virtuoso—a captivating pianist. A handsome blue-eyed Indian. A six-foot-nine nineteen-year-old who played semiprofessional basketball and was sponsored by the big swish symbol, well on his way to the NBA. The mammoth could dunk and dribble and defend. The big and tall perpetual client snorted amphetamines to improve his game. He was caught. He. Lost. It. All. My uncle moved in with my parents, young newlyweds, full of Jesus and hope for rehabilitation (a state of "habilitation" revisited, returned, reconstructed because words without the prefix "re-" or "un-" no longer applied). One day my uncle stomps in smelling heavily of reefer, a pyroclast of unorganized verbiage spewing out his throat. The CIA is on his tail . . . he might hurt somebody. My father takes him to the police station, where a policewoman refuses to incarcerate him—for what? *What if I hit you*, 275 pounds of blue-eyed Indian leans over the counter, *you'd have to take me then. You'd have to take me then.* Fast forward two years. I'm a baby, in my uncle's car, strapped into a child seat, and I shit everywhere. Shit on the baby seat. Shit leaking down the kid's seat onto blue pleather. Shit on this beautiful man's hands. A schizophrenic manic-depressive changed my diaper between Salem and Seattle. It's Thanksgiving in Lewiston, Idaho, and I'm six years old. There's some kind of commotion in the living room, a swell of panicked good intention reacting to a malfunctioned life, enough movement and somber voices to pull me away from coonskin-cap-wearing Davy Crockett. My uncle has to go the hospital. He quit his meds (unsupervised). I go to visit him with my father and grandfather after buying him a pair of shoes. *He can't have steel-toed boots*, my grandfather says, steep hills rolling behind tinted windows. The sign says

No Firearms. No Knives. Nothing that can be turned against staff (sanity didn't count). They lock me in the computer room to wait alone. *If someone comes in here and grabs you, start screaming*, a man in white scrubs tells me. *Start screaming.* I play pinball and wonder. My uncle walks in, looking like a blue-eyed Indian Jesus. I hug him and don't scream . . . I don't scream. It's Tuesday morning and I watch a second plane crash through steel and glass and flesh. Black dots tumble down skyscrapers, flailing, automata. I go in to tell my uncle but can't wake him. He's Seroquelled into his mind, snoring under medicated water weight. He slept through 9/11. I'm twelve years old, *NSYNC blonde, and playing Halo 2 in my grandparents' basement with my father's tranquilized brother. He picks up a shotgun (in game) and says, *This is a kickass gun.* And I (since I'm not allowed to swear) think he's a kickass uncle. Mr. Seattle Streets buys a beagle—Scooter, a long-eared dope who howls at the moon when it's overcast. Hell, it's Seattle. My uncle goes through women like insulin needles (unknowingly locking forty-six chromosomes together: lava to magma to obsidian), tells my grandfather he's always puddled because he's Indian—always one-fourth-of-alcohol intolerant, subjugated. He gives Scooter to Grandpa and Grandma. They consign the mutt to a friend. Scooter disappears somewhere half past adolescence—blurred between seasons and I can't answer my uncle's phone calls any more. Lie. I don't answer his phone calls anymore. Last family reunion (well past the surprise new cousin and my uncle's multiple baptisms in heavily chlorinated hotel pools): I offer him Nicorette cuz I hate watching his fingers shake, shake, shake rolling spliffs. I go to bed and am shaken awake in the dark. My cousin David says my uncle is a preacher. Says the mammoth just waxed poetic about grace and love and forgiveness and anal sex. Says he said *conviction* was the thing. My father comes in red-faced, apologizing for part of his DNA manifested outside himself, *He doesn't know what he's saying.* My uncle died alone in his apartment in a pool of shit . . . shit on this beautiful man's hands . . . he erupted, praying let us recreate ourselves after that superhuman promise that promise that madness violent elegance silence.[1] ∎

---

1 Arthur Rimbaud, "Drunken Morning"

ARMITAGE GHOST MURAL
Steven Carrelli

—preparatory drawing, graphite on paper, 2017

—mineral silicate paint on masonry wall,
Armitage Avenue CTA Station, 939 W. Armitage Avenue, Chicago, 2017.

PUBLIC WORK
Steven Carrelli

In June of last year, I received a cryptic email: "Dear Artists, please remember to return your contracts to me by this Friday." It was from an administrator of Chicago's Public Art Program, and I assumed it was an error. I had applied several months earlier to be considered for a public commission from the City of Chicago's Department of Cultural Affairs and Special Events (DCASE), but the accepted artists were to have been notified by May, and I had not received any notice. So I wrote back to the program administrator to say that I had never been offered a contract, and I was answered with some unexpected good news: I had indeed been awarded a public commission, and could I get that contract signed and notarized? I had been tapped to do a mural.

For the past twenty-eight years I've made a career of exhibiting paintings and drawings. Most of my work, though, has been small in scale. In fact, most of it is absolutely tiny: whole shows of 6-inch-by-6-inch paintings, often painted in egg tempera. I make my own paint by breaking an egg and grinding powdered pigment into the yolk. My studio looks like what you might imagine a miniaturist's studio to look like. When I recently did some 32-by-44-inch drawings, I joked that I was making billboards. While my work often addresses themes of our relationship to place and history, it usually does so by inviting viewers into a relationship that is intimate and tactile.

I had applied to the Public Art Program because I wanted to engage with these ideas in a new way. I was looking for a chance to deal with the specifics of place, history and identity in a public space. It represented a new challenge, a new chapter, and I was a little afraid of it. Perhaps I was a little relieved—disappointed but relieved—when I thought I'd been rejected. Or maybe I was hoping that it wouldn't be too different from my usual practice. In any case, I didn't expect to be assigned a mural. I imagined I might get invited to make a design that would be digitally enlarged and printed on an exterior tile wall, or maybe a series of architectural drawings that would be installed in a public interior space. But a straight-up mural, painted directly on a wall with big brushes Diego Rivera-style while standing on a scaffold with a team of assistants: it had never occurred to me that someone would want me to do that.

I soon learned the location of the wall that I was to paint. The building itself was a beautiful greystone four-flat that had been built in the late nineteenth century, but it had been altered as a result of construction on the Armitage Avenue elevated train stop just west of it. When the L platform was widened about a decade ago, the building had to be narrowed by about a third to accommodate the new structure. The western part of the building was sliced off and a new wall built. This was my wall. It was ugly: a former partition wall, probably of coarse bricks, that had been covered with concrete plaster and scored to look like cinder blocks, an apparent attempt at beautification. It was in okay condition, but not a perfect surface to paint on. It had some cracks and holes and was exceptionally rough and absorbent. It and the small plaza west of it sat directly under the L tracks and were in shadow all day. Still, it was exciting. I began to think of this project as an opportunity to experiment artistically with content and form. Rather than make a large outdoor version of what I normally make in the studio, this could be a new and truly site-specific piece whose form responded to the location.

In early July, my father died at the age of eighty-six. Because of this, my memories of beginning this public project—the first of my career—are linked to the loss of my father: the four days spent in the hospital with family, keeping each other company while Dad drifted away, traveling to and from the funeral in Ohio, writing a eulogy, worrying about my mother, thinking about the arc of my father's life. For me, these became inseparable from the birth of the mural.

My father was a small guy—five feet four inches tall—but strong, and he knew how to work. He was a skilled tradesman, trained as a shoemaker in Italy. For a while he worked at a shoe repair shop in the States, but there wasn't a lot of work for shoemakers here, so he spent a lot of time doing heavy labor. He worked at a brickyard, a loading dock, and he spent over a decade working at the Hoover vacuum cleaner plant in North Canton, Ohio. He was used to heavy work, and as a child I used to ask him to flex his biceps and show off his muscled arm. He would oblige me, blowing on his thumb as if to inflate the muscle. Age eventually weakened him, of course, but even in his old age it wasn't hard to see his former strength or to imagine the work his hands had done.

In the months following his death, I gave my mother regular reports on the mural's progress. It cheered her, I think, to envision her son working on a large, important project. It was a chance to think about the future, not the past.

The day after my father's funeral, I met the alderman of the 43rd Ward and a committee of community leaders from Chicago's Lincoln

Park neighborhood. They had been thinking about putting a mural on this wall for a long time. The stretch of Armitage Avenue where it is located had been designated the Armitage-Halsted Landmark District, and the committee wanted a mural to celebrate the historic architecture of the neighborhood. They had selected me because they liked the realism of my studio paintings and the precision of my architectural drawings. This was good, but complicated. Sure, they liked my prior work, but I feared that they wanted me to paint a nostalgic, sepia-toned picture of Armitage Avenue in the nineteenth century, with horse-drawn carriages in the street. That was not the exciting experiment I had been planning. But they were also a thoughtful group of people, and they listened to my ideas about situating the mural in the present while also addressing the history of the place.

I researched the neighborhood, sketched ideas, did studies of the architecture. Over a two-week period, I generated a scale rendering of my initial design. I stylized the architecture of the district, distilling it into a composition composed of the neighborhood's rooflines, a bulkhead-height frieze of architectural motifs, and the faded ghost images of painted wall advertisements.

At a contentious meeting in the alderman's office, the committee rejected the design and asked me to revise it. While some on the committee were pleased with it, the most vocal members disliked the liberties I had taken with the historic architecture that they were so proud of. I was, of course, disappointed, but I also had qualms about the design. To me, it felt too much like a theatrical backdrop: a clever design suggesting a period piece but lacking the presence necessary for a stand-alone public artwork. It had good design and good intentions, but I wanted it to have soul and depth. I realized that I had made a compromise design, attempting to offer the committee what I thought they wanted while using some of the visual devices that I was accustomed to using. Still, I didn't have a better idea. The committee's feedback was earnest, but it was also self-contradictory and reflected the conflicting interests of different committee members. I listened to their comments willingly, but while their input helped me understand what they saw, it did not provide the unity of vision needed to turn this idea into a good painting. That would have to come from me, and it would have to be visual, not verbal.

What I needed, and what I didn't know how to find, was a genuine way into the subject. I needed to identify something about this neighborhood, its architecture and history, that would allow me to interpret it, not merely repeat it. Despite the beauty of the subject—or perhaps because of it—I found it difficult to take inspiration from it. I wasn't interested in cultivating nostalgia for the nineteenth century, and I wasn't sure the neighborhood needed more of what was already there. How could I both respect the place and contribute something fresh and alive to it? The street is not a museum. It's a commercial district and has been since its founding, full of busy people working for a living, alive with a vibrant public. If this mural was going to work, it needed to find visual poetry in that life. I banged around my studio for a week, messing up sheets of paper. I walked around the neighborhood some more and read whatever I could find about its history. Then I found my opening. I began to realize that those buildings do in fact embody a great deal of life.

Those ornate buildings with their cast-iron pilasters and pressed-tin cornices, decorative brickwork and Italianate carved-stone window lintels represent a sense of craft that is familiar to me. Many had been built by immigrant craftspeople: metalsmiths and stonemasons from Germany and Ireland, Italy and Poland. I thought of my parents: a seamstress and a shoemaker who had immigrated to the US from Italy. They had quit school after the fifth grade in order to apprentice in their respective trades, and they were proud of their skills. The people who had built this place had different accents than my parents, but I saw their values and experiences as those of my family. I knew those people, and they were going to be my way in.

I also learned that many of the streets in Lincoln Park had once been paved in Nicholson paving: wooden-block pavers covered in pitch and tar and pounded by hand into the ground. I'd grown up seeing that kind of labor, and I'd learned to see it as graceful: a sort of working-class ballet. In my eulogy for my father, I had told the story of seeing him break up our concrete driveway with a sledgehammer. I vividly recalled the grace and force with which he dropped the hammer back almost to his heels, swung it in a big round arc, shifting his weight and sliding his hands smoothly to the very end of the handle, then folded his compact body nearly in half at the waist to slam the hammerhead down onto the block. The gridwork of those pavers—and the labor that they implied— would provide a unifying visual motif linking the ground plane to the architecture, defining perspective space while forming a bold graphic language of surface ornament. The painting would be a monumental wall drawing of painted lines and stained color fields—a sort of graphic tapestry—and the pavers, windows, pilasters and moldings would be its warp and weft.

Once the committee approved the design, I began my own version of this labor ballet. The execution of a project like this is not like my usual studio practice. It's more like construction than easel painting: building up and tearing down the scaffold each day, climbing up and down it, scrubbing the thick primer into a thirsty concrete wall with stiff bristle brushes. It's loud and dirty under the L tracks, with trains rumbling overhead every few minutes. My assistant, Brian, and I wore earplugs while painting, and dust sifted down onto us from the tracks above. It was physical and exhausting, and we were sore at the end of the day. I joked that I should have done this when I was thirty instead of waiting until I was almost fifty to do my first mural, but it also felt good to be pushed this way.

The work site had no water source, so we had to fill five-gallon buckets in the janitor's closet in the L station across the street. This put me in regular contact with all of the workers at the station, a few of whom were exceptionally involved in my project. Sandra, the evening station manager, let us store and lock my scaffold inside the station, and Janet, the morning station manager, would let us in to retrieve it each morning. They both came out to the wall regularly to check on my progress, and they kept an eye on the mural and my equipment when I wasn't there. Sandra talked with me about her love of calligraphy. Janet greeted nearly everybody on the street by name, and I learned that she's known as the mayor of Armitage Avenue.

A mural attracts a public, and the community members quickly became as invested in it as I was. There was Randy at the masonry supply shop, who supplied me with my paints. I'm sure I was Randy's smallest client, since he sells thousands of gallons of this stuff to industrial campuses, where whole buildings are stained with it. Yet he took such an interest in my project that he personally delivered two pints of primer to me at the job site. And there was the CTA worker who was painting over graffiti and who chatted with me about the design, showed me images of street art that he liked, lent me some tools to fix my scaffold and gave me a spare drop cloth. People stopped to watch and many asked questions. (They rarely noticed the earplugs.) Who were we? What were we making? Who was paying for this? Was the city involved? The alderman? A young boy going to a music lesson at the Old Town School of Folk Music cheered when I showed him the roofline of the school's building in the mural. While I was sitting on the ground drawing, a young girl whose mother was looking at her phone walked over to me and asked if I was homeless. (I told her this was my job, but she didn't seem convinced.) There were the regulars who passed by at the same time each day. One evening-rush-hour regular noticed I had gotten new glasses halfway through the project, and he asked for the name of my optical shop.

I finished the mural on a Saturday in October, after about six weeks of painting under the tracks and almost four months after that initial email. At the end of the previous day's work, Brian told me that he thought the major work was done and that I should spend some time alone with it to give it whatever finishing touches it might need. I adjusted some lines and tones, backing up frequently to take in the whole composition, then approaching the wall again to make a few more refinements. It was as close as that project ever got to my studio painting practice. It felt quiet. Except, of course, the trains were still rumbling overhead, and the traffic din was constant. A few people honked their horns and gave me a thumbs-up, and the usual pedestrians and CTA staff stopped to comment. In the late afternoon, I set up the scaffold on the other side of the plaza and climbed onto it to look at the mural from a little distance. The painting felt done.

At the end of a public project, the artist leaves and the public stays. I called it my wall, but it's theirs. Sandra and Janet are still there every day, and so are the alderman and the ward residents who argued with me about it. The CTA passengers pass it on their way to work and again on their way home. Kids on the way to music lessons walk by it with their parents and point.

On November ninth, my fiftieth birthday, we held a public dedication. There was a ribbon-cutting with the alderman. (We used four-foot-long scissors—where do you buy those?) The community leaders were there, along with representatives of DCASE and the CTA, my friends and colleagues, my wife, my in-laws, my mother, and my brother. There were speeches and pictures, drinks and doughnuts. It was cold and loud. There was traffic and the noise of the trains. There was the new mural at the east end of the plaza. And at the center, there was the public. ∎

FEELING OUT OF PLACE AT HOME

Bryce Berkowitz

Where I monitor what my father eats,
where the corporate cubicle's minor regrets
reflect off Lake Michigan like dim stars.
The sunset bleeds toward another planet
while sailboats bob on the water.
The sky is cloudy; our future cloudy.
But let's shoot the barrel rim,
hammer weathervanes, wake up happy
from this dream where we're falling
between the gaps in the leaves
between the branches, we stay.
Let's get twisted like cocktails
between the sheets of the afternoon,
tattoo sunflowers inside our dreams.
It's summer again, and I'm kayaking
with my father, unsure if I want kids,
but on the lake the dusk is lovely.
I feel lost between clouds and their reflection,
here at home, hoping the song's final note
echoes inside someone long after I'm gone.

ANGELS DON'T HAVE WINGS
Chika Onyenezi

It was my first day at the labor hall. I arrived very early in the morning, and needed a job. Theo dropped me off and wished me good luck. He drove back to downtown to pick up people for the blood bank and other medical experiments in Houston. Even though I lived in the same house with Theo, I didn't know what he was into until I met him one morning while looking for a job at the labor hall. He usually waits until there isn't anyone hiring for the day before walking up to people to propose his quick-money venture. He walked up to me and told me that I could offer my blood or answer a few medical questions for fifty dollars. When he looked at me again, he realized that I was the new guy at the bunkhouse (he lives there too). We laughed. He told me about a place I could be sure to find something to do each day. That was how I got here.

The dew was falling, and it was still dark. I walked into the door of the labor hall. I looked inside and it was already filled up, about fifty men and ten women already inside. I signed in and walked to the last man and asked him to reserve a seat for me. He looked at me and nodded. I walked outside to smoke. I stood outside and lit a cigarette. Several cars drove in and dropped men whose world seemed over by the look on their faces; old, grumpy, and fatigued, wounded and barely walking, tattered beards and tired smiles. I watched them walk inside with their dirty old jackets and old boots. I watched the sun come out of the clouds like a rat through a hole, it was orange and beautiful.

I finished smoking and walked back inside. They hadn't started giving jobs still. I sat down and thanked the man that had looked out for me. I slept for a while. When I woke, it was seven o'clock; they had begun to allocate work for the day with the sign-in sheet. They needed the women to go to high schools and work in the cafeteria. I watched them get on a bus and drive off. After that, only the men were left. Several batches were sent off until it got to me.

"You, and you . . ." the old man pointed at me and a lanky black man. "Take you and you and you," he pointed at three other men, "and you will drive to this address." He showed the lanky man the address on his phone, "There they will show you what to do." From all indications, he had already known the lanky man for a while, and he knew that he had a car.

"Follow me, man," the lanky man said to the four of us in a thick Caribbean accent. It was funny how he referred to the four of us as *man*, but I was in no mood for laughter. I was hungry and had had nothing but coffee and cigarettes since yesterday's evening. My hope was to work today, pay for daily rent, and eat food too. I lived in a dreadful place with dreadful men like Theo, who spent most of his days scamming people off blood donation and fighting at night with other tenants. Theo had knocked a man's teeth out three days ago. But there was something nice about Theo. Something soft. That was why he drove me this morning without asking me for money. There was pity in his eyes for me even though he didn't have much himself. I hated pity, but I couldn't do anything either but accept the pity I was given. Since I had arrived in the city, I had begun to learn about men; the lifestyle of ex-convicts, despicable people, men abandoned by their families and the society.

The lanky man counted us, instinctively the four of us stood in a single row. I was the first in line. I moved my fat self in line. The second was a black boy that looked like he could snap a neck in seconds, all his muscles jolting out. He had a gold tooth and wore a gold bracelet on his wrist. He wore big jean trousers that made me laugh. The third was an old man, whom I later came to know as Mike. Mike was a truck driver and was caught drinking on the highway by a policeman and his license was revoked. He told me that it was almost the best thing that had happened to him. Apart from the fact that he had to make money and pay for rent, he was just sitting at home fucking his new girlfriend every day. The third was a fat white man but unfortunately we never did have any conversation. He looked tired like most men here. I bet life weighed tons on his shoulders too.

We picked up tools for the day from a man who noted which items were being given out to us: a glove, a shovel, a digger, yellow jacket and helmet, and a contractor broom. We grabbed our items and walked with the lanky man to his car. He opened the trunk of his truck, and we threw in all our work tools. We all sat in the car and drove into the street.

Down by wheat farms, down by the church, down by the double-lighted street into Katy Freeway. We drove silently for miles, and miles, and miles of frosty wind that blew across our faces because one of the windows wouldn't wind up. Soon we got to the construction site. My mind wandered about. I imagined what home might look like now, what mum was doing. Maybe my father's shadows still filled every space of the house. Maybe he still woke up with his snuff in his hand, and sneezed, and sneezed. I had always wanted to see the world, I had always wanted to see what was out there, for this I was joyed deep, deep, deep, inside of me.

I arrived here from Botswana in August of 2009 with two bags and a mind to live the American dream. Knowing no one, I rented a place for myself and began life. I had run out of money and needed something to keep me going when Dan suggested I go work at the labor house because they barely looked at the employment papers and other things. Dan was a drunk white man I had met at the bunkhouse. He was drunk and good. The only time I saw him talk to me with a cleared eye, he offered to help me get a job with his own social security number, which was how I was able to be here. Three times I had seen Dan pee on himself.

Dan was in his midforties and poor. He liked me because he thought I was different and could listen to all his stories. He told me about how he had robbed a bank without a gun when he worked there as an accountant, and up until today, they weren't able to prosecute him because he cleaned his footprints, neatly. I liked the way he said *neatly* while I held him by the shoulder and walked him to his bed, staggering, his blood filled with liquor. He pissed most the money he stole away and gambled in Cuba even when it was outlawed to visit Cuba. Dan said that on special arrangement, one could go to Cuba from Key West. Back then, he had the special arrangement. Dan was smart: street smart, life smart, and all the smart a smart man can be. He could be a drunk, but that angel had no wings.

We waited for another hour until the site manager arrived and told us what to do.

"Now, you have to clear the third and second floors for today," he said.

He took the lanky man upstairs and showed him everything. Our unskilled selves started clearing debris and planks, and carved-out wood, and broken bits of tile, nail, and removing buckets filled with urine. Two men, the big guy and Mike, stayed downstairs, throwing dirt into the dumpster, while we flung some of the debris from upstairs. The white guy was tasked with lifting the things we couldn't fling down the stairs.

"I knew this was going to be easier, man, that why I put you here," the lanky man said to me.

"Thank you." I smiled.

"You are so respectful, man, where are you from?" he asked.

"Nigeria," I said, "But I have spent a couple of years traveling. I quit my job back home to travel," I said with a sense of pride and dignity.

"Then you must have degree, I guess?" he asked.

"Yes, I do," I said.

"Don't talk about it, man, here it makes no meaning. Just between you and me, man," he said, and flashed his tobacco-stained teeth.

Maybe I shouldn't have answered yes, I thought. I felt as though there was something not too good about me being a university graduate and working manual labor, something that shouldn't be spoken of. I never said anything about being a graduate ever after. I realized that the most important thing was becoming one with wherever I was, or found myself. Today, I was at the labor work, and that was me.

"No problem, I don't. I said it because you asked," I said.

"My name is Marcus, man," he said, smiling. There was this meekness in his eyes, a visible kindness. Afterwards, we felt at ease with one another. Like we'd known each other for a long time.

"My name is Emeka," I said.

"Man, I watched Nigeria in the Olympics in Atlanta, man. The dream team, what's his name again . . . Jay-Jay . . ." he said.

"Jay-Jay Okocha," I said.

He threw the planks down towards the truck downstairs and punched his fist into the air in excitement.

"Jay-Jay Okocha, man, that guy was a terror. He held that midfield like a master. He powered it. He dribbled . . ." he shifted his left foot to the right, "dribbled," he shifted his right foot to the left, imitating Jay-Jay Okocha's fast leg flip and leg work to my own admiration. He smiled at himself, looked at me, and smiled at himself again.

I noticed that he wasn't focused on me, but he was replaying the match between Brazil and Nigeria in his head, which might still be one of the greatest comebacks in the history of soccer, and it ended with a win for Nigeria. He talked to me about his home in Saint Vincent and the Grenadines, where he grew up. He talked to me about how he arrived in America with his soccer team many years ago and had since settled here. He had a home, a wife, and children and had always worked with his hands.

"Man, this is only eight dollars an hour, how do you manage?" I asked curiously, beginning to use his manner of speaking in addressing him back.

"Man, you see, America gives to you and wants to take back, you must never let it take back all, man. Avoid loans, man, live within your means. Love your woman. I love my woman." A crooked smile flashed across his face. I wondered how loving his woman became part of our discussion. I realized that the human mind was a machine of possibilities, and never sequential. Maybe, while he was addressing me, the image of his wife bumped into his head, and that was more important than everything he had ever possessed.

Maybe, love was a bigger topic to the brain so that once it flew in, everything, every thought, was weighed down. I had once felt this way before. I had once been in love, and whenever I remembered her, every useful thought danced into that basket of thoughtlessness. I myself was beginning to muse over my ex-lover, her ivory skin in the sun of Namibia. She could have been everything to me, but a man on a journey cannot carry the whole world with him, and these days, girls were impatient, they easily moved on. But yes, she had been the whole world to me.

"You must love her so much," I said.

He said nothing. He only looked at his watch and reminded me that it was time for break. I had no money for food, but went along with them anyways. I was hungry but I couldn't say it to anyone. He drove to the closest McDonald's. I couldn't tell if Marcus could read my heart. The way he looked at me, his eyes were filled with compassion. Poor me, I swear.

"Yo, man, I buy you food," he said.

I smiled and thanked him. He didn't even ask me if I was hungry, if he had, I would have declined the offer in order to sound modest and dignified. I walked with him to order the food, Mike and the big black fellow were already eating at the other corner. We took our hamburgers and walked into another cubicle.

"So, you've been in love, man?" he asked me, his big brows rowed up. I consciously rowed up my right brow and twisted my head to the right. My thought, my being, my senses journeyed a thousand miles to the deserts of Namibia and the pretty skin of Ndali absorbing the sun and reflecting it. Her arms flanked like wings of an angel as she ran around the farm. The last time she asked me how I was, I told her fine. I was ashamed to tell her that things weren't going as planned, that I still had no job, and that I was a vagrant. Yes, a vagrant.

I told her to move on with her life. I told her to find someone else that could love her. She cried, and yet I couldn't stay. At first, the hunger to see a new place took all the pain away. When the hangover was over, reality set in. Today seemed like one of those days steeped in the hangover of leaving.

"Yes, I was, I . . ." I stuttered, no matter how hard I tried to hide, it showed all over my face. Love was the language of the soul, and the eyes would always betray the soul.

"Man, I know. It can be hard, I know. I fought hard, man. Man, I left America the first time and fought hard until I returned and married my wife. We love each other, man," he said. The more he talked about love, the more his accent disappeared, and he sounded American.

We talked about love, what it could do to us, and how it could change us. We talked about the women we'd loved. We finished eating and left.

While the four of us rode in the car, we talked about love again. It was then that I learned the name of the black muscular fellow: Darius. Darius told us his story of love, and we listened. His tiny feminine voice sounded like a little bell ringing. I wanted to laugh that such a muscular fellow could possess such a tiny voice, but I held myself.

"Man, I saw my motherfucking cousin fucking my woman. Banging the shit out of her . . ." Darius said, the muscles on his face tightened, the agony and pain of that day had not left him still, "man, I held him and punched him twice in the mouth. Slapped my wife and she flew under the table," he stopped for a little and continued, "shiiiiiiiiiiiiiiiiiiiit," he stopped again.

"Man, I broke that nigger's ribs. Three. He sustained other injuries, man. That was how I went to jail. I am still on parole. I can't find any job, so I have to take whatever comes by to survive. Shiiiiiiiiiiiiiiiit," he said again. His eyes were bloodshot. His hair neatly shaved. He had tattoos peering out of his sleeves and collar.

We let him talk as though we were holding a therapy session. After his story, they car was so emotionally charged that none of us said anything until we got back to work. We all gently walked to our work stations and resumed. Marcus and I spent the rest of the evening cleaning the rooms and talking about soccer. Everything about him was soccer. He invited me to come play soccer on Sunday at his house. I said yes, that I would come, but I knew I couldn't get there because I had no car, and I hated taking public transport.

After work, we reported and signed off. It was getting dark, and it rained lightly. Marcus drove all of us back to the labor house and we signed off there too. I collected my check of sixty-five dollars and walked into the street to wait for a bus. Marcus saw me standing at the bus stop, weary, and offered to take me home. I was ashamed of where I was living, I was ashamed of even showing my fellow laborer that corner of the earth, tucked in between two high risings, more like shop than a house, and housing tens of men.

* * *

When I got home in the evening, I paid my rent of fifty dollars and had only ten dollars left. I promised the landlord that I would complete it later, and he admitted that I had never owed the house a dime before. Dan came back drunk as usual, but with a cheerful face that I got had something to do with his social security. He smiled at me and sat with me outside of the building. We smoked from my pack of cigarettes and talked about the city.

"Man, I have been in this city for five years. I used to have it all, a house, a car, and women every day. All those good shits, man. I am not fucking boasting. I don't play like Dave . . ." He belched loudly.

Dave was another man that lived in the building with us who often prided himself for going to the Olympics as an athlete, and who later became a coach. He made lots of money from gambling, until he had a stroke that left him bankrupt and his family disappeared with all of his money. Dave told me the story with tears in his eyes the very first day that I came into the house, just like he had told the others too. After telling the story, Dave limped away from me and said: "I will get back on my feet."

I had been there for three months and every day Dave boasted of being able to get back on his feet and never did. Dave taught me the most important lesson of life: that reality wasn't a fairy tale. Once in a man's life, he must face himself, accept the way he is, and speak the truth. There was never a way Dave, with half of his body dead, was going to be the man he used to be. Sometimes I wondered what became of him. The last time I saw Dave, he was walking into the cold night with a torn umbrella towards a dark alley that harbored the homeless. His tall frame stooped a little while he limped. I wanted to run to him and give him something, but I had nothing with me. I still beat myself for not at least stopping to say hello, I was saddened as I sat in the light-rail. I knew his fate, everyone knew his fate, apart from Dave himself. But the truth was that whenever Dave would boldly face himself, he wouldn't survive the next day. Sometimes, dreams kept us alive. No matter what, his hustle was still valid.

"Man . . . oh man . . . are you hungry?" Dan asked me.

"Yes," I said, "I got paid today, Dan, let's go find something to eat." I saw a big smile rise on his drunken face. I had only ten dollars left in my pocket and in the world, but I felt that I owed him a meal. Dan stood up and walked unsteady for a few seconds, regained his balance, and started walking majestically towards the busy road. I cautiously walked beside him. An angel might be drunk, but he was still an angel.

"Man, someone stole all my food from the fridge yesterday," he said from the corner of his mouth.

"I don't leave my food in the fridge. What do you expect with that number of people in one place?" I said. The light turned green, and we crossed the road. It was night, but one could barely notice. The streetlight illuminated our path. We talked and talked about the other men at the bunkhouse; the ones that snored at night, the ones that bullied others, the ones that worked hard enough every day just to afford a prostitute. We talked about us being inmates with our own money, and we laughed.

We laughed as though we didn't belong there. We laughed with lightness. The world and our pains seemed easier to bear. We walked towards the bridge and crossed it. By the mobile gas station, there was a Chinese restaurant. A Chinese lady owned the place. I had often heard about Chinese people being shrewd businesspeople. But this place was different, and this was my second visit here. She had the same kindness in her eyes as I walked inside. She had the biggest smile I had ever seen on someone's face. Even though she only spoke a few words of English, she always tried to ask me questions.

"Seat. Seat," she said, smiling. I sat down with Dan. We ran through the menu and ordered pork fried rice with two sodas.

"You. Family. Here?" she asked me.

"No, far away in Nigeria," I said, smiling.

"I like how you smile. You. Hardworking. Good man. I give you free today. Free," she said.

Dan and I thanked her immensely for being so kind on my account. We ate and talked and thanked her whenever she turned and smiled at us. She had a heart of gold, and from her I learned about a different kind of love. The love that came with kindness and mercy. I learned through her hard work, and stress, and life challenges that one could spare for the less privileged.

After the meal, we thanked her again and walked back to the house. Dan drank his liquor along the way from a flask he tucked in his pocket. We laughed, talked, and walked. Light showers of rain sprinkled on us. We laughed. With Dan, life was about the moment, about where he found himself, about those he could love until he could love them no more. Life was about everything he had ever had and lost, even his children in Memphis growing without him. I could be his son. I could be one. I was that young, and yet he looked at me with kindness.

"Try not to end here, my friend. You have the whole world ahead of you. For us, it's almost over," he said and drunkenly climbed on his bed and slept it off. I removed my clothes, showered, and lay on my bed.

I thought about the beautiful things that had happened to me. The kindness of men, ordinary men, who found it so easy to share whatever little they had. Men who said, "Damn the consequences, I will be my brother's keeper."

Men who wouldn't betray you easily for their ambitions, their ambition was the love. Men filled with so much compassion. I remembered the Chinese woman. Deep inside her eyes I saw my mother watching over me. Then it all made sense to me that all these angels had been watching over me and kept me away from harm. I remembered them. I closed my eyes and slept. ∎

GREAT THINGS
Wayne Conti

The fact that Matthew had no wife didn't make his existence with her any easier. He sometimes had to shout back at her when he was alone in his house. Nonexistent wives were changeable and he often had to remind her that she misunderstood him. Even when he stayed out at late hours drinking, it was only because he was off looking to find such a one as she. She would argue back for she sometimes displayed a terrible temper—her eyes often a light brown—staring into his eyes.

"Don't you see that?" he asked her. "You know me, if anyone does. I only do these things for you. I'm basically lazy. What I do, I do just for you. When I work I think of you."

And when he worked he *did* think of her. How jealous his friends would be, how surprised his coworkers would be, who thought him a hopeless middle-aged loner. A bachelor? Why he had two children, he fantasized. They were the fruits of his and his wife's grand passion for each other. The first child, a boy, who wasn't getting older—oh how he could remember Timothy's birth, he'd imagined it dozens of times: the dash for the hospital, the near accident in the rain or in the snow depending on the season of the reverie, but finally always with the old-style doctor with the pointed beard coming down the ancient hospital corridor to tell him, "It's a boy, my lad." Aside from those imaginings, Timothy was perpetually four or five or six years old. He could take Timothy anywhere. When Matthew sat alone at dinner in a restaurant, he imagined Timothy at his left. He never made any trouble, he was so well brought up.

His daughter was always three and blond and always dressed in a blue smock with tiny polka dots. He—well, he and his wife—never quite found a name for her. When Matthew felt particularly lonely, she would sense it and come up to him and give him a hug and he would order another drink. He and his wife had their moments, but all in all they were a happy, handsome family.

Of course Matthew wasn't fooling himself. Though his wife often accompanied him shopping, he never asked her out loud what she wanted tonight. He only bought food for one—well except sometimes he'd sort of "forget," but that was more to fool a checkout girl into thinking he was more than he seemed. Who knew if maybe that checkout girl might not *be her*, his wife. The checkout girl's hair was long and dark brown. He could see her standing beside him at their wedding, *his wife*, her imaginary hair, which had been blond recently, shifting then to dark brown, and he would take care of her.

"Twenty-seven dollars and twenty cents," she said to him.

"Really," he smiled.

She looked at him, and he paid her, then he pushed his handcart and imagined their marriage, little Timothy in a suit and their daughter still with blond hair.

He lived in a house he had bought. It was smallish, but bigger than he alone needed. He knew the family would grow into it. He had a terrible time making the payments. And his wife was pressing him to find a better house. He couldn't imagine how he would manage, though with his wife behind him, he was sure he'd soon be making more. He certainly hoped so.

In the office he had his own small room. He was cooped up with his computers, which he alone could operate. But people came into his office all the time demanding his aid. The first time they did so they always started by insisting their problem was a "system problem," meaning his fault, but it never was. After that they were a little more respectful of him, less dismissive, but with all that coming and going, he couldn't put up pictures in gold frames like other married employees, and he didn't want pictures of himself alone or of him with strangers or pictures of a dog, that would be too much. And more and more often he would fall behind on a critical backup of sensitive material when he sat with the door closed and dreamt of his wife, the program manual spread open facedown in his lap, and he dreamt of the two of them together in a rocky stream, secluded and beautiful, her laughing and throwing her bra to the shore and taking him in her arms and their skin touching and the golden retriever swimming, sticking his nose in their faces to their laughter, and the door slamming against the backup server and he'd jump to have his boss ask him in her very unpleasant way, "What are you doing?"

"There's a problem in their code," he said, shaken, and it *was* true. More or less.

"Well, I'm going to lunch now. See if you can have the investor side up by two."

She never invited him to lunch anymore, unless it was a lunch for the "team," and he would sit at the round table, where he was the only one to eat with chopsticks. They were surprised by that. He showed them how he did it, how to hold the chopsticks, and to start with one grain of rice, but somehow they seemed to think, if he caught it right, eating Chinese food with chopsticks was still somehow very weird. They ate with silver forks and knives. They talked among themselves and he imagined how his wife might just pop in and they'd have to make room for her and they would be so nice to him then—she was very good-looking!

But when he got home, well, they were having problems. His wife wanted a nicer house or at least a nicer street. And the neighbors! She was always fighting with them. He thought they were perfectly nice, kind of like his family when he was growing up. They were a little simple, yes, but his wife was like every woman he had ever dated, they wanted to be upper-middle or better. She nagged him if he even had a beer with one of them. Of course he was, as always, just off looking for someone like her, but she wouldn't listen. She insisted to the point where he'd stopped talking to them and no one that he'd known ever called except once in a while to complain about the garbage, if his wife had forgotten to put it out, and he'd had to put it out himself, but on the wrong day, and the neighborhood kids or something knocked it over. Fortunately none of this bickering ever happened in front of the children.

Nighttimes were long—he'd come home a little drunk—and often the next morning he dressed for work by undressing. He'd awakened to find himself with coat and tie and shoes still on, the lamps around his bed still lit and the DVD player asking if he'd like to watch the film again. Film? Sometimes, a little tipsy at the video store, he had chosen movie classics, while other times—well, his wife had a little bit of a taste for spicy stuff—with her figure she beat them cold so she wasn't jealous at all. It was fun. Once in a while you can put on a show for the neighbors. With neighbors like these who cared anyway?

On the dining room table one such morning he found a rolled-up real estate newspaper. A subtle hint from the night before. He could just *imagine* her nagging him again. She was always annoyed because as she said, "I know you can do great things." And maybe she was right. Maybe he *could* take on a part-time weekend job for some start-up. He didn't want her to work. He decided to skip breakfast.

Not too far from their house was Normandy Way. His wife thought that was the nicest street around. Most of the houses there were big with a great deal of land around them. Those were out of reach for someone with his present income, though there was one he had his eye on. In reality it probably wasn't any larger than the home they had, but he wasn't going to mention that. His wife had to admit it was "pretty nice," and she had a pretty nice way of saying it. The small house had sort of a Grecian look to it. He'd heard it was owned by an old professor of

Latin. Matthew smiled. He always looked at it when he drove by, and he drove by often. To his surprise that morning, he saw a For Sale sign in the road in front of the house. His smile faded. It was for sale. He looked at the sign again and again as he passed. Was the sign exactly in front of that house? No question—it was. There it was, For Sale, for everyone to see.

When he got to work he closed himself in his office. He picked up the phone. He found he had memorized the phone number on the For Sale sign. The woman on the other end didn't seem very friendly. He asked her about the house, was it still available, did it need work—he wasn't fussy—he could fix it up. The woman didn't seem to want to tell him much. She wanted him to come in. But he insisted he had a lot to do and his wife didn't have any time on her hands at all. Before he could come in he needed some information. He didn't want to waste his time or the real estate agent's. He wouldn't dare waste his wife's time. Reluctantly the woman answered his questions. At the end of the conversation he asked her the price.

After that he hung up the phone. He stared down at his desk. Maybe if he took two weekend jobs. What would a man not do for a wife and children? A beautiful wife who had her heart set on a house like that? What would he not do?

He left his office and crossed the floor. He saw his boss arriving, attaché case in hand.

Matthew asked her if he could speak to her a minute.

"Not right now," she said, turning her back on him. She said, "Maybe later this afternoon. Probably tomorrow is better."

She opened the door to her office and stepped inside.

"But," Matthew said.

She seemed to ignore him. Matthew took a breath, squeezed his hands into fists for a moment and walked into the office behind her. In fact he bumped into her slightly, which startled her.

"What are you doing?" she asked him.

"I have to ask you something." he said. "It can't wait."

"What!" she said.

"I-I-have to ask you. But I need a raise."

"At this time of year?"

"I think I'm due a raise. I think you know what a good job I do," he said.

"With the delays to the rollout of the new system?"

Matt looked her in the eye and he tried his best to smile as he said, "I'm not asking for myself." ∎

LEVITICUS
Mitchell Untch

Cousin Billy lights a cigarette,
cups the flame in front of his mouth.
Don't tell my wife, Janet.
She doesn't know I smoke.
He takes a drag.
She'd kill me if she knew.
Billy is filled with minor disturbances.

I'm really sorry about yesterday.
We don't care what you are.
We've all got our sins he says
and stands silent.
It seems like forever.
This type of silence never marries.

Billy examines the Johnson grass by the porch.
It'll kill everything if you let it.
Better start bush hogging, otherwise.
He flicks his cigarette and goes indoors.
Don't tell Janet 'bout the bourbon neither.
The screen door slams shut.
An hour's heat chases after him.

Janet approaches me from the other side of the yard.
We're really sorry about what the minister said yesterday.
You know Billy and I don't feel that way.
Janet's vowels are long and drawn and sweet.
Janet does not suffer minor disturbances.
Complications do not rifle her.

She sits down, folds the hem of her dress over her knees.
No one cares who's gay, but why do they
always have to rub it in our faces she asks.
I mean it's their choice. Her vowels: long, drawn, sweet.
She says she loves me because I am family.

It's the way we are here honey, forgiving.
Come inside before dinner gets cold!

You don't waste time chatting in the Midwest.
At dinner, you learn to pass the plates
before the gravy begins to settle
and conversations turn to silence.
You learn just how close to family
you're ever going to be.

Myrtles cast their net
of shadows over the lawn.
I pick up a stone, roll it in my hand,
throw it as hard as I can,
out of my sight I throw it goddam hard as I can.
What I had to come to find
will lie in the field for years.

A SUITABLE REPRIEVE
Jim Ringley

I remember spending the whole rain-wet spring burdened with a constant and sober longing. I'd heaped fault for this on Pee Dee Creek, where we lived: on the dumb cows who spent their days standing in drizzle, thinking about grass; on the shaggy, soggy chickens who shit on our porch steps; and on miles of road, nothing but mud. I was fourteen, and, to me, everything around me was ugly and no-good, and anything but what I had was what I craved most.

Ten miles away, a monastery and all-boys Catholic high school stood on top of a hill, overlooking the Arkansas cow pastures and dairy barns. You'd do a double take the first time, so out of place it seemed, the cluster of high stone buildings with arched windows and turrets on some of the corners. From the narrow strip of rural highway, Subiaco Abbey and Academy was a vision of postcard foreignness and fairy-tale brilliance. The abbey church rose out of the misty landscape like an improbable castle, its bell tower and sharp peaks pointing heavenward.

There was nothing homespun about Subiaco, no spliced fence wires or slipshod plywood patchwork. Its order and rectitude expressed to me that goodness was beautiful and that beauty had a noble purpose. I only dared apply to the school because we lived nearby, because my grades at the public school had been good, and because I knew if I did maintenance chores for the monks, I could work off the seven-hundred-dollar days-only tuition. So far, my fourteen years had amounted to nothing. I hoped that if I became a Subiaco Trojan I could be rescued from some vaguely awful and lifelong mediocrity. I *needed* to go there.

One afternoon in April I came home to our gap-jointed and bent-nail farmhouse to find a large butterscotch envelope on the kitchen table. Bernie had brought it. Bernie doubled as a part-time hay hauler and our regular postman, driving the farm roads to sell Skylab stamps out the passenger window of his sunburnt pickup. From the envelope, I pulled a navy-blue-and-orange T-shirt along with a letter of invitation to begin ninth grade at the academy. I was elated—and relieved.

* * *

At summer's tail end, when Subiaco Academy held its freshman orientation, we new students gathered in the field house on neat, bristly Astroturf. There, under caged lights that buzzed high in the metal trusses, the monks took turns laying out for us what privileges and pleasures we could look forward to and what would be expected in return. When school began, there were pep rallies and bonfires to boost our Trojan spirit, and during these swells of esprit de corps, I felt confident that I'd found my tribe. I learned the football cheers and made friends with a couple of classmates. Still, I didn't really fit as part of the group. There were a half dozen of us local students in my class—"Day Dogs," they called us, for going home each night to our families. We were a ragtag subset. We didn't wear fashionable polo shirts or docksider shoes. Even among the Day Dogs, I felt as though I were circling in some outer orbit. I wasn't even Catholic.

Heavy homework was new to me, as was the presence of doctrine and ritual in school. On saints' days, we broke our schedule for mass in the church, a vast, marbled place of kneeler-knock and coin-clink echoes, of kaleidoscope windows spilling wine-stained light. I tried to see the divine connection between suffering and devotion, injury and unconditional love, but without luck. Gradually, instead, I picked up the words to hymns and Gregorian chants and synchronized myself with the patterns of standing, sitting, and kneeling. I understood the great value the monks placed on the eucharist and confession, though there was no pressure on me, no expectations. As a non-Catholic, I had no obligation to confess anything. I was exempt from the unburdening and free to keep my sins to myself, whatever the consequences.

From the beginning, I felt overly small and exposed. I felt isolated too, by my hand-me-down clothes and by what I knew and the other boys didn't: that I smoked cigarettes in a toolshed when I went home at night; that my dad made me nervous on weekends, the way his hands crimped and folded one beer can after the next, as if one by one, they had let him down and someone would hear about it. I didn't want my classmates to know my mom washed the clothes in our bathtub and hung them, underwear and all, over lines she rigged around the coal stove in the living room.

I concentrated hard on my studies, praying I wouldn't fall behind. So many civilizations and overpopulated histories poured from Brother Jude's lectures; Babylonians and Etruscans, Normans and Huns invaded my mind, pushing and clamoring with details of their lives, crowding like refugees of the past into swamped rescue boats. And cryptic algebra tormented me. Week by week, I felt sucked backward in an undertow of increasingly complicated formulas. Even though I had made the honor roll the first quarter, I worried I might not make it at the academy. I had enough sense to know that anything was possible.

Now, in mid-December, I felt thankful that my first semester was almost over. While the tables in the school cafeteria were being cleared from lunch, the polished halls of the academy's Main Building echoed with a fever-like mash-up of voices and the reverberating clatter and slam of metal lockers. I flung my own locker door shut and crossed the lobby to the double glass doors. They parted with a breathy gasp. *So cold outside* . . . The winter air had a finer, cleaner edge to it, even crisper now than during our morning classes. It smelled brisk too, earthy with gutter-damp leaves and dead grass, moist clouds, and although I didn't see anyone smoking nearby, I picked up the pale blue fragrance of a cigarette, recently snubbed. Over lunch the dull clouds had grown heavier and seemed so low now that a tall monk with a broom might be able to bat them if he could get a foothold on the steep, red tiles above the fourth-floor dorms. Normally, the portico and patio in front of the lobby would have been lively with students, their voices all bouncing around the tan stone walls of the campus. Instead, only a few boys made beelines like spokes across the circular drive, shoulders hunched, puffs of white breath scuffing their cheeks.

Most of the students here had come far from home, from places like Dallas, Costa Rica, Iran, and they stayed on campus for weeks and months at a stretch. They hunched over their work in the second-floor halls, making notes while the radiators dozed. Studying together, eating, showering, and sleeping; privacy barely existed, and with final exams looming, the collective mood had grown edgy and sullen. Some of the taller, stronger boys still shoved and teased, calling each other *pussy* and *faggot*, horseplay that after nearly a full semester had become tiresome. Most of us steered clear of their jockeying. We were sick of it.

Less than a week away now, Christmas vacation glimmered like a mirage. I found myself hearing fragments of carols behind the closed doors of the piano practice rooms or whistled softly in hollow stairwells. I counted the days until my time would be free of so much thinking and memorizing, when I could lie on my bed at home and read mysteries and forget everything, and no one would care.

I headed toward Alumni Hall for Father Camillus's Freshman Composition class just as bells began to ring from the church tower. I abandoned the sidewalk and cut across the parched winter grass, keeping one fist nested tightly in my pocket, the other hand locked around a small stack of books. I held them hard against the bony jut of my hip. When the bells stopped, cold silence surrounded the last wavering note, gathering it into a merest hum that trembled like the last bead of a candle's flame and finally blinked into nothingness. I shivered.

The air in Alumni Hall was stuffy and faintly sweet with a scent like floor wax, cough drops, and aftershave. Both sides of the long hall were hung with photographs of each graduating class since the early 1900s. The older, sepia-toned students wore dark suits and bow ties at one end. At the other, recent graduates of the midseventies let their hair go puffy and sported pastel suit coats with wide lapels. I couldn't imagine myself as a graduate of anything, but then, I couldn't know what future I was slipping into. The old-timers in Pee Dee Creek kept telling me how fast I was growing. I knew I was changing—being changed—but into what? Like some hapless serf in a Grimm tale, I'd wake to discover beastly hair in the most private places, my chin cursed with pimples, my voice turned awkwardly froggy and unreliable. Thoughts of nakedness and sex were nearly always in mind, and where did *those* come from, and where might they lead? What did their insistence say about me?

I made my way to our classroom. The cover of my textbook was still cold while the back of my hand prickled warm. My cheeks, too, burned flush after coming inside and my coat collar held on to the vaguest whiff of winter air, a bitter smell like frost on cold tin. I took a seat among the rows of mostly empty desks and waited. What to make of these thoughts I never asked for? Even as I wrestled the most vexing algebraic riddles, Brooke Shields might appear in my mind with her smoldering I-dare-you teen stare and bare skin to derail me. I lacked all fortitude. Wasn't that evidence enough that my nature was corrupt? And here: when I was in first grade, my peewee soul yearned for a classmate named Penny, a dark-eyed girl with fine features and pink lips. For some reason, I made the childish decision that she would be even prettier with tears in her eyes. One afternoon, our teacher called us students one at a time to the front of the class to receive some sort of holiday treat from her. I remember Penny's turn. I remember the rounded toes of her patent leather shoes approaching me between the rows of desks. I remember that as she passed me, my right foot jabbed out to tangle her feet. I tripped sweet Penny on purpose, and it was a terrible crime. She *was* lovely in her sorrow, but the festive air in the room had been spoiled, and our teacher—a teacher whom I admired—was very disappointed, frustrated, and herself wounded by the senselessness of it. She demanded to know who, *who*? No one answered. Nothing came of it.

* * *

When the classroom was nearly filled, Father Camillus walked in and laid a handful of books on the desk at the front of the room. He stood tall and staid in his black cardigan buttoned over starched black clerics. "Good afternoon," he said. Lanky white hair strayed across his forehead. He picked up the felt eraser and began to clear the blackboard, sweeping it in high arcs around his head. And, as the scribbles on the board were replaced by emptiness, calm began to settle among the desks in the classroom. Scuffling shoes and zippers, sniffling, and whispers—all of it quieted until I could even hear the last, soft passes of the eraser.

This class had gradually and unassumingly become my favorite. English class was more a sanctuary to me than the elegant church with its lofty barrel arches. I took our *Christensen Rhetoric* workbook to be my sacred text. Few things pleased me as much as opening a brand-new book. I would part its immaculate pages from the center, feeling stiff glue bend in the spine. I would lift the paper to my cheeks and bury my nose in the crease. With my eyes closed I took long, slow breaths, drawing in the thrilling perfume of the binding, brand-new ink, and paper. It cleansed me. Any textbook, any example of fine literature, I imagined, had the power to save me from my sorry commonness. In these pages was my redemption, I could smell it.

Father Camillus's chalk ticked against the board as he started uncoupling coordinate adjectives from free modifiers and wrote them one under the other in spidery gusts. He spoke the words aloud in his sturdy baritone as they formed under his hand, "Across his nose . . . from left . . . to right . . ."

The room seemed too warm, perhaps. Pirani sat sleepy eyed and slump shouldered in his Trojan jacket, his pudgy hands piled one across the other like puppies napping on the pages of his workbook. "Pirani," Father Camillus said. "What's the subject of this one?" Pirani fumbled with his book, smoothing the splayed pages with his hands and squinting at it. I looked in my own workbook at the sentence by Wright Morris:

Across his nose, from left to right, he dragged the sleeve of his Davy Crockett jerkin, leaving the mica-like trail of a snail on his cuff.

Father Camillus went to the long bank of windows that looked out on the campus and stood there. I knew that sight—"the mica-like trail of a snail . . ." I had seen those shimmery traces at home, on the flagstone walk and across the cellar doors. I had watched kids wipe their noses that way, and I also knew the pearly luster of mica from the small rock collection in the top drawer of my brother's dresser. Like a wizard, the writer had taken three separate experiences I knew firsthand and had transfigured them, fusing them into a single, astonishing sentence that itself drew slowly from nose to cuff.

Father Camillus gazed outside, waiting. The gray day was dimming, closing around the hill like a wool overcoat.

"Brooks?" he said.

Brooks gave the answer. Father Camillus unlatched one of the windows and tugged it open an inch or two for fresh air. Next to one of the monastery's farm buildings, a monk's black cassock stood out against the blanched landscape, a dab dark as ink on grainy parchment. He fussed with a gate and disappeared.

"Because," Father Camillus explained. "'Davy Crockett' is an adjective here, not a person." This ruling caused sighs and soft groans of hopeless confusion. All the while, as we parsed these phrases, moisture particles were clinging to dust and pollen far above us in the somber sky. That moisture froze into flecks of crazed crystal and began to sink through the high atmosphere, tiny splintered looms laced with vapor. They drifted lower, gathering weight and whiteness, blooming into bits of downy fluff.

"Yes, it's a proper name, but it *describes* the boy's jerkin."

From the back corner came the sound of poorly stifled snickering and a chuckle that misfired as a single, phlegm-clotted cough. Father Camillus ignored them and looked around the room to gauge whether these grammatical distinctions were sinking in. "Let's look at the next one."

When Miss Emily Grierson died, our whole town went to her funeral: the men through a sort of respectful affection for a fallen monument, the women mostly out of curiosity to see the inside of her house, which no one save an old manservant—a combined gardener and cook—had seen in at least ten years. —William Faulkner

I had read a lot of books, but I read them only to know their endings. Now I began to feel the pulse of good words. I could sense the proper fit of one clause against another. As some boys could look at a car's engine and understand the logical relationship of the carburetor to the crankshaft, so I knew subjects and verbs. I started seeing to the bones of sentences, not just to name their functions, but to appreciate their shape and shading.

Beyond the windows, revealing themselves in a peripheral way, the first snowflakes of the season appeared, winking here and there like stray dust on film. Then more came down, fatter and brighter against the dark elbows of the elms and the curving shore of the asphalt drive. They fell with the grace of stars. Father Camillus didn't notice. His chalk stayed busy at the board while we students poked each other with pencil erasers and pointed to the windows. Over the roofs of town to the fading blue ranges of the Ouachita Mountains, the world appeared marvelously transformed. We stared. On the far side of the room, Briscio half-stood out of his seat, craning as his eyes darted over the view. The snow didn't fall only in the yard, nor only on the tennis courts or on the soccer field behind Heard Hall. It fell on the row of low houses and the feed mill in the distance. Its arrival was purest benediction, a gift for everything equally, for the privileged and the lesser alike. Father Camillus stopped writing in midsentence and turned around. Then he looked outside, too. "Ah," he said. "There it is."

For a moment, we watched and no one spoke. Then Briscio asked him, "Is it snow?"

"Indeed, it is." Father Camillus looked at Briscio intently. "Have you seen snow before?"

Briscio, whose home was Belize, shook his head.

"Then go out," Father Camillus told him. "Go see it."

"Now?"

"Yes, now." he said, casting a hand toward the door. "Go ahead."

Briscio grinned wide and lifted his umber corduroy jacket from the ladder-back of his desk chair. He hurried out of the room, closing the door very softly behind him.

The rest of us glanced at each other and blinked at Father Camillus. He returned to the blackboard. In his hand, the chalk made quick dashes and curls like comets in space. Letters begat words and the words blossomed into clauses. I began to feel swept up in the surge of history— history as an accumulation not of facts, but of people and their common urge to tell what happened. I had the sudden inkling that every molecule in the universe was working intently on some fantastic project and that they had started at the instant of creation, and that they had never lost momentum, nor could they, ever.

Briscio appeared below us in the yard. He did not run or laugh, but walked reverently among the flurries. Mostly he stood still with his hands and face upturned. He looked around. Delicate snowflakes spilled over him like a practical joke on a miraculous scale. I imagined their cold sparkle on my cheeks and lashes. I remembered the tinge of ice and zinc, the taste of snowflakes like winter starlight on the tongue. A rush of giddiness welled up in me. I tried to tamp this unexpected joy before it yanked me out of myself, but Briscio walked and snowflakes tumbled over the world. Then Father Camillus called us back to the board and all I could think was how wondrous, how lucky, how *beautiful*, everything. ■

EIGHTEEN
Lisa Taddeo

I see the way you look at me. I don't want you to feel shame and read the rest of this red-faced. But it's important, you've lectured, to begin with the *raison*.

You asked us to write about our deepest secret. Any length, you said, so long as we made it into a story. You didn't provide any more direction than that. The assignment was delivered orally. You didn't write it on the board like you usually do, or send a follow-up email after class.

Is it solipsistic of me to think that the sole purpose of this assignment was so that you could hear something sordid about me? I was assaulted by my stepfather. I was fingered by him in a horse barn, my rubber boots sinking, not without pleasure, into the muck. Something you could use to know me, and also to think about in the evening, when you get into bed next to your cold, latent wife, in her Ralph Lauren outlet pajamas.

I never had a stepfather and the only terrible thing my father did to me was die. I was sixteen so I've had the requisite couple of years of looking for saviors. Our newspaperman was Qatari. His name was Mohammed. Shortly after the event I was up before sunrise, crying on the front lawn. Our grass was still emerald, still verdant; it would take months before his absence would be felt on all living things outside our home as well as within.

Mohammed saw me and came over and put his arms around my shoulders. My father had been in a car accident but the details were slurred. We didn't know how my father—who was perfect and all-powerful—could have made such a mistake. Changing lanes recklessly in front of a long-haul truck. You want to hear something funny? The trucking company was called G.O.D., for Guaranteed Overnight Delivery. It was wild to see the letters G.O.D. emblazoned on the truck that took my father's life. I looked at the accident pictures because I have always played this game, daring myself to do the scariest thing. As a child I used to take drags of my mother's cigarette when she left the room for a moment. I never got caught, or experienced a greater thrill.

Mohammed told me he saw my father one morning, on one of his walks. He said my father was sitting down on the side of the road, on a sewer ledge. Mohammed stopped his car and got out. He said, Dr. Judson, what is wrong? Apparently my father replied, I am very sick, Mohammed.

This was unbelievable to me; my father was an ox but more than that, he would never have confided in our newspaperman. It was unbelievable, but I believed it. I told my mother that night. We smoked cigarettes at each other across our glass kitchen table. She cleaned both sides of it. Every week my father would help her flip it over, balancing it carefully on its beveled edge. The only thing that rang true was that my father used Mohammed's name when he spoke to him. He used everyone's name at them.

Mohammed invited me to a cocktail party at his family home. The butter-yellow invitation was included with our *Star-Ledger* the following week. I wanted to be closer to the last person my father had confided in, so I went. I wore a black lace dress with cap sleeves. I drove my Volkswagen Cabriolet, the one my father bought me the month before his accident, I drove it into a tony old community in South Orange. Big gaping manors with cornices and columns and dark brick and hedges. Rich, elderly people homes. Piss and dust.

I was shocked to discover that the paper delivery man's house was one of these stately mansions. I parked the car down the street and walked in my clunky heels to the door. A woman opened the door, his mother. Inside I smelled biryani and curry and it was so fine, to smell homemade food that had nothing to do with the kind of food my own family ate. She had a generous smile and took my bottle of wine from me very politely but I could see by the way she handled it that it was against her religion.

Mohammed came forward to receive me. He introduced me around the room, to other white people from my town who were on his paper route. Wealthy old doctors, a financier, some surgeon's widow. Everybody wore black and their mouths were all exceedingly dark, their lips vermilion. Maybe it was just my eyes that were translating it that way. When Mohammed went to help his mother in the kitchen, I leaned against an oak pillar and sipped lime-flavored seltzer. At length I arranged myself a plate of biryani and spooned a small amount of chicken tikka masala over it. I dipped naan in the mixture and ate daintily. The feeling of missing my father in the context of that strange home, it was like being bitten by a tiger. You cannot, actually, survive.

Mohammed was twenty-five if he was forty. I never asked. He wasn't attractive but he was very clean. He had a large nose and that night wore a fine pique shirt with cuff links. I never asked why he kept up a newspaper route in his dusty little Honda, when his family lived in such an estate. For that matter, I also never asked why he invited the people on his paper route to a cocktail party.

He crossed the parquet to find me whenever I was alone, which wasn't too often. You know with old people around, they always include you, they always bring you into the folds of their conversation. They like the smell of young blood, and to hear the names of the universities to which you are applying. I talked to the surgeon's widow about my father. Those were the early days of the loss, when I thought random people might have the key to healing. She wore a pin, a peony made of pink pearls with a ruby center. I couldn't stop looking at it.

Mohammed's mother brought me another plate of biryani with tender chicken bites in their savory orange sauce. She must not have seen me eat the first plate. I had the distinct feeling they were trying to drug me, or at least lull me into a queer submission with their rich, piquant food.

The surgeon's widow touched the nape of my neck with her cold fingers. I was surprised by her touch, but I didn't jump back or anything. When you are very broken by grief, you can feel like a cloud, and if a stranger touches your body without asking, it won't affect you the same way. In any case, she wasn't being fresh really, or strange. I wore a necklace I'd forgotten I had on. A little pair of garnet cherries with gold stems, on a very thin 14 karat gold chain. It was the first piece of jewelry my father had ever bought me. I was twelve years old, we were in a mall in the western part of the state—I used to think New Jersey was continent-wide, the way we'd visit so many towns, there was always a new town we hadn't yet seen, we would never, it seemed, exhaust New Jersey—and I saw the necklace on one of those light-gray velvet busts, behind security glass. It wasn't expensive, I realize now, but then it seemed like the ultimate act of devotion, my father saying, You like that? You want it?

Part of what made the necklace so precious is how angry my mother was when we came home. I think it is impossible to not feel slutty when your father has purchased something for you and you come home wearing it and your mother gets angry. Or perhaps it is only me.

Isn't that lovely, the surgeon's widow said, fingering my pendant.

Oh, I said.

Mohammed told us you recently lost your father, she said. Her hair was the silver of fairy godmothers but her manner did not align.

I nodded, swallowing.

Loss is more a part of life than we want to believe it is, she said. That's the trouble.

She came closer to me, I had the thought of smelling mice on her breath, but there were so many new and interesting odors in that house that of course it was just my imagination.

My first real loss was not Harry, she confided. Harry was my husband. Harry Joel, the brilliant neurosurgeon. My first real loss was my son, Jed. He was not Harry's, he was from my first marriage, to a man named Eddie, who worked construction. My mother told me from the beginning what a mistake I was making, but back then we didn't know as much as your generation does. Anyway, I didn't know how much of a mistake it would turn out to be. Jed was five when Eddie took him to work one day. I was over my marriage by then, and feeling beautiful, and there was a man I'd begun to see, a man with money and a summer home already. I made Eddie take Jed to work, because I wanted to go to a party at this man's lake house. I was afraid another woman would snatch him up before I'd gotten up the courage to leave Eddie. I was resentful of what Eddie had let me become. A woman caring all day for a child. A woman without the resources to hire a nanny. I loved Jed of course, with every bone in my body, but what I loved even more was the vision I had of Jed as a rich man's stepson. I loved who I would be and who Jed would be once Eddie was out of the picture. I imagined this man I was seeing would be benevolent and kingly and make Jed his rightful heir. Finally I would glide around a home the way I was supposed to, my brain freed enough of financial stressors and housekeeping duties to be the perfect mother I knew I could be. And so on that day I wore my best sundress and perfume at my wrists and attended the party at the lake, meanwhile Jed and Eddie went to the site and, it's amazing, truly, that you have the stupidest men working the most dangerous jobs. I have always marveled. And the alcohol they drink, the cans of beer, and some of them hard liquor. You can guess what came next.

I shook my head.

My young son was crushed under the wheel of a crane. Eddie'd taken his eyes off him for a moment. Five years old. That's the age when you begin to trust them, when they are finally less stupid.

She took a sip of her seltzer and I could nearly see the liquid going down her throat.

For a very long time, she continued, I tried to isolate the precise instant, what I was doing at the lake house. I made love to the man I was seeing, during the party, in the pantry off the kitchen while some waitstaff were bumbling about just outside. I think it was that exact moment. The moment of my orgasm, you see. Because that is how God likes to do it.

Another sip went down the translucent neck.

It took some time, but I regrouped. You must, you see. Because at first suicide seems the obvious choice but then two weeks go by and then three, and later it has been six months and—Harry came at the exact time men like Harry come. Just when you need them. We were married for thirty-five years. No children. Lots of travel. Brazil, Berlin, Italy, of course. Skiing in Saint Moritz every winter, until just last year, when his second hip gave out. Last month, a heart attack over a warm bone broth at home. As it should be. And now, I've had enough, you see. You must know when to say when.

I thought to embrace her. My mother was a very fragile woman and so I was always trying to take care of them.

At length, I spoke to the other guests. They were nearly all doctors—we lived in a neighborhood full of them—and mustachioed and goateed as my father had been. Salt-and-pepper wiry hair on their slack but erudite faces. None of them offered any solace. From across the room, I could always count on Mohammed to be checking up on me. That night it seemed that he alone in the world understood my pain. Our newspaper delivery man.

Later in the evening, Mohammed and I sat at the wrought iron bistro set on the lower patio. We looked out at the full moon, the bright tin stars in the black sky. It took him almost a half hour to place his palm on top of mine. His hand was ringless, smooth, I felt certain I could push it away and there would be nothing awkward. He wouldn't pretend it hadn't happened. I could feel his safety from the manner of his hand. At the very same time, can you believe I was deathly afraid?

You wear a ring, a golden lion with sapphire eyes. You could say it was my fault, my doing, that first day you asked us to describe an *objet.* And I wrote one thousand words about your ring. With my perfect vision from the first row I could see the etchings, the dull shine of the eyes. But can you tell me in complete honesty that you did not wear the ring on purpose, and brandish it on purpose, and then proceed to wear it for the hundred days that followed, so that I wouldn't think anything was amiss? I can practically hear your wife say, When did you start wearing that ring again? I can practically smell her veal meatballs going round and round in the sauce.

I asked him about my father, this man who hadn't known him at all. His lips were dark meat. He applied pressure to my hand. Inside, the minimal guests were moving about, perhaps getting ready to leave. My legs were cold so I crossed them. It was the first week of October, which had always been my favorite time of year. Of course by that point autumn had become the season of my father's death.

I don't know how the newspaperman came to have me. That wasn't even the strangest part of the night. The startling thing came later. But outside in that chilly courtyard, looking out at the city lights of Manhattan from a sterile suburban perch, Mohammed certainly had me. It wasn't terrible but it didn't make me feel good. It wasn't entirely consensual, but it definitely wasn't rape. He didn't move in and out of me in any perceptible manner. I don't think my underwear came off. I remember his breath tasted like lipstick, but I don't know that we kissed. When it was over we were two slugs in the cold grass. I felt very open to the world.

Christina, Mohammed said.

I turned to meet his gaze. Like all men's faces after sex, his was hideous.

Hmm?

Your father loved you more than he loved anyone.

I nodded. It was something I knew but had forgotten, like everything.

Mohammed reached with his womanly finger and grazed my nipple. During intercourse he'd pulled the neck of my dress down, along with my bra, to expose my yellow rack. Now he brought the dress back to cover me. I've always wondered why men were so intent on dressing you after they'd come. It's like the red squirrel, needing to replace a nut it takes with an oak leaf.

I imagine you now, the prim golf hole of your mouth, the row of tough white teeth in there, as you lick your lips, reading this. I know from your books that you're the type who gets off on other men having their way with women you know you can never have. You must have had a cold mother. Did she keep her nipples from you?

* * *

I don't want you to pleasure yourself to the thought of me with the newspaperman, nor do I want you to move on to someone else. In many ways I only feel alive when someone like you thinks about me that way. That clean, obsessive way. It's like putting a stone in a sacred spot, and I glow.

Besides, I admire you! There was that day that I was worried you thought the Canadian girl was smarter than I, when you said what you did about Nabokov . . . "However unrelenting, however unforgiving of his characters, he was, indeed, a rapist of a certain kind," I thrilled to that. You seemed that day to be a protector of good little girls.

I've thought of you often, from that point on. Like after we came back from spring break, during which time I'd read the essay you wrote about you and your wife on holiday—you used that word, though you are not British—at the Italian seaside resort, with the crow-colored waters and the large sun rocks. You and your wife were walking on the dock one evening when you heard a scuffle. On the floor of a fishing boat a man was taking advantage of a woman. You shone the light of your phone on the scene, and the man barely looked up. He kept undoing his belt. Your wife held fast to your elbow. Don't, she hissed. Leave it be! But you hollered at them. You said, Stop! in your remedial Italian. You acted as though the man were a bear and the more noise you made, the better. The man stood in the boat. You could see he was much bigger than you, and stronger. His belt buckle hung slack in the darkness. Your wife was pulling on you, hissing, and then you noticed the woman, cowering at the man's feet. Her dress was torn, and you could see through her legs to the dark thatch between. The essay ends there, in that considerable darkness; you did not say if you'd saved the woman or not, or ran back to your safe hotel with its hard bed and congenital Americans. I both admired that it ended like that and was disgusted by your immorality. Your snakehood.

You probably don't want to know, anyway, what I think of you. It would be enough for you to know I admire you and look up to you. But I'm going to tell you what I think. It's not all bad or good, which you're probably not enough of an adult to understand. What I mean by that is, you may be erudite and schooled and well traveled, but you are sad inside. You are brittle. You aren't a protector of little children. And so, because I don't owe you my protection, not after you withheld yours from me, here goes:

Your breath up close sometimes smells of cats. You drive a white Jaguar with dead leather seats. The idea of your car depresses me, its tape deck, its grandmother morbidity. Sometimes when I look at you I am very disgusted. Other times, in crowded places, like train stations and bus stations and anyplace where people my age are drinking cheap beer, I imagine you walking through the scrum to save me from the impotence of anonymity. From being half drunk with people who are full drunk. I know that with you I would drink orange wine and eat crisp scallops in glassy, green sauces. I know you know where they have good olive oil, even in this college town. I don't think you're ugly, but you are. Objectively speaking, your face is oddly shaped, your nose is disturbing, your cheeks are hollow like Depression-era despair, your neck sags, your hair is sparse and not intellectually so, and I can see the wiry hair in your ears from across the quad, when the sun shines and you smile at me and give a queer half wave. You are the color of cold egg salad.

I know what you think of me. I'm objectively beautiful. I'm eighteen. My skin is apricot tan and it moves over my bones like horses. My hair, I know how to swing it behind my shoulders when I know you're watching. I want you to think I don't notice. I want you to think it's okay.

I want everyone else in the class to think I don't know it's going on, I want them to think I'm so inviolable, so fair, so snow, so primly stupid, that I don't know you are worshipping me, hating me, in that damp head of yours. That's the part of me you don't know, and I'm telling you now. That's one secret. A small one.

* * *

My mother used to be magical, all-knowing and all-seeing. After my father died, the magic vamoosed. I'm not sure why or how, but she stopped knowing things. She stopped caring, too. That's why I could smoke around her suddenly. The night I went to the Qatari party, I came home past one and she was asleep. I smelled of curry and I was covered in the sort of postcoital paste that glows in the right light, if a mother is looking at you hard. But mine was sleeping. Likely she'd been sleeping for a very long time. She didn't hear me come in, and she didn't know what had happened, my having intercourse of a kind with the man who whipped our newspaper onto our driveway. Anyway, it's what happened *after* he had me is the secret I've never told.

The word *secret.*

I wonder why you did this. On what day did you become the sort of person who gives out such an assignment to a classroom of young, nubile minds? To stroke your own self to the tune of us, to the tune of little children in the palm of your hand. To, in effect, become a rapist of a certain kind.

When I was a little girl, I became obsessed with a strange couple that lived across the creek from our house. We didn't live in the country, but in the firefly suburbs of New York City, and the creek was not anything grand, just a pleasant burbling one that gasped through the perimeter of woods. There were wind chimes outside this house, which was smaller than ours and ugly. The yard was the kind that attracted bugs, there was a bug lamp that turned on in the evenings, hot and blue.

One bored summer day, I wrote a note, I was nine or ten years old. Perhaps eleven. My friends were all at summer camp and I was at home all day, accompanying my mother to the grocery store, my father to the Sears. I typed up a note on my word processor and slipped it into an envelope. I stepped on mossy rocks to cross the creek and left the note on their doorstep. Then I sloshed through the water back to my house, panting, excited. In my note I said a variety of strange and irresponsible and psychotic things. *I miss you and I am sorry and I hope the family is all right. I still think of you every day.* Things of that nature. Nothing too inspired, but in a way it was brilliant, because it was general enough that it could have been anyone, writing to anyone else. Perhaps I wanted the wife to think I'd had an affair with the husband, I really don't know. All I know is that it was a disturbed thing to do. I was strange in these ways, but otherwise normal, well-adjusted. I wanted for romantic love, like any girl that age, like any girl any age.

I asked them to leave me a note in the same spot. Two days later, I waited until I heard a car leave the driveway—it's important for me to say that I never saw the occupants of the house, only their lights on or off, only their car in the driveway or not. There could have been two people who lived there, or one, but from the note they left for me, I believe it was two. Sure enough, there was a note tied to a rock with pastry string.

Dear Cynthia, it began, and my name as you know is not and never was Cynthia, and it said, *We are so happy you have made contact again. We don't want to frighten you away again, and we want you to come home and have it be the way that it was.*

I don't know if they were fucking with me, because I was fucking with them, or if there had been a young girl, a daughter or stepchild, or someone one or both of them had assaulted. I pictured a house full of stained rugs, old pots and pans, and a child's bedroom with a patchwork quilt and dusty Raggedy Ann dolls from the seventies. Back then my mind swam with the possibilities, these days it swims even more.

I didn't tell my parents of course, because I would have had to tell them the creepy thing I'd done to start it. I can't help thinking now that the road to hell is paved with little girls like me.

I have a little document where I collect quotes. Some of yours are in there, but most of them are from people who will long be quoted after you yourself are forgotten.

* * *

I wonder if you and your wife fuck and if so how.

Do you each read your books then set them aside. Does she keep her silk pajamas on, do you merely allow for enough space for your pale, cold cock to find its way. Did you tell us (me) so many details about her because it inured you to being a filth bag?

It's not amazing to me that you teach this class only for me. Only *to* me. That is sex, after all, isn't it? It is everything. You were denied a certain amount of rosy cheeks in your youth, and now you seek to recreate it with me. You were greasy and sloppy and old before your time. Men who were boys like you will never be faithful to a woman.

I can only hope my father was not like this about some girl. I can only hope he never did what you will do to me.

Because we are going to fuck, of course. We both know it. Or you only don't know it because once you know it it will ruin your days, you'll have too much. I'm more perfect like this, ounces of pretty meat behind the cool counter. But you're too keen, with this assignment you see, you've already gone too far.

I tell you the story about the newspaperman, because I want you to know—this is my only power, you see? If I am lamed in the future, if I am buying Lucky for Life in Stoughton, Massachusetts, or wearing high heels on a corner of some not-pretty mountain town. If I am a supermarket cashier in in a slender Arizona town, yes of course some fault will come from what happens between us, but know that it won't only be you. It will be Mohammed, of course, and my father, of course. And the man on the beach in Puerto Rico when I was thirteen and wearing a butterfly bikini, who said such things to me, and my cousin's friend, the eighteen-year-old boy with the thick lips who would grow into a very good-looking man, who turned to my cousin and said, She has a phenomenal little body, look at those legs, you can already tell. When I was three years old. It won't only be you, you see?

Or perhaps because my father died and I was had by several strange men, none of whom were boyfriends, perhaps I will be saved from the middling future. Perhaps sleeping with men like you, I will avoid the Park Slope mothers, the Litchfield County mothers. Sitting around a table with these women, tender as saltines, as they over and over ask the question, But can a child, I wonder, eat *too* healthy?

The other reason I tell you the story is because you are smart, because I look up to you, and because I wanted to ask you, in a way that you would have to pay close attention, I think about that night, that strange cocktail party, and you know? Sometimes I think they were all dead, those people at the newspaperman's cocktail party. Sometimes I think *I* died that night. Or that I was in the car with my father when it flipped in the air like a toy. What if that is my biggest secret in the world? That I am dead. That's what you fantasize about every evening, while your wife reads Sybille Bedford and you turn away into that mad fetus of your brain, that this strong, tough body you hold in your mind's eye, this body you eat gelato with on future rocky beaches, is the body of a dead woman? The body of a woman even more used than you can imagine. Would that make you feel worse? Or would you, then, be able to forgive yourself? To imagine what we will soon do will never have actually happened. ∎

DEAD SPIDER
Heather Cousins

Legs an empty setting
waiting for a jewel

YOU ALWAYS HAVE BEEN CENTAURS

Richard B. Simon

Your guitar is in its flight case under the plane, the custom redwood Mano built for you that cost so much it nearly broke your marriage. You keep replaying the fight with the band in Tokyo. Mostly over money. But also over music. Over control. Chafing at how you ride them. But you need everything to be just where you want it. Just where it needs to be. To make art. To get big. To make some money and take better care of Cin and rise up out of the goddamn grind so every record, every tour doesn't have to be an existential crisis. Maybe finally have a kid.

The sun is up before they finally deplane you. You step out onto the wing and the heat blasts you. The plane's skin is scored with tiny fractal curlicues, serrated rainbow holograms that seem to burrow infinitely into the steel. The flight attendant ushers you to the emergency slide. She is perfectly crisp in her dolphin-grey suit. Her feet are sheathed in fine silk stockings. You can see her French-painted toenails through the sheer. A toe ring. The tiniest glint of rebellion. You leap out onto the yellow like the foldout says, bounce, and slip slowly down to the tarmac. But it's not tarmac. It's a mosaic of hexagonal glass tiles, shot through with circuits. It stretches out across the vast plain. Solar panels. Hundreds of thousands of them. You don't remember hearing about this.

You are surrounded by high-techno emergency vehicles that have formed a wide perimeter around the plane. They are round and glassy. They look like no cars you've ever seen. Some are so black they seem to absorb light. Others are so white you can't look at them. Their flashing lights, dark, rich blues and reds that you've been watching all night, seem to emerge from nowhere, like they're being projected from the vehicles' roofs. You are greeted by government men backed by riot cops in full black armor, their face shields opaque. Some are carrying long cattle prods, truncheons, their tips dripping with electricity. A few are in space suits. They've been circling the plane for hours. There are ambulances and fire trucks. Your sense for estimating crowd size is sharp from tour. You count about a hundred people surrounding the two hundred who get off the plane. Not a bad night here at SFO. Thanks for coming out, folks.

You've never seen the international terminal from this angle—it looks much bigger. There's more glass than you remember. It looks more like Denver than SFO, big swooping tents of steel and glass rising up like a range of sharp-peaked Fujis. It glows like a new copper penny in the deep red of the rising sun. It looks like it is hovering over water. A mirage.

It is unusually hot for so early in the morning. Humid for San Francisco at the peak of summer. You wonder whether this is actually San Francisco, or whether maybe the plane has been hijacked to someplace like Singapore or Dubai. You breathe in deep and it tastes like California. The ocean, the bay, the heat off the hills. You hope Cin hasn't been sitting in the airport all this time waiting. You stick your shades onto your face. The cracked temple pokes the bone behind your ear. It broke three tours ago. You'll replace them when you can spare the money. The Texan who was holding forth all night about sunspots is demanding that someone tell him just-what-in-hell's-name-is-going-on, trying to foment a rebellion on principle. You want to talk to your dad but your folks are off the grid at some yoga campout up in Ukiah. They're old hippies. They live in their own chaotic dust storm, never with their shit together.

A Japanese woman faints and falls to the solar tile. The world seems to undulate around you. The glass Fujis of the international terminal are bobbing subtly down and up, like the whole terrain is moving. An earthquake. Why not. You squat to your haunches and press your hands to the tile. It's cooler than you expected. Round pips pop up from its surface for traction. You feel the ground roll below your hands and feet, a long waveform passing. It's not an earthquake, you realize. The runway is floating on the bay. You remember Feinstein saying something about this in the paper—but you don't remember hearing that they were actually doing it. You wonder where you've been. Wrapped up in recording, project after project, gig after gig, tour after tour, trying desperately to make ends meet in the maelstrom of the tech boom that is gobbling up your entire rock-and-roll world.

They load you onto buses, more streamlined versions of the ones that shuttle the kids down to the tech campuses. Inside, they are even more high-tech than you had imagined. The seats are impossibly thin, pressed from laminated bamboo. Scandinavian. The ceiling is a glass vault, almost like there's no roof at all. The conditioned air is cool and dry and sweet. An ethereal music plays, barely loud enough to make out, a sort of organic electronic harmony of the spheres, like nothing you've ever heard. There's a melody in there, just out of reach. Something familiar. You tune your ears but you can't place it. You get seated and you look straight ahead. You're not ready to talk to the woman next to you. You keep your shades on and you try to lock in on that melody line. And you realize, with a shock and a horror, that it's one of yours. Someone ripped you off. Adrenaline and cortisol course through you. But it's not just your melody. It's the whole goddamn song. It's "Dreams of Forgotten Futures." From your brand-new record. Transposed into this electro-organic technomuzik and burbling out of the bus from unseen speakers, like the sound is just materializing in the breath.

You don't remember hearing about this.

* * *

Government agents debrief you for weeks in the old zeppelin hangar at NASA Ames. They give you medical tests and scans and take blood and urine, stool, semen, and lymph. You're not allowed to contact your family, but they let you walk around Moffett Field, which is surrounded by a twenty-foot levee that holds the bay out. Everything is covered with photovoltaics—down to, they tell you, the steel-and-glass skyscrapers that rim most of the bay, many of them built to house people displaced by the rising sea.

They tell you that in the twenty years since your plane disappeared into a sort of fistula between two folds in the fabric of space and time, the world slipped past the lurch toward authoritarianism that had felt like a dull gnawing at your marrow. Fossil fuels are only used to make nanopolymers. Planes run on electrolyzed hydrogen. Humans finally got it together. But sea levels have risen eight feet, and they're still rising, despite a lot of geoengineering, some of which has gone badly wrong, some of which has gone right. The latter includes a retractable solar parasol at the Lagrange point between the sun and Earth. A lot of the Bay Area is gone, including your childhood home in San Leandro—one of the zones that was deconstructed and left to revert to tidal marsh, along with much of low-lying San Francisco and Oakland and everywhere. And that's with the battery of Thames Barriers they installed throughout the Golden Gate like locks to generate electricity and regulate the storm surges. People call them the Electric Potatoes. It's a great band name.

They tell you that Americans and citizens of most industrialized countries have a guaranteed basic income now. They tell you it was the only way to keep the global economy flowing in the wake of what they now call the Tech Leap.

* * *

When Cinnamon finally picks you up, she's driving a jet-black pod. "This is really weird," she says, and she gives you a hug and a kiss, but it's not a real kiss. She's crying. She was thirty-five six weeks ago and now she's fifty-five. She's even more gorgeous. She's dressed like a serious woman. She's wearing pearls, and a wedding band that's not the one you put on her ten years ago.

She lays it on you slow as she winds up the solar causeway they hung on cables above the old 101, which is now a tidal marsh.

Your friends and big deal musicians you've never met did benefit gigs. The record sold. The straights ate it up because they thought it was a terrorist attack. The guys were all torn up with guilt. If it hadn't been for their little intervention in Tokyo, you would have been on the flight with them. Rohelio stopped playing and left the Bay, moved up to some nothing town by the Canadian border. Magnus blew his brains out. Chong lost his marbles for about ten years, then he made a record about the whole thing and it blew up, in a bigger-than-your-typical-indie-rock way. Like he was one of those old crazy diamonds with a comeback. Getting interviewed on public radio and barely able to talk, laughing at those cryptic jokes that go over everyone's head but his. Your old records got looked at again, started selling again, the whole catalog. *Wire and Wood* resonated with the kids in their rebellion against their techboomer parents. They made a folk legend out of you, stenciled your face everywhere. Money came in.

The car sounds like a whooshing, whistling zipper across the solar road. A richly colored yellow lightning bolt in the windshield display is pulsing in the rhythm of the dotted line.

"It drives itself," she says, "but I still like to be in control."

"That's what I love about you, darlin'."

"I can't remember," she says. "Did we have that before you—um."

"Just a couple weeks ago," you say. "It was just getting started."

She's not looking at you. She's looking straight ahead.

"It charges itself from the road," she says. "Grid takes it out of your GBI."

"*No comprendo,*" you say. You're trying to will her into making eye contact with you.

"They all merged into one giant entity that moves money and power around," she says. "You really don't have to do anything with money anymore. It sort of all happens automatically with credits. GBI goes into your account, plus anything extra, like my—like our—or, your. The. The royalties. The AIs talk to each other and divvy it all up and send it where it needs to go. It's not bad. Ten K DC a month GBI. The royalties are . . . a lot more."

You don't understand half of what Cin is saying but you realize she's doing better without you. You love her so goddamn much, you're happy for her.

The city is taller than it was. You can hardly tell where the hills are under all the skyscrapers. They're whimsical, pyramids and toruses and cylinders and twists. Organic shapes. They all seem to have some kind of wind turbine. They are terraced and bursting with plants and trees, dangling vegetables, flowers, and fruits. You didn't think it was possible to grow bananas in San Francisco.

"I'm married," she tells you as the pod whispers off the solar freeway and onto city streets. Your heart cracks, even though you knew this was coming.

"I saw the ring," you say and your voice barely comes out of you. "My parents?"

"They died," she says. "Years ago. Of grief. I'm so sorry."

The major streets are walled with steel-skinned towers, their facades warped in surreal geometries. The lights are timed so that you never have to stop. You want her to drive it out to Ocean Beach and over the top of whatever fucking solar seawall they have out there and just keep driving, to oblivion, to Tokyo, to 2017, to the bottom of the ocean where they buried you.

She drives you out to the Haight, out to the end where it slams into Stanyan. The record store is gone. The whole block has been replaced by a stainless steel apartment tower, a mirror-polished rectangle that twists up to echo the de Young and looks west across the park to the onrushing Pacific, which Cin says is turning the Outer Sunset back into a sea of dunes. She points to the parking lot wall that was always painted with murals of tragic rock heroes who meant something here. Garcia. Hendrix. Janis. Bob Marley. They've added Tupac and a Filipina trans DJ named 6. And then there is you, looking just like you look now in the rearview. The image is based on a publicity shot that Suzy took a few weeks ago, the mural faded and weathered, worn down by the acid fog. It's thronged with tourists. With candles and flowers and wreaths.

* * *

You're in the cavernous green room and you're drinking coffee and tuning the Mano, which they have finally managed to deliver, just before showtime. You can't help but think that its molecules have been rearranged by the time warp. You don't change the strings. Your rig is already onstage. You hear the low thrum of the crowd out in the Ovary. The arena sits above what used to be Treasure Island like a cluster of titanic glass grapes, a godzillian kelp pod thrown up by the advancing sea. A thick, brushed-steel tunnel slinks from it like a tentacle and drops into the bay, connecting the Ovary by subhyperloop to the Transbay Terminal. But you've had enough of getting too far too fast. You walked it through the foot-and-bike tunnel, beside the moving sidewalk, down a glass wall that looks out into the bay. You found an octopus clinging to the glass, picking off mussels, and you watched her pulse in the tide until Shep called to hustle you along.

Rohelio has, in fact, kept playing. His chops are as tasty as ever but less wild. Less muscular. More subtle and complex. Mature. And he's in good shape. Chong is like an ancient warrior, a master of his instrument. His beard is long and wild and wispy and black. Age has thickened his body. He's got a B3 onstage, and a Moog, and some instrument that bends air that you don't really understand. "You'll see," he says. It's almost the only thing he says to you. He's fused to his machinery, a musical cyborg. You all are. You always have been centaurs.

You brought Storm in on bass. You've never played in a band with him, but you've gigged together plenty. He's a monster player, his style instantly recognizable. One of the best in rock. And still totally unknown outside the underground. Which apparently still exists.

Cin stops in with her husband and her two girls, one of whom is in college studying quantum biology. The girls are brown and lean and long legged. They're starstruck. They're like your kids in a way. The kids you should have had years ago. Years before. You put them in the front row, even though you don't want to look at any of them. But all these goddamn songs are for her.

Shep's stage manager, Julie, comes in. She's a pro. It's time, she says. There's no opening act. You want the anticipation to build without interruption or distraction. You did the solo acoustic thing at the Fillmore for friends and promoters and industry folks to hear the new songs. People were stoked and the buzz was global. So Shep put this together. He played up the man-who-flew-through-time thing. You've never liked that kind of hype. You argued against it. "Man," he said. "You and that old-fashioned phone. You're kidding, right?"

You've played big festivals, but never this. Never an arena. Never headlining for fifteen thousand. It's everything you've ever wanted. You only had to lose everything to get it.

The Ovary was built for music by some hot Chinese architect whose brain is wired for structure and sound, a genius at symphony halls doing her first high-capacity shed. The beams are bent redwoods, the joints some indestructible elastic nanopolymer so the room can expand and contract and flex. There's a warmth to the space that you've never experienced in a venue this size. It feels like it's alive.

They bring the lights down and you stand in an awkward cluster in the wing while the crowd whistles and hoots. Rohelio's wife and kids are behind you. Storm's two girlfriends. Chong's husband, Howl. Many of your friends. Artists and musicians and promoters and writers, blasted by the paunched, wrinkled laser of time. The stage is set out from the back, so there are seats in the round. There are no speaker stacks, no lighting trusses. Just your rigs onstage. A metallic sphere hovers on a maglev plinth center stage and is somehow the key to the PA system. The arena is dark. But you can see the dark-blue glow of people's VRSE lenses shining in their eyes. You can feel their anticipation in your gut. The hair on your arms is standing on end.

You take the stage and the crowd roars.

You strap the Mano across your chest. It hasn't been plugged in since its journey through the rip in the universe. You wonder how its body, built from a dense, purple old-growth redwood door, will resonate with the hall's redwood timbers. It's already two thousand years old, cut from a clone of an organism born 240 million years before. Twenty years ain't no thing to a redwood.

You raise your arm and hold it up in the air and you let it build and build. Your left hand waits on the E chord. You can feel them waiting for it to drop. You let 'em wait, let the years catch up. The crowd roars, louder and louder until they are almost screaming for it, then you plough your right arm like a bomb into the strings and the band is on you like an extension of your body. You blaze into "Kit-R-Grr," channel all that energy into your fingers. Your skin is gooseflesh, sending every vibration from every hair right into your central nervous system. You squeeze it out of the neck, twist and wrench it and it torques your body back. You end it quick but your timing is off and the guys don't follow and it falls apart onto the floor. They roar but it's dull and short and you can feel them wondering whether you've still got it, like you're some old fuck who hasn't played in those twenty years and not the exact guy walked through the goddamn rip from yesterday. The rage gurgles up in you.

You launch into "Wind and Water," another old one from the first record. You keep it tight to get the band in line. You feel their disgruntlement behind you. It sounds like a rattletrap. It's all coming back to you. Chong rubbing against you with the B3, stepping on your leads, Rohelio reversing time and throwing you off.

You do "Anteater" and they are all over the place. It's dissonant and rhythmically off in the hall. It's a mess. Fraud sweats out of you like a tsunami. You're sure they're streaming for the exits. You turn around so they are with you when you end it and you give them a look to kill. Chong grins at you like some twisted Buddha. His black shirt unbuttoned, his chest glistening with sweat, his hair blowing in the fan. He's trying to undo you. You count off the ending this time. Try to pull your shit together.

Chong and Rohelio lock eyes and nod. You look to Storm, thirty feet across the stage, and he shrugs. You wish Magnus were here. You chase away the image of Magnus with his head blown open. Rohelio starts trickling in across his rims and cymbals and snare and he kicks the bass a few times. Chong has one hand on the synth and the other on his air machine. He starts playing the intro to "It's About Fracking Time," the centerpiece of the new record. He's going off-setlist. He's taking control. Playing the climax too early. Trying to motherfuck you. Him and Rohelio, always together. The two of them. There's nothing you can do about it. The guitar doesn't come in for the first twenty bars. You're right back there in Tokyo and you stand there and you wait and you boil and you feel the gravity of all those years that you lost, sucking you in. You find Cin front and center with her arms around her husband and their two girls right on the rail in front of them and you rip apart. You feel yourself whirling around, the blood rushing chaos to your head. You stalk over to Chong and he is still grinning that goddamn Buddha grin and you're taking your guitar off and you're lifting it off your body and you are going to knock him off that goddamn bench. He closes his eyes slowly and he's still laying out the groove and your guitar is up over your head and his eyes open and meet yours.

Let go, he says.

You stand there stock-still like a soldier in an old Civil War painting with a bayonet.

Eleven, Chong says and he nods his head to the arena and you turn around and there are fifteen thousand people on the edge of their teeth waiting for you.

Twelve, Chong says, and you realize you're trembling.

You reach out and put your palm on the metallic sphere and it thups out in the hall when you touch it and you feel it ground you, the charge slip out to Earth. The maglev pushes against your pulse. Your pulse is galloping out there off-time, filling the hall, pushing air into thirty thousand tympanic membranes. You close your eyes and you breathe deep and your heartbeat slows and you feel it slowing in the air and it feeds back into you, slows back into you, slows you until it's perfectly in time with the groove. You're still holding your guitar up above your head and you've got two measures so you let it fall onto your body. Nineteen. You check the strap and step to the mic. Twenty, you

twist the time rip into the strings you feel it coming from out there in the hall like you're tearing the fabric of time and space and the groove deepens into an ocean of breath and the air mass hovering above the hall lights up deep dark red and you can see the sound emanating synesthetically from thin air above the crowd, the molecular lasers sculpting what the sphere picks up in negative space, pushing against the waves from your stack behind you. Sound is coming from nowhere, from everywhere. Chong's keys are nebula, Storm and Rohelio stone and sea, you bring the shattering light sky to ground, ground to sky. The lights are purple and red, they're sculpting the passage of time above the crowd like a soft and curving flower blossom. Glowing, feeling it, feeling Chong and Rohelio, Storm and Cin and everybody around you holding you up, you're on the edge of the envelope between the air your amp is pushing and what's emanating midair above the hall, and for the first time since you fell through that flower, you feel your molecules align. For the first time you feel you are in perfect balance. The guys, the crowd, Cin and fuckface and their girls, Shep and Julie and the whole crew and everybody. They're all holding you up. They always have been.

So you let go. ∎

TO DOOR
Noah Dobin-Bernstein

Y ou must understand me! Sometimes the indignities of the city, of living among so many absurd creatures swarming . . . Yes "swarming," that's the word. Like the bees, too stupid to avoid their own demise, buzzing and swarming towards the pesticides, towards the deep freezes. Drone bees, they used to call them, hovering around the queen, unproductive, good for nothing but reproducing. Not even capable of ending their pathetic lives with a glorious sting. But God had a plan for the bees, didn't he! I was stung as a child, I remember that brief agony. But I am still here, my stupid little bee friends. Where are you?

Sorry, I am sometimes distracted by my own metaphor. But extinction, that ultimate justice, has an allure, doesn't it? I often wonder when our time will come. Especially with men like Igor Boyko among us. Savages like Igor Boyko throughout this insufferable city!

Ah, yes, I should have begun there, with Igor. Then you would clearly understand. You will cheer me on, in fact. Prepare your little *heart* emojis, your little *thumbs up* for this story I am going to tell. For Igor Boyko, and the many men like him, they bring us all down, don't they? But not today, today he learned his lesson!

My unhappy collision with Igor Boyko came only today, just this morning, when he threw open his car door on Milwaukee Avenue— what kind of brute opens a door like that? In fact, such stupidity, such vicious indifference is so common now that we have made a verb of it—"to door." To door! To use your car door as a weapon against your better neighbors who travel without fossil fuels, without your antiquated disregard for humanity's self-destruction. A double crime. To guzzle gasoline and throw your door like a bomb!

So that's how I came across Igor Boyko, that unrepentant terrorist, as I skidded on the slick, snow-dusted street and whack! Right into the door of his Chevrolet. An old one, not even a hybrid, not even a decent car. My bike is worth more, I'm sure. Thank God I saw him open it and squeezed the brakes. But we who brave the Chicago winter streets on two wheels, we know the care it requires. The impact bounced me, as if my bike and I were so much rubber, towards the gauntlet of traffic.

If I had not begun to brake, if I had not seen it coming, would I even now be telling this story? Would I not instead be planted on a hospital bed, unhusked by the scrape of concrete and tires, sprouting IV tubes at each wrist? Imagine, instead of my testimony, the quiet beeps of machines tracking my vitals!

As it happened, I did brake. And, though I bounced, I fell close. Other than the shock and a tear in my slim-cut wool pants, I arose unscathed. And perhaps then—perhaps if Igor Boyko had admitted his sin, had begged my forgiveness—perhaps this day would have continued without significance. But I have warned you about the scoundrel, Igor Boyko, and now he will show his ugly face.

"My door! You need watch where you're going!" Those were his words. I swear! No apology, no concern. Just clutching the flapping door of his pathetic car. One of the hinges had split with the impact, and the door hung at a slight angle, as if ashamed.

I sent him to hell, of course, in so many words. To the deepest, hottest level. And I took a picture of his license, just in case. That's where I learned his cursed name. Still when I think of his reaction, his "my door," still I feel the fury burn inside me. And though I tried to go about my day, to sort my spreadsheets and attend my projection conferences, I could not calm the flame. "My door!" I drank my four cups of morning coffee to steady my mind. "My door!" I strove to concentrate on the IRS Form 1065. "My door!" I took an early lunch and trudged through the snow to Nordstrom Rack to replace the wreckage of my pants. "My door!" Returning to the office in new pants, I treated myself to fresh-cut potato chips fried in duck fat with chimichurri flavoring. "My door!"

Nothing, nothing could erase the crime from my mind. Now I will grant you that I can be sensitive, that at times my skin proves thin. My mother laments, to anyone foolish enough to listen, how she spoiled me as a child. She calls it entitlement. Hah! I wish everyone felt so entitled to justice!

And so I gave up the vain effort to forget and turned the full tide of my focus upon Igor Boyko and the siren call of revenge. As the workday came to a close, I invited the other bikers of my office for a drink. Our office is small, and of the eleven employees, five of us arrive each day on narrow wheels (you can tell which ones by our absence of overflowing gut). We five assemble regularly around a table at the Postapocalypse Microbrewery on Randolph to blur the cells of our spreadsheets. To feel alive after eight hours of incubation in that den of fluorescent lights and computer screens.

This time, even before we had ordered, I told them of Igor Boyko and his unatoned offense. Their mouths hung open, more in shock than thirst, and each swore to aid me in my quest for retribution.

"We bikers must defend ourselves! Or who will defend us? If only we knew where he lived!" said Douglas Parker as he sipped his Soma Holiday Saison.

"But we do, don't we?" answered Tommy Buffone, nursing a pint of Aunt Lydia's Red Ale. "You have the picture of his license. We know! We know where that little bastard lives!"

Thank god for Tommy and his brilliant realization. For once we mapped our route, a little less than seven miles, taking Grand Avenue to his Belmont Cragin address, we could all taste the pending satisfaction of revenge beneath the sharp hops of our beers.

"So we go to his home, but then what?" I asked. "We must make an indelible mark, a clear sign. We must warn all the Igor Boykos of this uncivilized city!"

Again Tommy spoke up. Perhaps he was best equipped for the vengeance business with his Sicilian heritage.

"The growlers! Everyone stop ordering pints. From now on we drink from growlers. Look."

We all admired a shelf of sixty-four ounce brown bottles designed to look like the original nuclear bombs. Yes, we thought. Perfect. We ordered three growlers, two of my favorite, Tessera Wheat Beer, and a third of the Soma Holiday.

As we drank, the plan came into clearer focus. Igor Boyko's wretched existence unraveled in our imaginations. The atomic growlers became more lethal as they drained into our glasses. We each sent messages to friends and acquaintances, other bike commuters, other potential victims of the door. We asked them to spread the word. By the time we mounted our bikes again, dark had fallen. We rode, a bit wobbly with drink, in our pant-clipped business suits, overcoats, and helmets, elegant like medieval knights.

The seven miles flew by through the warehouses turned wedding venues, the barred windows of corner bodegas and the stubbed-out smokestacks to Igor Boyko's home. We rode in silence, except for the muffled bass oozing from steamy dive bars and the occasional cursing of a pothole. Despite the freezing air, we each had the alcohol and layered wool to keep us warm. And the weighty purpose, the imminent glory of our mission, lent strength to our weary legs.

Soon enough we arrived at the unsightly yellow box that Igor Boyko calls home. It was surrounded by low bushes that winter had stripped of foliage and left as a collection of fragile sticks. I could imagine the musty smell inside, the threadbare furniture and the inevitable creep of bedbugs. Men like Igor Boyko bring the old world with them, don't they?

We leaned our bikes along a neighboring fence and began to fill the growlers with stones and dirt. As the glass bombs grew heavy, other bikers appeared—soon there were dozens, loosening their neckties as they dismounted. The buzz of spinning spokes becoming overwhelming. More and more bikers arrived, a whole community wronged by Igor Boyko. Yes, I thought. This will bring change; these are the good people, the proper citizens of Chicago standing up for themselves at last!

As I was the victim of the day's attack, I was charged to throw the first growler. It was heavy, and I allowed myself the indulgence of a dramatic windup before releasing the bottle. It flew soundly through the first-floor window, breaking the drone of bicycle wheels with a scream of shattered glass. Laughter and cheers erupted from all around me.

Soon Igor Boyko, the villain, appeared at the ruptured window, terror and confusion in his eyes.

"What, what are you doing? No, no! Go away. What are you doing?" A small girl approached from behind him in the house. She nuzzled her unkempt tangle of blonde hair into his side. He gathered her in his arms and looked back at our crowd. For a moment I hesitated. But no, she too must learn. She must know the truth of her father's crime!

"Igor Boyko," I responded, "today you nearly killed me with your door. We have come for justice!" Again the cheers rang out. Igor shooed the girl back away from the window and disappeared himself just as the other growlers came rocketing through.

A friend of mine, himself once the victim of a turning car with no signal, arrived as promised with an axe. He handed it to me and smiled. With the first swing, I split the cheap wood of the house's door.

"No!" came the villain's voice from inside. "Please, we rent. They will kick us out. Please!"

I swung again, and a chunk of wood fell to the concrete beneath me.

"Please," he said again.

"Say it!" I replied, giddy with the perfection of my plan.

"Say what, say what?"

I swung again, and the whole door shook on its hinges.

"Say what you said this morning!"

"What, what did I say?"

Another blow. Now a hole opened the size of a football.

"You remember! You said, 'My door!'"

"Okay, god. I forgot. Why, why are you doing . . ."

"Say it!"

"My door! I said it." His voice split and trembled like the wood. "I said it. Please. My door. My door."

There it was! The same words, but turned from the offensive shout of their first utterance to an apology, to a plea for mercy. Words made sweet like honey, that bequest of the disappeared bees. And had the sirens not then begun, the flashing lights approaching from down the avenue, I don't know if I would have shown mercy. Maybe, maybe not.

But as it happened, I grabbed a splinter of his door and ran, mounting my bike and scattering with the other riders, down the side streets and alleys, untraceable in the night.

When I arrived home, I placed the scrap of wood on the mantel above my fireplace. It looks elegant, almost sculpted, on the marble shelf. As I admire it now, my mind replays, over and over, the triumphant sound of Igor Boyko's broken voice, whispering, "My door!" ∎

PEPPER'S GHOST
Theadora Siranian

Before night swarms across the sky—brief slash
of winter citrus at the horizon, then evicted
by darkness. I'm in love again with the idea

of being beautiful, spying my mirrored self
in the dusky half-light. As if only at day's end
may I be content with my own physicality.

But what I see darts past, sidles in and out,
is vague, porous, not to be trusted. In sleep
I dream an egg cratered as the moon floating

in my palm. Obsidian carapace hovering,
murmuring, cracking open to reveal a yolk black
and dense as an animal's pupil. Limitless

universe, starless galaxy. Midmornings as
a child I watched my mother pray, crouching
in the bedroom doorway, myself suppliant.

Other language, other voice, her face bathed
in tears. Her words like slivered grafts of light
spilling into her steepled hands. The earth

pushing itself round with ancient, fatal patience.
The day swelling, the cicadas beginning
their metal-thresh hum. Always inexplicable:

the cheap plastic statue of the Virgin
on the nightstand—how she kept her face
placid while the arch of one foot remained

planted firmly on the snake's back. Once,
a neighbor set her house on fire, running
toward us across the field cradling a honey

jar filled with bees, the flames behind her
framing her hair like a halo. I hear
the nothing whisper, palpable as the blood

moving beneath my skin. I break the egg,
lean forward, openmouthed. I am godless.

NAKED LADIES
Teresa Burns Murphy

Driving toward BJ Dunnegan's trailer on the outskirts of Kennerly, Arkansas, Ruthie Clayton wanted nothing more than to turn around and go home. She'd spent the afternoon wrangling Dr. Andrea Klein. A former theater professor at Byrne College, Dr. Andrea was now a patient in the nursing home where Ruthie worked as an aide. Ruthie generally kept a close watch over her favorite patient, but Dr. Andrea had escaped from her room while Ruthie was attending a reception for all the residents and staff who had August birthdays. Ruthie would have gladly skipped the party, but the social activities director had made her a special cake, white coconut topped with six yellow candles—one for each decade. Just as Ruthie had been ready to blow out the candles, a woman in a wheelchair had screamed and pointed to the windows that stretched along the cafeteria wall. Ruthie had turned around and there stood Dr. Andrea, bare breasts pressed against the glass, hand between her legs, fingering herself. Ruthie was a big woman but quick on her feet. She'd grabbed a blanket from a supply closet and headed for the door.

Ruthie'd had a devil of a time getting Dr. Andrea back to her room. She'd thought about texting BJ before she left work, letting her know she couldn't come out. But Ruthie had made a promise to herself the night before—she was going to break up with BJ.

As Ruthie's car bumped along the shady gravel lane that led to BJ's property, she leaned forward and pulled her smock away from her sweaty back. She rounded a curve and made her way up the hill where BJ's trailer was set in a clearing just off the road. Ruthie parked in the yard and sat staring at the rust bleeding down the corrugated metal siding of the beige-with-brown trim 1980s Skyline mobile home until BJ flung open the front door.

Acid rose from Ruthie's stomach and filled her mouth with a sour taste as she watched BJ sprint down the cinderblock steps. BJ was a broad-backed, fat-bellied woman of fifty. Her breasts spilled from the armholes of the white tank top she wore with a pair of gray cut-off sweatpants. Her blue eyes shone beneath crescents of flesh, her right eye more hooded than the left, the result of an old wound BJ's mother had inflicted with a belt buckle. Ruthie released her seat belt and got out of the car.

BJ hustled across the parched grass and wrapped her arms around Ruthie. "Honey, have I got a surprise for you!"

"What?" Ruthie said, wriggling out of BJ's embrace.

"Come on."

BJ grabbed Ruthie's hand and pulled her around to the back of the trailer. As the concrete foundation for a house came into view, Ruthie's eyes widened and her pulse quickened.

"You didn't think I was serious, did you?" BJ said, slapping her dimpled thigh and laughing.

"I didn't think you were going to start until this fall."

"Rick finished his other job quicker than he thought he would."

The smell of freshly turned soil and cement filled the air of the hilltop clearance, leaving Ruthie scarcely able to breathe.

BJ grinned. "You better call old Suzie Langston. Tell her you're ready to sell your house."

"I doubt her offer's still good."

"Oh, hell, Ruthie, you know that grasping bitch'll buy it quick as you call her. You told me she's been after you to sell ever since your mama died."

"She'll just sell it to Old Man Crews, and he'll rent it out like he has half the other houses in the neighborhood."

"So what, Ruthie. We been dating for nearly five years now. I been saving for this house for God knows how long. We could even get married. We *better* before they take it away from us."

"I don't know if I can do that."

"You could if you wanted to," BJ said, tipping her chin and raising her eyebrows.

Ruthie looked down at her hands. She'd had her mother's wedding band stretched to fit her right ring finger. The row of tiny diamonds caught the late afternoon sunlight, and for a second she saw how the ring had looked on her mother's slender hand. The last time she'd touched her mother was when the funeral director asked if she wanted any jewelry removed before he closed the coffin.

BJ puffed out her cheeks and exhaled. "Ruthie, are you ever going to let go of the past?"

* * *

The next morning, when Ruthie backed away from the only house she'd ever lived in, her head throbbed, a steady reminder of the guilt she felt for giving in to sex with BJ. After supper and too many margaritas, Ruthie had taken hold of BJ's outstretched hand and allowed herself to be led across the cracked linoleum floor into the dark-paneled bedroom. An air conditioner inside a tiny window had whirred steadily as BJ slid her hands underneath Ruthie's smock and lifted it over her head. Kissing Ruthie's neck, her breasts, her belly, BJ had murmured, "You're so beautiful."

Ruthie rolled up her car window to shut out the rotten smell emanating from the chicken processing plant and drove in the opposite direction toward downtown Kennerly. As she passed her former neighbors' houses, she remembered how proud she'd been as a child to live on such a nice street. Ruthie shook her head as a gray rock house came into view. If Brother Campbell were still alive, he'd have a fit over how rundown his old place had become—grass knee deep, a washing machine (lid up) sitting on the carport. His wife had died almost a year ago, and their heirs had sold the house to Old Man Crews. He'd rented it out to a skinny, tattooed man who appeared to do nothing all day except sit in the house, music blaring, the smell of weed wafting through the air. Some of Ruthie's old neighbors were still around, but more of them were gone with each passing year. The ones left griped about the Mexicans renting houses and littering the yards with kids' toys and gaudy religious statues. With both of Ruthie's parents deceased, she figured most of them would be happy if she left the neighborhood too.

Ruthie drove past the old laundromat, now a florist, where an elderly man named Carlton Noland had died decades earlier. As a teenager, BJ had been involved in his death. Ruthie remembered it being the talk of the town though she hadn't known any of the girls involved, including BJ. Ruthie had met her five years ago at Big Chuck's Diner where BJ worked as a cook. At first, Ruthie had been fascinated by BJ's stories of running wild with tough girls who called her Big Dog. BJ said even though the old man's death was ruled an accident, it should have been a wake-up call for her. But she kept having run-ins with the law until a judge finally told her she could either go to jail or join the army. The army had settled BJ down, and now all she seemed to want was a peaceful life with Ruthie.

Ruthie turned onto a side street so she could drive past the World War II memorial fountain situated in a triangle of grass where the old water tower had once stood. That spot made Ruthie think of sitting in the back seat of her family's Galaxie 500 with her older sister, Carol, her mother in the front seat, her father's steady hand on the steering wheel. Seeing the water tower had always reassured Ruthie that her family was on the last leg of whatever journey they'd taken and would soon be home. Ruthie turned right onto the highway that cut through the heart of her hometown and fixed her eyes on the road ahead.

The sun about blinded Ruthie as she whipped her car into a parking space behind the nursing home. She picked up the aluminum lunchbox her father had carried to his job at Patterson Electric. That plant was gone now too—jobs shipped to Mexico. Ruthie's father had worked there for twenty-five years until his hands started shaking so badly he could no longer grip the tools he needed to fix the machines. Parkinson's disease had made him an old man at fifty. Ruthie had been about to graduate from Kennerly High when he got the diagnosis. Carol had just wrapped up her sophomore year at the University of Arkansas. Ruthie had planned to work for a year as an aide at the hospital and then go to nursing school. But as her father's limbs became increasingly rigid, he required more and more assistance. Carol had gone back to the university, but Ruthie had stayed in Kennerly to help her mother, working nights at the hospital while her mother worked days at a clothing store downtown. Ruthie figured there would be time to go to nursing school later. But the years had turned into decades, transforming Ruthie from a voluptuous teenage brunette to a gray-haired woman in wire-framed bifocals, her chin rapidly receding into her flabby neck. Holding her father's lunchbox, Ruthie headed for the door.

As soon as Ruthie was inside the building, beautiful, blond Marla Sims, the director of social activities, rushed toward her. "Ruthie, thank God you're here. Andrea Klein's in the music room nekkid as a jaybird. A group of schoolkids are going to be here to sing in thirty minutes!"

"Put this in the break room," Ruthie said, handing Marla her lunchbox. "I'll see what I can do."

Before Ruthie got to the door of the music room, she heard Dr. Andrea's high-pitched voice crooning "Light My Fire."

"Her favorite song," Ruthie whispered.

Ruthie squared her shoulders and pushed open the door. Dr. Andrea was perched on the piano bench, clothes strewn across the beige carpet, banging on the piano like a child. Former students still came to visit Dr. Andrea, though she was often confused as to who they were. Some of them had told Ruthie that Dr. Andrea had always been a handful, but she'd been a brilliant teacher until Alzheimer's disease took hold of her brain. Sixty-three years old—it just didn't seem fair.

"Come on, Dr. Andrea. Let's get your clothes on."

Dr. Andrea lifted a pale shoulder as she turned her head toward Ruthie. "I'm too hot for clothes."

"It is a bit warm today," Ruthie said. "But you don't want to turn the old men on too much."

Dr. Andrea lay across the piano bench, her thin legs straddling it, her fluffy white hair trailing off the edge, as she gazed up at Ruthie with those chicory-blossom blue eyes. "Don't you think I'm sexy?"

"Sure I do. But if you keep pulling stunts like this, Dr. Lawson's going to order restraints."

"Hmph!" Dr. Andrea said, sitting upright. "He wants to fuck me."

Dr. Andrea's indignation turned to terror as she looked around the room, crying, "Where are the costumes? We've got a show to do and nobody's made the costumes!"

"Come on, hon, let's get your clothes back on."

* * *

About the time Ruthie got Dr. Andrea settled in her room, she heard someone screaming down the hallway. Ruthie almost ran into one of the nurses as she went to see what the commotion was.

"Who is that?"

"New patient," the nurse said, twisting her mouth to one side and making a clicking sound. "They brought her over from the hospital this morning. Better double-glove, Ruthie.

Chart says she's being treated for syphilitic meningitis."

"Ruthie!" Jason, another aide, yelled from the doorway of the room. "Could I get some help down here?"

"Be right there," Ruthie said, hurrying toward the room.

"Maybe you can do something with her. When I tried to take her vitals, she hit me and started screaming about Trooper Glover."

"He's been dead for years."

"She's bat-shit, Ruthie."

"What's her name?"

"Moore. Juanita Moore."

Panic rippled through Ruthie's body, but she kept her voice calm when she said, "I'll deal with this, Jason."

The odor of feces permeated the room, and the occupant of the bed writhed beneath the covers, shrieking, "Goddamn you, Trooper Glover. How many times have I told you not in the ass!"

"Juanita," Ruthie said, inching closer to the bed. "Trooper Glover's not here. He's dead. Remember?"

"Who are you and what do you want?" Juanita said, pushing the covers away from her face.

Ruthie stifled a gasp. Juanita's face was skeletal and splotched with a purplish rash. Her brassy red hair, cut short, was patchy and faded at the roots. She peered at Ruthie, her brown eyes widening inside their nests of wrinkles. Raising her head and lifting her sharp little nose, she smiled, revealing a mouthful of chipped teeth, darkened along the gum line. Then Juanita fell back against the pillow, slipping into another world.

Ruthie's hands trembled as she put on fresh gloves. When she pulled back the sheet, she gripped the side rail to keep her knees from buckling. Dark pits dotted Juanita's crepey thighs. BJ had old cigarette burns like this on her breasts, left there by her stepfather. The only time Ruthie had ever seen BJ cry was when she talked about how the man had entered her bedroom at night while her mother worked the graveyard shift at Patterson Electric. Ruthie steeled herself as she opened Juanita's briefs and wiped excrement from her bottom, careful not to injure the bulbous hemorrhoids.

"Son of a bitch! I told you not in the ass!"

By the time Ruthie left the room, there wasn't a dry thread on her body. She could hear the schoolkids singing in the music room, their sweet voices trilling "America the Beautiful."

Ruthie kept her head down, hoping no one would stop her as she walked toward the break room.

It wasn't anywhere near break time, but Ruthie needed to process what had just happened. She scrubbed her hands raw before filling a Styrofoam cup with coffee and sitting down.

For years Ruthie had seen Juanita standing in front of Big Chuck's Diner or outside the Hi-Way Motel. Ruthie had gone often to the motel parking lot at night and watched Juanita, trying to get up the nerve to approach her. Finally, on the eve of her fortieth birthday, Ruthie had driven to Fairport and bought a fifth of Jim Beam. Ruthie remembered everything about that night—how when it had started sprinkling rain, Juanita had walked from the side of the motel to the awning-covered driveway, the curve of her bottom slipping from beneath her black skirt with each step. Standing beneath the light, Juanita had wrapped her arms across her chest, pushing her small breasts up over the top of her cream-colored camisole, rubbing her forearms as if she were freezing despite the August heat. Tears slipped down Ruthie's cheeks as she remembered how she'd longed to take Juanita inside the motel, where she'd rent a room and fill the bathtub with warm water; how she'd wanted to gently remove Juanita's clothing and wash the black eyeliner and mascara from Juanita's face while the water warmed and cleansed her. When the rain had become so heavy she could no longer see Juanita, Ruthie had looked down at her own hulking body, her wrinkled décolletage, her breasts sagging inside the new bra the saleslady at Penney's had said would lift them. The saleslady had also recommended a spandex undergarment to suck in Ruthie's gut, but she'd offered no advice for minimizing the cellulite visible through the fabric of Ruthie's pants. Ruthie had worried that Juanita might laugh at her and turn her down despite the thick wad of cash she had stuffed into her hip pocket. But it had been her fear about who Juanita might tell that kept Ruthie inside her car. Turning the key in the ignition and flipping on her windshield wipers, Ruthie had glanced at Juanita one last time before driving away.

That night she'd dreamed of kissing Juanita's maroon lips, returning them to the pink rosebud hue they'd been years ago when she'd sat across from Ruthie in the school lunchroom. Like the other free-and-reduced-lunch kids, Juanita had eaten whatever the lunchroom ladies ladled onto her tray. Ruthie could still see the orange stain around Juanita's mouth after she'd devoured the ground beef and macaroni and cheese drenched in tomato sauce the school called Chili Mac. Ruthie had never seen anyone eat so greedily. She'd tried not to stare at Juanita, tried to keep her eyes on the saddle-bag-brown Roy Rogers lunchbox her father had gotten for her at the dime store downtown. Ruthie had loved the sky-blue oval across the front where Roy, wearing a white cowboy hat and a jaunty neckerchief, smiled at her as he stood next to his horse, Trigger. Every day Ruthie's mother had filled her lunchbox with tuna or ham sandwiches, cut into little triangles and wrapped in wax paper. She'd put in a piece of fruit and always something she'd baked—cookies or a brownie. Swallowing and licking her lips, Juanita had watched Ruthie remove each item from her lunchbox.

One day after Ruthie had eaten her sandwiches and banana, she'd rubbed her tummy and said, "I'm too full for this brownie. Could you eat it?"

Ruthie had been shocked by how quickly Juanita had shot out her grimy little hand and snatched the brownie, all the while eyeing Ruthie as if she was afraid Ruthie would take it back.

Ruthie remembered how she'd sat and watched Juanita stuff the brownie into her mouth.

Even from the distance of more than fifty years, shame flooded Ruthie's body as she recalled why she'd stopped giving Juanita part of her lunch.

Carol had caught wind of what Ruthie was doing and had come up to her on the playground, grabbing the sleeve of Ruthie's sweater, practically yanking it off her. She'd put her face right next to Ruthie's and hissed, "You better stop giving that Juanita girl food, Ruthie, or I'm going to tell Mama."

"Why?"

Carol had narrowed her brown eyes and flipped a long, cinnamon-colored curl over her shoulder. "Her mother's a bad woman. You better stay away from her."

"What do you mean?"

"Shut up, Ruthie, or I'll slap your head off," Carol had said, and then she'd flounced back across the playground to join her laughing friends.

* * *

That afternoon, when Ruthie pulled into her driveway, she saw her neighbor's grandson, Harrison, coming down the sidewalk behind a huge, tawny-colored dog with a black face. The dog strained at the leash, dragging the little boy along.

"Hey, Ruthie," Harrison called, shaking his blond bangs out of his eyes as he tugged the dog to a halt.

"Hey, Harrison. You got yourself a new dog?"

"I wish. She belongs to Merry Dell. She's back here living with her mama now. She's letting me walk her dog. Her name's Ursula. She's an English maskiff."

"Kind of looks like she's wearing a mask, doesn't it?" Ruthie said, suppressing a smile.

"Yep," Harrison said. "I figure that's why they call her a maskiff. Hey, Ruthie, want to walk with us?"

"Not right now, hon. Maybe later."

The dog yanked Harrison forward as she lurched toward a squirrel darting across Ruthie's front lawn. "All right then, Ruthie. I better get going."

"Be careful," Ruthie said as she watched Harrison trot down the sidewalk behind the dog.

Sometimes when Ruthie saw Harrison, she thought if things had been different for her, she might have had a boy like him, a boy who loved to pretend pirates were lurking behind every tree in her backyard. "No use thinking about that now," Ruthie muttered as she unlocked the side door and went into the house. She grabbed a can of Coke from the refrigerator, carried it out to the backyard, and sat down in the swing. Her father had built the white, wooden frame before his hands had gotten too shaky to hold a hammer. The frame was beginning to rot, but Ruthie couldn't bring herself to replace it, just as she'd been unable to remove her mother's glasses from the table next to the chair she always sat in to read her Bible. Ruthie's eyes teared up when she noticed the surprise lilies blooming along the back fencerow. "Naked ladies," her mother had always called them.

"I got myself a real naked lady now, Mama," Ruthie said out loud, thinking about how many nights she'd sat in this swing with her mother, telling stories about her patients. Other people's problems always seemed easier to talk about. Ruthie would have told her mother about Dr. Andrea, but she would never have said a word about Juanita Moore. Ruthie had once made the mistake of asking BJ if she'd seen Juanita outside of Big Chuck's. BJ had narrowed her eyes and scowled when she said, "What you asking about that old whore for, Ruthie?" Ruthie had said she'd gone to school with Juanita, refusing to meet BJ's gaze. "No," BJ had said, "I ain't seen her in a long time."

Ruthie's face burned with shame as she remembered how Juanita had tried to get back in her good graces after she'd stopped sharing her food. Or maybe Juanita had known all along who Ruthie was and had done what she did to punish her. That sense of shame had never left her since she was a little girl, sitting across from Juanita in Miss Garnett's third-grade classroom. Juanita used to watch Ruthie, constantly cutting her brown eyes over at Ruthie—waiting, waiting, always waiting—and then she'd strike the minute Miss Garnett called the kids who sat in front of them up to her desk for their reading group's lesson. Ruthie tried to ignore her, tried to dismiss the tingling heat rushing up her thighs.

"Pssst, Ruthie. Watch this."

When Ruthie looked up, a smile would play across Juanita's rosy lips, and she would look at Ruthie the way barmaids looked at cowboys who came into saloons in the television westerns Ruthie and her father watched on Saturday afternoons. Juanita would shimmy her shoulders. Her wrinkled dresses had plain sleeves, unlike the crisp, puff-sleeved dresses with full skirts Ruthie's mother made for her. Juanita would run her tongue over her top lip and turn sideways in her seat so that her skinny, white legs were in the aisle between her desk and Ruthie's. Juanita, her eyes still fixed on Ruthie, would push air through her teeth in a way that sounded like a wire brush hitting cymbals on a trap set. *CH chchCH chchCH* came Juanita's voice as she extended one leg and, beginning at her thigh, pretended to remove a stocking.

CH chchCH chchCH. Juanita's voice seemed to get louder and louder, and Ruthie wondered why the other students didn't turn around. Once Juanita had slid the invisible stocking off the scuffed patent-leather shoe she wore without an anklet, she'd pretend to fling it around her head like a lasso, gyrating her hips, keeping her eyes on Ruthie. *CH chchCH chchCH.* Ruthie always ducked when Juanita flung the imaginary stocking at her.

Juanita would giggle and start the striptease all over again with the other leg. Ruthie's face would redden and she'd feel sick, the way she did when she drank milk that had gotten too warm in those little cartons they sold at school. But she couldn't take her eyes off Juanita.

Ruthie took a swallow of the Coke and looked out at the place that had always been her refuge. Every inch held a memory of something or someone she'd lost—her father holding a cigarette between his lips as he walked behind a push mower; her mother, on her hands and knees, patting down the dirt around her pansies. Now that Ruthie was sixty, it seemed that loss surrounded her. When she first met BJ, she'd felt hopeful that things would work out between them. It hadn't taken Ruthie long to realize they were from different worlds. Even as Ruthie had become increasingly disgusted by BJ's very presence, she pretended to love her, believing she could stave off that sense of loss. But loss was engulfing her. She was only three years younger than Dr. Andrea and even older than some of her other patients. Ruthie's mother used to tell her she would be a late bloomer. But Ruthie had never bloomed. Fertile soil had turned into graves until, one by one, Ruthie had buried most of the people and things she loved.

Ruthie scanned the backyard. She wasn't sure she could ever leave this place. Carol had made it clear she didn't want it. Ruthie had paid Carol for her half of the property the day after their mother's funeral. Carol had to rush back to her job in California, where she'd transformed herself into a "liberal." With a sideways glance Carol had told Ruthie about all the "LGBTQ" people she knew.

"You ever slept with one of them?" Ruthie had said, just to get Carol to shut her know-it-all mouth.

Ruthie looked at the koi pond their father had dug years ago. She could almost see herself as a young girl standing next to Carol at the pond's edge, tossing pebbles at the fish to get them to move from behind the rocks. The backyard had once looked so big and lush to Ruthie, alive with the fragrance of her mother's flowers and the splash of frogs as they leapt into the little pond. Now weeds were overtaking her mother's flowerbeds, and the pond was full of dirt and moldering leaves.

Ruthie swiped at her eyes, not trusting what she saw through the blur of tears. A cluster of surprise lilies seemed to float over the koi pond. She rose from the swing, keeping her eyes on the pink, trumpet-shaped blossoms as if, were she to look away for an instant, they would vanish. Ruthie waded into the muck, gazing into the open face of a single bloom. She imagined herself entering the stamen, traveling through the yellow core at the center of the pink petals, down through its narrow stalk until she reached the roots. As she leaned toward the flower, she was startled by the sound of the gate latch clicking open. Her foot slipped on a slimy rock, and she sloshed Coke down the front of her smock. Regaining her footing, Ruthie turned to see Harrison entering the yard, accompanied by the massive dog.

"There you are, Ruthie. I should've known you'd be out here. I gotta show you what Ursula dug up in Mrs. Campbell's old yard."

Harrison moved closer to Ruthie while the dog sniffed at the grass around the pond.

"Looks like some kind of key, but I hadn't never seen one like it before. Maybe it's to a buried treasure chest."

He held up a rusty roller skate key, and Ruthie's heart ached for the things she knew were ahead of him, but she smiled. "That's an old roller skate key."

"A what?"

"We used to use them to tighten up our shoe skates."

"You mean like wheelies?" Harrison said, frowning and pulling back his head.

"No. Our skates were metal. They fit over our shoes. Maybe I can hunt up a pair and teach you how to skate on them."

"That'd be cool. But Ruthie, can I ask you a question?"

"Shoot."

"What you wadin' around in that old pond for?"

"I was trying to get a better look at these flowers."

"We got some of them in our yard. Grandma calls them surrection lilies."

"Resurrection lilies?"

"Uh-huh. That's it."

The dog pulled Harrison closer to the pond's edge, and he had to hold the leash tight to keep her from getting into it. He shook his head as he peered into the murky water. "Ruthie, you ought to clean this old pond out. Get you some goldfish like that hippie that moved into Mrs. Campbell's old house done. The front yard's a mess, but he's got his backyard fixed up real nice."

"You know, Harrison. I might do that."

"Well, if you're not too tired out, maybe you'd like to walk up to the fountain with me and Ursula. The water up there's real clean."

"I'd like that," Ruthie said, slogging her way out of the pond. "But I'd have to change first."

Harrison shrugged. "Me and Ursula can wait. But you better hurry up, Ruthie. It's not gonna be daylight that much longer." ■

RICE PADDY
Florence Homolka

Banana trees,
their trunks hollow like dreams,
like no mind,

offer quiet shade
beyond the rice paddy.

You steam the fruit,
cut chunks into coconut milk
with salt and *pandanus* leaves,

offer sweet pudding to the belly
of the clay fire goddess,
frangipani at her toes.

Beyond the paddy,
the wind tunes her seven strings,
sings a song from Guangling.

In September, we will harvest rice,
thresh grain from the husk,
eat it sticky with sesame and mango,
then gather the straw for bedding,

but this day in July,
the milk cow may roam along
the Mekong River,
lowing to the South China Sea,
before she returns.

THE SERPENT'S DANCE
Christopher Blasdel

Ryuji had always felt the presence of the Shintō deities. The hills and mountains around Nara, his hometown, were full of shrines, both large and small, and even in the city itself tiny sanctuaries were tucked away in places one would least expect: beside pachinko parlors, next to one-hundred-yen shops and in the shopping arcades. Around the main station were numerous shrines housing kami deities to greet the arriving passengers. Like the ubiquitous crows that flew overhead, the city coexisted with the gods. Everywhere one went in Nara, the past deeply informed the present, but so much was it a part of daily routine that the townspeople had mostly stopped noticing.

Not Ryuji, however. He loved the sense of serenity and purpose of the old shrines, with their numerous festivals and legends. It was silly, he knew, no one really believed those old stories of the kami anymore, but he often recalled the tales his grandmother told him when he was a boy. One story he liked especially was the tale of the youthful god Wakanomiya, the son of the two main deities at Kasuga, the vermillion-colored shrine built centuries ago on the small mountain above Nara.

His grandmother said that the young deity Wakanomiya originally appeared as a snake by his parents' shrine during a particularly bad drought, and so the elders built him his own shrine further up the mountain. After that, she said, the rains fell and crops grew in abundance.

Though Ryuji's school friends never thought much about the old shrines that dotted the forest paths around Nara, Ryuji, even now as a worldly twenty-two-year-old, still held his childlike feeling of awe toward them. That was why, a few years back, he had joined Kasuga Shrine's traditional music ensemble and began to learn Bugaku dance so he could perform for Wakanomiya's yearly festival in mid-December, the On-Matsuri.

His friends couldn't understand this. Though nominally proud of their city's heritage, they were only vaguely interested in it. They were more interested in the latest fashion, cars or girls. On their free days they all went to Osaka to shop or hang out. Ryuji joined them when he could, but lately he felt distant from them, especially as the festival approached and the rehearsals took up more and more of his time.

The final rehearsal was tonight, and Ryuji rushed through the streets of Nara so he wouldn't be late. He rode his skateboard—his preferred means of transportation—to the rehearsal hall, feeling the cold December wind sting his face as he raced along the winding pathways through Nara Park, past the ancient ponds, towering old pines and rows of stone lanterns. He arrived at the Kasuga Shrine hall, flipped his skateboard up, deftly caught it as it spun around and walked in. He tried to look nonchalant in front of the others, but inside he was excited and nervous about the rehearsal.

This was because he had been chosen this year to dance the solo Serpent Dance at the festival. It was a coveted role and the most demanding piece of the entire repertory. Not many of the ensemble members—especially those as young as Ryuji—were asked to dance it. He practiced hard to perfect the movements, but he was still unsure of himself.

The musicians had already taken their places along the side of the rehearsal room. They faced the hard, polished cypress floor where Ryuji would dance. Ryuji put on a simple robe and took his place among the gagaku musicians. As they prepared to begin, the ensemble sensei stood up to announce the presence of a visitor from Tokyo. Ryuji glanced to his side and was startled to see a young foreigner, about his own age, sitting right next to him. The sensei then turned to Ryuji and said, "Please look after our new guest."

Foreigners often came to Nara to study the festival music and dance, and sometimes they observed the rehearsals. But there was something different about this one. Most of the foreign visitors were older, professorial-looking men or women who, although obviously interested in the subject, always seemed a bit out of place. This one was different. He was dressed in loose jeans and a colorful sweater and had bleached his long, curly hair in the local fashion. Ryuji, who rarely spoke to foreigners, thought he was probably handsome, but then Ryuji didn't really know how to judge a foreigner's looks. Perhaps he was a model here for a photo shoot?

But no. He was holding a ryūteki flute and was studying the score, so he must be here to perform. Ryuji's eyes wandered to backpack lying behind him. On top of the backpack was a skateboard, exactly the same brand as Ryuji's.

The only foreigner among a group of Japanese, this young man would normally have stood out, but he looked so at ease and comfortable sitting there that no one seemed to take any notice of him. Ryuji, suddenly remembering his duties, thought he should at least try to begin a conversation and started to introduce himself, but then halted, wondering if the foreigner could speak Japanese. But before Ryuji could continue, the young man announced:

"Hi. I'm Andrew. I'm studying gagaku music at the university in Tokyo and I'll be playing flute for this year's festival."

That was in perfect Japanese.

"Oh, I'm Ryuji."

Ryuji looked into the Andrew's eyes and was greeted with a warm but slightly mischievous smile. That put him somewhat at ease, but he still felt a bit self-conscious. Andrew then furrowed his brow and looked like he wanted to ask questions about the music.

"Would you mind if I ask a few questions?"

Ryuji hoped they would not be difficult ones. Although he knew the movements for the dance and could follow the music, he wasn't sure he could explain, at least not in a way that Andrew might be able to understand. But before he could reply, Andrew continued: "It's about the music for the Serpent's Dance. I was taught that the dancer comes in when the lead drummer cues a beat around the third round of the opening flute canon, but I was also told that it may be done differently here . . ."

Ryuji was stunned. He didn't expect the foreigner would be so fluent in Japanese or know so much about the music. Most visiting foreigners spoke in a halting, formal Japanese—if they spoke it at all—and to his knowledge, none of them had actually tried to play the music, although many of them came to hear it.

Normally, Ryuji felt self-conscious talking about the dance or music, especially in front of his older colleagues, since they might think he was trying to show off. But there was something immediate and even reassuring about Andrew's question, so Ryuji answered naturally and automatically.

"Well, the dancer just takes the cue from the group leader who plays the small drum. Usually it occurs about two rounds into the flute canon, but depending on the dancer and the size of the stage, it can differ. You just have to listen for it."

"Who's dancing the solo part in this performance?"

"I am," Ryuji said, trying to sound as if he performed it every year.

"Wow, I heard that's one of the hardest dances. That's great!"

Ryuji didn't quite know how to react to Andrew's sudden enthusiasm; his modesty prevented him from smiling, but yet he didn't want to seem indifferent. Fortunately, the sensei signaled for the rehearsal to begin, and Ryuji excused himself and got up to prepare for the dance.

Ryuji waited for his entrance. The musicians began with a simple four-beat rhythm marked by the hard, leathery raps of the lead drum and metallic clang of a suspended cymbal. Soon, the solo flutist played a single pitch that soared up an octave and gained in intensity until it seemed to pierce the walls of the room. The tone then cascaded back into the lower octave and began a simple melodic pattern. A few bars later, a second flute player began the same pattern, like a canon, and a few bars after that, the third player joined in until six flutes, including Andrew's, were all playing the same melody out of synch. The simple melody, disjointed as it was, became a cacophony of flutes, defying any sense of sequence. This sonic chaos prepared the stage for the dancer's entrance.

Ryuji loved this part. When he was little, the violent disorder of the flutes frightened him, but he had learned to appreciate the cacophony, and now it excited him and sent sharp, energetic shivers through his body.

For the Serpent's Dance, the dancer had to circle a small wooden snake placed in stage center, pick it up and hold it aloft, then exit. This dance was transmitted to Japan over a thousand years ago, and the explanation was that these simple movements were supposed to depict the story of a man from far-west China who was an expert in hunting and devouring snakes.

Ryuji went through the dance, concentrating on each movement just as he had been taught. It didn't look so difficult when his teacher did it, but now there was so much to remember. He had to keep his arms parallel, head at just the right angle, and make long enough strides that took him exactly to the edge of the stage. At the climax, he had to feign surprise at discovering the snake, lean down, pick it up and hold it above his head. The final movements expressed joy and victory.

Ryuji finished the dance and returned to where Andrew was sitting.

"That was awesome!" Andrew exclaimed.

"This time was easy," Ryuji said. Although the rehearsal room was cold, Ryuji had broken out into a sweat. "I was just in this light kimono, but when we perform it for the festival tomorrow night, I'll be wearing a heavy costume along with a mask. I hope I can see what I'm doing."

Again, Ryuji suddenly remembered his manners. "By the way, Andrew-san, you play the flute very well. Did you study long?"

"Only a bit, but it's nowhere as good as your dancing," he demurred.

There were a few moments of silence, then Andrew looked at Ryuji and said, "I like best the part where you lift the snake up. It's amazing, like you have discovered some special, natural power. I think lifting it up high above your head like that signifies that you have somehow made that power part of yourself. One of my professors told me that this dance probably originated from an old Indian religion that worshipped serpents.

Picking up the snake in the dance maybe signifies the discovery and mastery of a powerful energy; you know, like, um, the so-called serpent power in Yoga."

This grabbed Ryuji's attention. He understood Andrew's words, but he wasn't sure what he had meant. No one else—his teachers or elders in the shrine—had ever said anything like this about this dance. He thought the dance was about a faraway man who was delighted to find and eat a delicious snake. But the idea of discovering a new power and making it one's own intrigued him. Maybe it was like learning not to be afraid of the flutes any longer. Ryuji decided he would have to think about it a bit more.

After Andrew said this, he put his hand on Ryuji's lower back and quickly rubbed it in an intimate gesture of friendliness. This move took Ryuji by surprise. Andrew's hand was warm and felt pleasant on his sweat-drenched back, which was quickly chilling in the unheated room. Once again Ryuji felt an energetic surge throughout his body.

Late the next day, on the eve of the festival, Ryuji and the other ensemble members gathered in the rehearsal room to prepare for the walk up to Wakanomiya's shrine. They had to accompany the deity down the mountain to the temporary shrine where he would be feted with food, dance, music and prayers. After exactly twenty-four hours, they would accompany the deity back to his home.

Preparations finished, the head priest entered and motioned for the group to follow. Ryuji, Andrew and the rest picked up their instruments and entered the cold December night.

The entourage walked past the main shrine and out the gate. Already, many tourists had arrived to watch the spectacle of this famous festival. They carried flashlights, chatted and slowly made their way up the hill to witness the ceremony. When the priests and musicians came out, they parted to allow them to pass.

The entourage soon arrived at the door of Wakanomiya's shrine. The priests gathered around the shrine door while the musicians warmed their instruments.

Ryuji kept his eye on the door of the shrine. He knew the head priest would open the door and remove the deity Wakanomiya precisely at the stroke of midnight. Only the head priest was allowed to look inside and touch the sacred object that represented the deity. What the sacred object actually consisted of, no one but the head priest knew.

Finally, as midnight approached, the priest in charge of the crowd told them to extinguish all lights and keep silent. One of the tourists, a young woman whose slick, urban fashion made her seem out of place in the ancient surroundings, ignored the warning and instead turned her flashlight on so she could see the activities. The priest ran over to her, grabbed her flashlight and threw it into the forest. She looked surprised and almost angry for a moment before she realized what she had done and hung her head in shame.

A hushed darkness fell over the crowd and only the illumination of the stars and half-moon remained. Out of the silence a very low, sonorous tone rose from the host of priests gathered around the shrine door. The chanting crescendoed, and the head priest opened the door and entered the sanctuary.

The chant climaxed, and the head priest emerged from the darkness holding the deity tightly to his chest. The other priests quickly surrounded him as if to offer protection. The lead flute player performed an opening stanza and the procession began. The entourage, headed by two large torches and brass censers, moved away from Wakanomiya's shrine and began its descent down the trail. Andrew heard his musical cue and lifted the flute to his lips and played. Ryuji walked next to him, playing the double-reed hichiriki. Soon its shrill sounds and the smooth harmonies of the shō bamboo mouth organs joined in and mingled with the gentle fragrance of the incense wafting in the cold air.

After about an hour, they arrived at their destination. The head priest mounted Wakanomiya into his temporary shrine that faced a grassy stage surrounded by bonfires and electric lamps. It was here, the following evening, that Ryuji would perform the Serpent's Dance.

The next afternoon, Ryuji arrived early to prepare. His costume was elaborate, heavy, and putting it on required the assistance of several of the elders. Andrew was there and offered to help.

With Andrew watching, Ryuji unwrapped his costume, took off his street clothes and put on the undergarments. These were the only parts of the costume that were modern and warm. Next came an under kimono, a soft, gray cotton garment tied with a simple sash around the waist. The outer costume consisted of multiple layers of colorful robes, made of finely woven silk embroidered with traditional family crests on a red background of cloud patterns. One of the robes had a long embroidered tail that swung with the movements of the dancer. Ryuji knew he had to take care not to step on it when he made sudden turns.

Andrew helped Ryuji into these clothes. The boy already looked splendid, but the most elaborate part of the costume—an orange outer vest—was yet to be fitted. Shaped like a poncho and suggesting a warrior's armor, it consisted of heavy, woven silk and was adorned with elaborate designs of dragons; two each on the front and back, floating on a background of multicolored clouds. Andrew picked it up and admired its richness and color. He then placed it on Ryuji's shoulders and bent down to fasten it.

Andrew put his arms around Ryuji's waist to tighten the band. The costume, dating back hundreds of years, was elegant but not very well insulated, and to Ryuji the warm proximity of another human, however fleeting, was a welcome relief from the cool night air.

It was time for the musicians to take their places. Andrew took a last look at Ryuji, smiled and then went to the musicians' tent. Ryuji paused before he donned the final but most important part of the costume, the mask. Carefully, he opened the old pine box where it was stored and lifted the centuries-old mask.

Ryuji placed the vermillion mask firmly on his head and went to the mirror. His young, smooth face was transformed into that of a grizzly warrior from ancient China: a man, certain of himself, who knew the secrets of hunting dragons or serpents and was about to begin his quest for one.

Waiting offstage, Ryuji felt nervous. The cold exacerbated his stage fright and he began to shiver. He remembered that had to dance facing the shrine. This performance was not for the townspeople or the tourists, but for the deity, Wakanomiya himself.

By the time Ryuji made his entrance to the sounds of the flutes, it was late afternoon and the sun had already set. Bonfires, set at four corners of the stage, filled the air with a scent of pine and provided illumination in the waning light. The grass was dry and brown, and the evening chill had created a light condensation on the grass that made footing precarious.

Ryuji began circling around the stage, each time getting a little closer to the coiled serpent prop placed in the center. During practice, he had imagined this part of the dance as a hunter closing in for the kill, but now he had a distinctly different sensation. This sensation had to do with the deity, which he could feel watching from his perch towering above the stage. It was an unmistakable presence, hovering over him and scrutinizing his every move, but it was familiar, if not a bit frightening. At one point in the dance he experienced a sudden jolt. Thinking that Wakanomiya had actually stirred, he momentarily turned to look, but all he saw was Andrew's face, intently looking at him while he played the flute.

Ryuji turned his head downwards to regard the serpent. He remembered what Andrew had said yesterday at rehearsal, and a connection between the deity and the serpent suddenly became apparent to him. The epiphany was as clear as the December night: picking up the snake meant that he was picking up the deity himself.

Ryuji experienced a moment of intense confusion and disorientation. He lost track of the music and forgot his movements. His mind went blank, but fortunately, before he had time to panic he heard the distinctive drum patterns, and these enabled him to regain composure.

He quickly remembered his choreography and reached down to pick up the snake. He lifted it to a position high above his head and tilted his mask upwards in an expression of victory. For a few moments, Ryuji held the snake aloft. The music stopped, and a single flute played a short segue into the opening of the next movement.

The moment of confusion past, Ryuji felt again a powerful and warm sensation in his lower back, slowly making its way up his torso. The remaining dance movements were crystal clear in his mind and he carried them out perfectly.

There was no more cacophony. The soft, harmonious chords of the mouth organ floated above the melody of the flutes and the reed pipes. The drums punctuated the dancer's final steps. In the last refrain, Ryuji brought the snake to his hips and faced the shrine. He bowed, made two steps in perfect time with the large drums, arched his hand one last time and briefly squatted. The flutes and drums stopped. It was time for the dancer's exit. Slowly, grandly, Ryuji made his way offstage.

* * *

The small local pub was tucked away in the little warren of shops below the main shrine complex. The festivities were complete, and Ryuji went out drinking with Andrew to celebrate their success.

Ryuji talked about the dance. He wanted to explain the extreme disorientation he had felt followed by a sudden enlightenment during the dance, but he couldn't quite find the right words to describe it to Andrew, so he just said the obvious.

"The grass was too wet. I thought I would slip."

"This sake should help you regain your balance." Andrew joked.

Ruyuji took a sip of the chilled local sake and he felt a rush shooting through his body, still tense from the dance. He deserved to relax: his dance had been successful, the festival was finished and he was with his new friend. Suddenly, it occurred to Ryuji that he didn't know much about Andrew, so he asked him why he came to Nara.

"Well," Andrew began, "it is like the sensei said. I'm a foreign exchange student at the Tokyo national conservatory. I was researching the Wakanomiya On festival, but I felt in order to grasp how such festival worked, I should actually experience it, not as an observer, but as a performer. My teacher in Tokyo introduced me to the sensei, who invited me down to participate. I was also very curious to observe how to the locals view the festival."

What Andrew couldn't really articulate to Ryuji was that his interest in the festival was because it was a symbol of all that in Japan which fascinated him—the beauty of ancient ceremony, the awareness of the awe-inspiring forces of nature, the elegant, otherworldly music and dance and, of course, the people who made the festival happen. Andrew grew up in the panhandle of Texas. It was a place of raw beauty and elemental power but sparsely populated. He understood the sway nature had on human activities and how one could both fear and respect it—indeed, the panhandle weather itself could at times feel like the wrath of the gods—but the relative newness of human inhabitation in his part of the world provided no cultural or historical insights for how one might understand one's relationship with nature. He hoped that the ancient city of Nara with its festivals and ceremonies might just provide him with a vital connection to the past for which he yearned, especially if he could participate in the festival that went back almost a thousand years. Whenever Andrew heard gagaku it conjured in him a certain longing, a desire to belong, a wish to hold on to it as long as he could.

Andrew had other longings that he yearned to share with Ryuji; a desire that two souls might connect in a common interest and work together like a dance, but this longing, although the most important and pressing on Andrew's heart, was even more difficult to articulate.

Ryuji, for his part, had always wanted to visit the US and could not quite fathom why Andrew might want to leave his home country to come to Nara. Wasn't the US the most modern and advanced country in the world? What could possibly be so attractive about Nara? But, yes, he realized that there was something special about the Wakanomiya festival, and Andrew seemed to share Ryuji's enthusiasm about dancing for the deity.

The pub, in the meantime, was getting full, and as more customers entered, Ryuji found himself crowded closer to Andrew until their shoulders were touching. For a while he tried to maintain a polite distance, but after a few more drinks it didn't seem to matter. They were both leaning into each other.

Ryuji drank much more than usual, and the boys stayed until late and were eventually turned out when the pub closed well after midnight.

They got on their skateboards and began riding down the street. Andrew was still somewhat sober, but Ryuji couldn't stand very steadily and felt relieved when Andrew pulled alongside him and put his arm around his shoulder to steady him. In fact, it was Andrew who was now leading the way, and Ryuji felt the curiously embarrassing sensation of having an outsider guide him through the familiar streets of his own city. He wasn't sure where they were going, but it seemed to Ryuji that they were heading back in the direction of Wakanomiya's temporary shrine.

But instead they arrived at Andrew's hostel, which was near the shrine. Ryuji turned to say goodbye, but Andrew remained silent. He then took Ryuji by his hand and led him into his room, saying only that since he was so drunk he should probably stay here for the night.

Ryuji was glad to be out of the cold air. He sat on the bed and nervously began talking about the dance. He was going to ask Andrew about the serpent and the strange sense disorientation that he had experienced onstage, but Andrew, without saying a word, walked over to the bed, sat down and put his arm around Ryuji's shoulder and drew him close. For a moment, Ryuji didn't know what to do. He felt the same kind of sudden confusion as during the dance: circumstances were once more spiraling out of control. What brought Ryuji back to awareness was the incredibly peaceful and reassuring feeling of Andrew's warm shoulder and strong arms. Ryuji relaxed and let his head fall against Andrew's shoulders. He felt Andrew's hand reach around to caress his face and closed his eyes as their lips joined. Andrew pulled him closer and their hands began exploring each other's bodies. At that moment, Ryuji thought he heard the flutes begin their canon.

The next morning Ryuji awoke alone. Andrew was nowhere to be found. What's more, Ryuji was not in a room, but lying next to the bonfire that was kept going near Wakanomiya's temporary shrine, his head propped on his skateboard. How had he gotten there? he wondered. As he roused himself, Ryuji thought about the previous night and then remembered what had transpired.

He heard that foreigners often did that sort of thing, and indeed it had been pleasurable—after all, Ryuji had been quite drunk. But where had Andrew gone? Then he remembered something Andrew had said in bed last night, a comment about a rising serpent, and how it looked like the one in the dance. They both laughed at this silly joke, but now Ryuji wondered if that might possibly be another interpretation of the dance as well. Perhaps, he thought, I should ask Andrew when I see him. As he picked up his skateboard and prepared to leave, he felt once more the unmistakable gaze of the deity on his back. ■

PRIDE NIGHT
Micah Ruelle

We're one of three couples slow-dancing,
attempting to grow a dance floor, & some
girl sticks a hand in our faces, mumbles,
"Here's a high-five—here's to loving women,"
then smiles. My girlfriend looks away,
holding my back a little closer. But I relent,
pulling one hand away. Smile. Give the stranger
the feeling that she helped a good cause
I hadn't realized I was campaigning for
by holding E—. The ever-lovely E—,
that gold star E—, the unstoppable E—
who is swaying in my arms like nothing
happened because it was beneath her.
& it is. I apologize, but it also falls
beneath her. Like that guy—from that time
we showed up at a throbbing house party
& I was one of two white people
in a group of sixty people speaking Spanish.
I was quiet, but happy. I refilled her drinks
as she conversed with old friends. I held her
hand & her back as we joined everyone
salsa dancing, until she said, "hang on a sec"
& was pulled off some guy—now beneath her
after she threw a punch because "he ruffied
our drinks." Later I found out it was because
he said that she shouldn't have brought
a white bitch. Oh, E—, who loved to lie
to protect me, the E— who scared me
when she said, "You don't care who is watching
& just do what you want—I love that." To which
I replied, "Doing what you want isn't political—
it's America." E— shook her head
because who was I? I was new, & this naiveté
was beneath her. Pride was just beginning
to writhe & grow within the city as we turned

out the lights, when beneath her,
I unbuttoned her blouse. "Say it again," she said,
& I drunkenly whispered to her, "this is political—
this isn't America," & we laughed
like we had in the pool that day the flowers
from a Texas redbud were shaken from the trees
landing on the water where E—was also floating,
& I was nowhere, & always beneath her.

DEATH IN ANDOVER
Frances Park

All I know about the boy is that he was seventeen, a student at Phillips Academy, and that he died at the train station. That he was of Asian descent made a gray day grayer. Atmospheric.

For me, New England is easy to romanticize. I was born outside Boston in Cambridge to parents who were part of a nearly invisible wave of well-groomed Korean grad students and their wives in the 1950s. You can tell from fading photos how well my dad fit in with the company of young foreign scholars who believed they would change the world. From generation to generation, we dream. Too soon my family moved south to the Virginia suburbs of DC—my dad got a job at the World Bank—but Boston was always there, my hometown sitting in some mythical mist up north, and in the back of my head, in my heart of hearts, I believed that had we stayed I would've grown up happier with a real feeling of home, far from the madding hicks and mean girls. Granted, many of our neighbors were fine and I loved the Lyle family next door, but telling people I was born in Cambridge, Massachusetts, was a source of pride for me as if I had planted the ivy or was one with the ivy. Some ivy connection.

I'd been back to the Boston area before but never in October and never here, to Andover, a prep school town so picturesque in collective memories surely it's always autumn. Staying at the Andover Inn, we'd flown in the day before for a post-wedding celebration—the daughter of my husband's good friends from college had recently wed in Tel Aviv, and now it was time for their stateside friends to get down and party in the old town hall. American Jews, Israeli Jews, Colombian Jews—no one made me feel like the odd one out but we are who we are, aren't we? Still, everything felt starry, in sky and spirit. People kicked off their dancing shoes and drank with abandon. Through it all, the bride was a vision. She wore a pearly thing in her hair.

The next morning my husband went out for breakfast. For me, the echoes of last night's loud hip-hop–rock–salsa meant a quiet coffee in the room would do.

"Take your time," I told him.

From the second-floor windows of our sweet corner room, the

town took on a gothic cast, looking more like a movie set than a place where real lives are lived. Peyton Place, if you're old enough to remember. I finished my coffee, then took a shower. When my husband returned:

"Well, I heard some sad news."

"Oh?"

"I noticed a crowd at the church next door so I asked the person at the front desk what was going on. Apparently, a student at Phillips Academy took his own life last week."

My heart sank. No one wants to hear that.

"His memorial service is today."

Last night, a song; this morning, a hymn. I took to Google to confirm a hunch: an Asian surname.

Momentarily, the pregnant sky's impending birth dashed our plans to get a good look at the village shops and restaurants in daylight before heading out to Logan Airport. My mood had changed anyway. A boy was dead. This was his town. The view from here was so close to the streets and sidewalks I felt like I was twelve again, peering out the window of my parents' bedroom upstairs to see if the coast was clear. If not, I'd stay holed up in my room writing stories. Many lives were lived up there.

But back to Andover. My eyes were hooked as I spied on a stream of young mourners coming back from the memorial in packs of twos and threes, heads down. The occasional loner, hands in pockets. It was all very hushed. Black-clad figures against old stone buildings provided a timeless optic; it could've been now or circa World War II. Were these the boy's friends? Or just classmates? Did they attend the memorial out of respect or because the masters insisted? Did anyone know his despair? Did anyone care? To be fair, the procession was somber but a little emotion would have been nice. A funeral face or two, my God. Finally, a girl collapsed in tears before tearing away from her friends. I wanted to take a picture but didn't.

Then the rain came, hard and heavy.

* * *

Maybe you can relate, but I think more about death now than I did a decade ago. In the past year I lost my soul-mama Tess, who was something, and my sweet dog Jefferson, who was everything. Sometimes when I think about getting old, the notion of checking out with a magic pill saves me. Not while I can still boogie in an old town hall but when

I'm frail and don't know night from day. True, it's tragic but not like a boy facing death head-on at a train station.

Generation after generation we dream, then die. But at seventeen?

* * *

On the dance floor, the younger guests had hoisted the bride into the air. She was light as a feather. Champagne bubbles.

Meanwhile, a few blocks away, preparations were in place for a morning memorial.

One body up, one body down.

A soiree, a suicide.

* * *

A couple of weeks later, I'm still haunted. Why am I writing about a death in Andover? The boy wasn't my son. All we shared was the earth and an Asian heritage. Whatever went wrong is out of my sphere. When I mentioned to my husband I was writing this little reverie, he looked at me as if through ancient New England fog.

"Oh—did someone die?"

* * *

One day in 1979, my family buried my dad. Much like that Andover morning, it was October and gray, not a miracle in the sky. Let me tell you something: the sound of rain hitting the tarp over your father's coffin will break you.

The funeral was attended by hundreds, mostly Korean scholars from the early days and international types from the World Bank. Many years later, they're all a blur in the rain. Only Mr. and Mrs. Lyle remain standing, strong and loyal.

My dad's sudden death at fifty-six was natural but he was still too young. His dream checklist only half-done. If anyone had the will to live, if only to take care of his family, it was him. He was our hero, our Hercules. But even he could crack.

A decade earlier—and here's where the story grows fuzzy because my memory is that my dad confided in me but considering I was only about fourteen, maybe I just overheard it—I learned there was an incident on a plane during his World Bank travels. A feeling came over him, the urge to jump off. The feeling was so powerful that when the plane landed, instead of catching his connecting flight back to the United States, to us, he took a taxi to a hospital. There he was sedated, having suffered what must have been a severe panic attack. At that age, I can't be sure how I coded it beyond a certain truth: My dad was more fragile than I thought. Maybe we all are. ■

WHAT YOU WANTED
Andrew Fague

You were taught wrong: we're moving away from the sun.
Chosen seeds of light, like you said, should tend their own fires.

The moon will drift off too, much sooner,
always so unresolved, thin, different, attracted to moss.

When the moon is gone, what becomes of the well?

Do the secrets get darker on the moor?
What becomes of whispers in the grasses,

or under the wharf, giggles like dew shivering
in cool, tidal breezes?

What becomes of prom night,

silk and tulle, pantomime, plump lives
lowering themselves down rusted chains

into watery light, into the gentle reflections of a wanderer,
wizened in memories, chastening desires

as if flushed, tussled, wandered grandchildren?

Without the silver necklaces left out by wild oceans
for you in the night, how to face the day?

At dawn, the light could be lauded into extinction,
palms lined for crucifixion. You wanted

to gaze back over history—rocks, water, the old plants,

unsanctified soil. You wanted the warm, deliberate eyes
of moody storms, lost soldiers

leaned over the deck rail or wobbling in grey-eyed light.
You wanted a shaky bench under a lilac overgrown onto a shed,

space and time for a local, neglected luminary.

NO PRECEDENT
Robert Leonard Reid

1

At least you could say that the generals appeared to be well-read.

General Bouton characterized the hostage situation at the university as "Kafkaesque." General Frieden allowed that it was "Dostoyevskian." General Loomis went overboard, opining that the descent into "the bowels of depravity" was worthy of the Marquis de Sade; then adding with a laugh that the Snopes family would, uncharacteristically, find itself right at home in the university library. There a mob had attacked and beaten twenty-eight students who had gathered to celebrate the life and work of the recently deceased poet, Marco Coulos. The twenty-eight had been bound, herded into a lecture hall, stripped of their clothing—the group included both men and women—and heaped like firewood in the open space at the front of the hall. Guards with assault rifles surrounded the bodies, which were then doused with gasoline. A communiqué went out, demanding that the teaching of poetry at the university be terminated at once.

The last speaker at the hastily convened press conference, General Klein, invoked both Nietzsche and Poe in his comments. He ended by making dark reference to two obscure nineteenth-century German texts by an insane mathematics professor named Heinrich Fürtweigle: the first a vicious manifesto declaring poetry to be Satanic; the second a novel banned throughout most of its history for its poisonous, philistinic ferocity.

2

Whether the generals had actually read the authors whose names they so smoothly invoked seemed beside the point; Kafkaesque or not, the situation was desperate; members of the media wanted hard news, but they knew that in order to accomplish their objective they had no choice but to indulge the military in its literary conceits. The same was true a day later when General Frieden, alone, returned to the podium to announce to an utterly silent room that the outcome all had feared had, in fact, come to pass, and with a virulence that exceeded even the most dire predictions.

"Our best information is that all are dead," he intoned in a steady voice, his gaze riveted on a scrap of paper clasped between his fingers. "I speak of the assailants as well."

He cleared his throat. Once again he mentioned Dostoyevski. A murmur ran through the room. Suddenly Murray of the *Register* was on his feet, determined to shatter the shabby pretensions of the press briefings at last. His face red with rage, his voice trembling, the veteran reporter pointed a finger at the general and demanded to know whether any of Dostoyevski's characters had ever, in fact, immolated twenty-eight innocent human beings; and then he had the indecency to point out that until General Klein had mentioned the insane German Heinrich Fürtweigle on the previous evening, the situation in the library had, by all accounts, been well under control.

3

Fürtweiglean: *Characterized by hatred and/or surreal distortion. Monstrous or grotesque, said of a political action, particularly when effected by a mob. Hopelessly dark and destructive, often with sexual overtones. Morbid or cruel, outwardly directed, but with the ultimate goal of self-destruction. Unbridled rage, usually directed toward one or more of the arts, in particular the literary arts, such as drama and poetry.*

4

Article 7

Now, in order to understand the nature of the poet, we must conceive for these pious individuals the names and concepts of a trinity of imposters; a polemical negation that, in Kantian terms, must be either willful or phenomenal and must either amplify or destroy the authority of the individual, together with perhaps his very person. The questions before us, then, are these: Is the bard man, beast, or God? If he is man, by what authority does he banish science, scholarship, mathematics, technology, enlightenment from his pathetic scribblings? If he is beast, why does he primp like a pink-cheeked schoolgirl? And if he is God, why does his breath smell like a sow's anus?

5

Rosse, the *Independent*: To the best of your knowledge, what time did it begin?

General Loomis: Knowledge by acquaintance or knowledge by description? I employ Bertrand Russell's distinction, which I find useful.

Rosse: By description.

General Loomis: Sometime after 7:00 p.m.

Creston, the *Observer*: How many are involved?

General Bouton: If the set is discrete and countable, perhaps thirty hostages, plus twice that many assailants. If it is continuous, an infinite number.

Creston: An infinite number?

General Bouton: I mean to suggest insects, not people. The situation borders on the Kafkaesque.

Weldon, the *Mirror*: General Frieden, is that how you would characterize what is going on—Kafkaesque?

General Frieden: General Bouton is a far more distinguished interpreter of the Austrian master than I, and I would hardly presume to question his statement. I have some familiarity with the Slavic texts, however—perhaps "Dostoyevskian" would be a useful referent. In any case, such terms are intended only to suggest a pathway by which the observer can begin to harmonize his inner and outer responses to objective reality.

Weldon: And what is that reality?

General Frieden: The library is surrounded by our forces. We have it on good authority that the aggressors are calm and that the hostages are being well-treated.

Weldon: You are optimistic, then?

General Frieden: With allowances for the possible cognitive discrepancy between relevant emotional and contextual antecedents and my ongoing evaluation of the current state of affairs, I would say . . . yes.

Weldon: General Loomis?

General Loomis: It would be irresponsible for me not to admit that, if earlier reports are true, we are observing a descent into the bowels of infamy that is worthy of the Marquis de Sade. If that is the case, you may be certain that the Snopes family would find itself right at home in the library. *(pauses)* I apologize for the antithetical transition. *(laughs self-consciously)* We have no corroboration of those reports, however, and at the moment, they must be labeled as rumors, if not outright lies. With that in mind, I would agree that, overall, the situation is under control.

Weldon: General Bouton?

General Bouton: I agree.

Tenney, the *Globe*: General Klein, do you agree? And do you have anything to add to your earlier comments relating to the literary models for these events?

General Klein: The situation is under control. As for models, I believe Nietzsche and Poe were poor choices, and I would forgive my colleagues for giving me a failing grade on my examination. If I may be given a second chance, I would direct you to the so-called Devil of Heidelberg, one Heinrich Fürtweigle. The so-called Ten Articles of his bizarre screed *The Heidelberg Manifesto* are instructive. And his quasi-novel *The Library* depicts events not unlike those we are observing. Of course, the work is fiction, and one must be careful about drawing parallels by labeling these events "Fürtweiglean." Still, the Devil's narrative is remarkably prescient, and though the author was quite mad, his understanding of human nature was, in my opinion, sound. One hopes we are witnessing a reenactment of only the opening scenes of Fürtweigle's nightmarish narrative and not the savage final chapters.

6

CHAPTER 43

Von Kuhlman resided on the third floor of a dilapidated building that reeked of old age and cat pee, and whose landlady was so ancient and so feculent that he sometimes fell behind in his rent—not because he lacked the ridiculously few coins she demanded for residence in her sumptuous palace, but because he could not bring himself to knock on her door and gaze upon the hideous countenance that greeted him when it opened. He had taken the room for the simple reason that it stood across the plaza from the library, giving an unobstructed view of the building's great western façade. He had spent the better part of this November day at his corner window, musing. Now he pulled a shaky table over to the window, collected a plate and a dirty fork, and sat down to his supper.

The sound of duty echoed in his ears—today no less harmonious or insistent in its demands than forty years before when, entering through the massive doors of the library, he had harkened to its unyielding call for the first time. How well he remembered that transcendent evening—the livid clouds, black clots in a blood-red sky; the pigeons flushing from the branches of a plane tree and circling three times before disappearing behind the cathedral tower, just then tolling its oppressive call to mass; the pale young girl playing alone on the walkway leading to the main entrance. Turning at the last moment, he had seen it all. Then the door closed behind him, and the precocious ten-year-old knew with certainty that the world of his childhood was closing with it.

He took his father's hand. Together the two stepped into the cavernous entryway. The bitter aroma of erudition and old books wafted into his nostrils, inducing in him a moment of panic. In a vast room to one side, surrounding scores of polished oak tables, hoards of lickspittles hunched over their tomes—abjectly he thought, as though questing for ignorance. What contempt he felt for those buffoons in their gowns and their quivering lips! What pity!

Father and son moved in the opposite direction, entering a lecture hall. In a hundred chairs sat an obsequious rabble, starstruck by the notable before them, a supposedly learned versifier with, alas, secret misgivings about himself; weak of soul but sparkling of insincerity. Ladylike in soft cloth, cold and contemptuous of eye, his cheeks pink, his thin lips carmine and glistening like the mouth of a common streetwalker, he bedazzled the simpering army of acolytes.

The child shuddered. The luminary raised his arm, thrust out his chin, opened his mouth. Out poured a cacophony of gibberish in a language so foreign, so foul, that the boy felt his ears bursting into flame.

Now in the dim light, picking absently at his miserable potatoes and his thin boiled beef, Von Kuhlman felt his blood raging through his veins, even as it had on that epiphanic day so long ago. He rested his fork and gazed across the plaza toward the wall, golden in the slanting light of the setting sun. He smiled as he pictured what had happened next. The boy abruptly dropped his father's finger and pressed on alone. Boldly he marched to the front of the room; then, continuing, the eyes of the hundred riveted upon him, fearful for his life yet jubilant for his brave heart . . . moving under the control of what seemed a supernatural force . . .

The bard sniffed, as though he had been assaulted by an offensive odor. Through scornful eyes he directed a withering glance at the child, then turned away.

The crowning arrogance of the gesture needed only a moment to register. The boy stiffened. Then he rushed forward, screaming . . .

7

—No one will believe it.

—That General Klein's mere mention of the word "Fürtweiglean" unleashed the mayhem in the library?

—Yes. As a plot device it doesn't hold up.

—What is the point of analogy? What is the point of literary parallel? Why bother to say that one thing is like another if the one is not *like* the other?

—Likeness is not precise. Likeness is inexact. Likeness draws attention only to similarities. In any case, you're going even further in this story by asking us to believe not only that the one thing is like the other, but that the one thing *caused* the other.

—Why do you traffic in words if you do not believe in their power to effect change? Perhaps you should pursue a career as a mime. Your experience is with likeness that is vague. I agree with you that such similarity is not likely to be causal. But what if likeness is precise? What if *The Library* is exactly like the events that unfolded? Who is to say that the mere mention of one will not set in motion the other?

—Your story is simplistic.

—Do you remember Messella, how it happened exactly like Tolstoy?

—Surely coincidence.

—Really? And Annagrepple?

—You fall back on anecdote. Where is your proof?

—Strips of copper that to a tolerance of one ten-thousandth of a centimeter are the same length will adhere utterly to one another. You cannot pull them apart. The atoms line up side by side and lock unyieldingly onto their partners on the opposite strip.

—Now you're a physicist. Now you propose to preach a comprehensive truth. Behold . . . not simply art but science too! Your story is not merely Fürtweiglean, it's Newtonian! It's Einsteinian! But how exactly does it shed light on justice or peace? How shall it help us to understand the terrible darkness of the human soul? ■

OUR HENDRINA
Lara Markstein

We all worked hard, not just Hendrina. So we didn't love her simply because she drove a wagon across the country at fourteen. If anything, we were embarrassed for our friend. Hendrina was a slight girl and when she gripped the riem, she had to double over to perch on the wagon's chest. Seated, she believed she possessed an air of competence. So she insisted on this acute and awkward angle between breast and knee as she called to all sixteen of the wide-horned oxen for hours on end: Kleintjie and Swartjie and Grootjie and Erasmus and Mompara and Moses and some others and Lui.

Hendrina was a *voorloper* for her parents, who did not have servants enough for her to wait in the back on lattice beds like us, stitching the hours into trousers and sheets (mended trousers, mended sheets; nothing was ever new). We envied her poverty. These were the same grass-stuffed mattresses on which we slept and on which we would likely give birth. We saw no evidence that they would not be the same beds on which we'd die. Indeed, Marta bore her first child in her parents' wagon and perished before they'd had time to wash the bedclothes of blood. Which would have been terribly sad were it not for the spectacular efficiency of such a demise.

Not that steering a wagon was easy; fording the Orange River, Hendrina's transom snapped. Though the waters were swollen and struck the boulders with great force, she did not scream. The muscles on her arms just hardened to the size of small apricots as she urged the oxen on; our Joshua crossing the Jordan. Hendrina commanded attention, all right. She could not help that her gestures made our own achievements look small. And we were not idle ourselves those two years we walked.

We came from the west. Mostly around Graaff-Reinet, where our fathers were farmers. Our mothers were sewers and menders and butchers and cooks and medics and farmhands and washers and God-fearing women who went to church and prayed each night before bed. They were dusty and sweaty, but their fingernails were clean. And so ours were, too, even with the chores. This far from a town, we all played our part. Sheep tails must be melted for candle wax. Cow shit collected to waterproof canvas walls. *It's a blue horse of a different color,* our mothers said when there was something they lacked. They also said, *The cock is king of his dungheap*, so. They had opinions about the trek.

Our party was a hundred wagons large with almost a thousand cattle churning the sweet grass to mud. What a sight we must have been, inspanning the oxen when the koppies were still shadows against a dull sky. A real *horde*. If a slow-moving one. We only ever eked out a few miles before the heat of the day obliged us to rest. Then we waited for the thunderstorms, which electrified the veld and turned the air to glass. By the time the temperature cooled, we'd add only two or three miles more before dark.

Most often, though, we didn't go anywhere. Our party stretched out haphazardly, marooned on a never-ending plain that was broken only by the long-deserted charred remains of kraals and scattered rock formations that had resisted the erosion of rain. After all, there were wagons to mend, oxen to rest, cattle to fatten and tend with a mix of grease and tar, which fixed broken bones and cuts and sprains equally. And these were the times Hendrina was beaten by her pa.

We were all beaten regularly and could guess the weapon and length of a flogging by the shape of the welts: thin strips for whips, stubby straps for canes, the compact geometry of a buckle repeated over again. Drinking *mampoer*, our fathers shook their heads at the discipline they'd been forced to instill. It was not easy beating goodness into a body the way you would hone your favorite knife. But they were fine Christian men and would not be faulted for lack of effort. Still, Hendrina's hidings were legendary.

We must add that Oom Bezuidenhout did not *only* beat Hendrina. He was generous with his punishment. His son, Hendrik, deserved a good thrashing, though. Hendrik had a unique talent for finishing his errands only when the last cattle had been corralled, but finding himself free when a bag of *beskuit* appeared. The boy was greedy, which we understood. We all wanted. But he was lazy, too, and that we could not abide.

Now when Hendrik was beat, the whole camp knew of it. His screams could be heard a laager away. Pleas to Jesus Almighty, apologies, promises; Hendrik was a model of Christian repentance while his ass was being flayed. Thank heavens for her sister Nella, our parents said. Petronella had golden ringlets and a pudding face and had memorized the entire book of Psalms at five. We hated her.

The marvel of Hendrina's beatings was not the noise then, which mostly consisted of her father's grunts, but the length. They did not end. While we quickly surrendered all scorn and dignity in snot-nosed groveling, Hendrina locked herself in a battle of wills. She *should* have wept. She *should* have screamed. She should have apologized for all the sins she'd yet to commit, like the rest of us. But she would not admit that her father was right and so he whipped her for insolence, harder and faster until he ran out of breath and the muscles in his arm turned to porridge fat.

The beatings were awful. By which we mean, filled with awe. Wagons away, we strained to hear the thwack of leather on skin, and conjured chains and marble amphitheaters and jeering crowds; an Old Testament spectacle demonstrating mankind's great capacity for suffering and the cruelty of God. We were at once sickened and excited by her nerve. How could you not love a girl like that, who did not know when to give up?

We traded biltong and rusks to see her scars. Sometimes stolen strings of tobacco, too; she charged extra to trace the mealie-silk lines down her spine. Or the swell of her cheek or the ruffle of melted skin. Hendrina was practical like that. We were never rich enough to touch the wounds themselves, weeping and raw, so we made do with endless dissections of her arguments.

Was Oom Bezuidenhout really so mad that Hendrina had asked him to fix the iron tire of the wagon? Perhaps he'd snapped, hearing her go on about mutton for dinner again when everyone else was eating antelope and bontebok and springbok and gnu. Hadn't Oom Lourens dragged a fat quagga through camp while her father nursed his head from the *mampoer* of the night before? You couldn't expect a man to give up his brandy. Not when he'd dragged his family to a strange and violent land that he did not understand.

And he'd warned her, right? Asking whether he'd requested her opinion. Hendrina must have known what awaited her when she said it was a good thing she'd offered her mind anyway. She must have considered lying, if just for a moment as her father reached for the sjambok, which he kept by his bedside because he was a man who dreamed, and his dreams bore a striking resemblance to this disordered earth. Just once, she must have imagined shutting up. But she wasn't sorry and she wouldn't let her father win.

Hendrina could hear the tokoloshe rooting around the beds at night, hyenas screaming and Zulu assegais scraping over shields. She heard the crack of flame when two years earlier our homes burned beneath a Xhosa raid, and she dared us to be afraid.

It was this we loved about our Hendrina. In the same way we loved kneeling beneath the lip of canvas in our wagons, watching those terrible summer storms. The sky full of wonder, but nothing good to come of it.

According to Hendrina, hunting and keeping the wagons in good repair were the least our fathers could do after they'd convinced our mothers to pack their Sunday best into chests they would not open for years. It was true our mothers were not fond of cramming knives and soap and bars of lead beneath their beds and that before we'd left there'd been a lot of arguing over taxes and slaves. But why they'd finally agreed to the whole endeavor remained for us one of life's great mysteries, like sun-showers and nightclothes.

"To have their say," Hendrina claimed. She'd heard that in the new country women would speak at the Volksraad. We'd heard nothing of the sort, though we slept beside the bed on which our brothers and sisters were made. Which just showed how remarkably good we all were at keeping secrets.

"We're better off here, anyway," Hendrina said. And she was right. We were forgotten on the trek and could slip away. We had the whole country beneath the white sky in which to play. Not that we noticed this freedom. We were concerned with boys.

Our mothers were already starting to talk of marriage, and we eyed the men with suspicion. Eyed each other, too, bickering over the handsome ones, the rich ones, the ones who rode a horse with that slack-backed sway, as though with a shift of his hips the whole universe would be his to command. "Why else do men have families?" Hendrina said.

It was true that no wife seemed pleased with her lot. Airing the bedding, our mothers did not need to strike the mattresses so keenly, as though each night the very linens collected the residue of regret. And while their gossip over suitors contained an uncharacteristic sympathy, this alternated with delight. "You'll see," they crowed. The mothers of toddlers said, "You, too, will grow old."

Hendrina swore that she'd not marry anyone. Though she spent a lot of time with Karel, we were quick to point out. Karel, who chewed tobacco like his spit was gold.

Karel had joined the party alone, having ridden hard across the eastern provinces with just a tent, a horse, and a few head of cattle that he'd stolen from his parents, who had refused to trek. We appreciated the patriotism of such a theft. What courage! What style! Our fathers cajoled him into eating the food their wives had made. Oom Bezuidenhout especially took a shine to the boy and Karel could be found at their wagon, smoking and reviewing the family disputes. They told each other tales, Karel's dark curls shaking beneath his hat as lions thickened and mountains grew and gold multiplied.

So Karel must have felt some kinship to the family and it was not surprising that when Hendrina's spokes broke he lent a hand, galloping across on his shaggy horse, a mix of Basuto and Arab stock, unbridled and unshod, like all the rest.

"It's more effective to travel with four wheels," he said over the squawking of the hens in their baskets, and Hendrina could have murdered him. But before she could contemplate the details of revenge, he winked and added, "We'll fix it before your pa finds out." Then he set to work chopping fresh wood from the assegai and carving a perfect replica of the broken spoke. Hendrina was proud but sensible and tightened her kappie and knelt at his side to help.

When they rode into camp later, Karel said he'd been ill. None of us believed him, of course, with Hendrina scowling at his side. Especially when he lingered by her wagon the next day to offer advice she'd rather he kept to himself.

"Don't try to wrestle the bastards," he informed her of her oxen. "You think you'll win against a thousand pounds of meat?"

"You've never seen me wrestle," Hendrina said through her teeth.

Karel said, "Wrestling only gets you so far. You've got to treat them as though you were in love . . ."

Precisely what that looked like, who can say? She did not abandon the soap she was making with fat and soda and wood ash when word spread through camp that the men who'd gone to hunt lions had been hurt. The lions had been devouring our cattle at night and Karel had joined a troupe of young warriors who fancied themselves David in the den—except they sought to slay the beasts with flintlocks instead of prayer.

Later, after the crowd receded, she visited the tent where the injured men lay. One boy was dead. The left side of his body had been shredded by claws and his innards stuffed back beneath the skin with just a dirty shirt to hold them in. Another lay moaning on the bed between a roughshod table and a grand stinkwood chair. From the pallor of his skin we knew he was not inheriting the chair. Downstream, the men dug two graves.

While our brothers sang psalms slow and serious, it was evident from their hurried efforts and the empty brandy bottles strewn by their bare feet that they all agreed Cornel had been a show-off, and his death only surprising in that it had arrived so late. Gerhardus's eye even wandered to the Prinsloos's tent, where pretty Sarah sat. There were plenty of girls who pretended they had to be held when a body was readied for the grave. So who could blame these boys for enjoying a good death?

At least we didn't have to worry that Hendrina's heart would break over Karel. For Karel was a helpful fellow, forever fetching pails of water for lovely girls. Our mothers didn't complain. An extra pair of hands never hurt, and what was so terrible about a bit of excitement anyway? They'd been such obedient daughters and look out over this great sea of green grass for what good that had done.

Karel seemed particularly fond of Magrietha, who, on behalf of Hendrina, we didn't like. She had neither the intelligence nor the personality to fill her too-tall frame, so that whole parts of her body appeared drained. She also had the face of a horse and an ugly laugh you could hear whenever Karel was near. She mended his linen jacket and his trousers, too, and we imagined her kissing the filthy fabric so often we knew it was true.

When we mentioned this to Hendrina—not to be mean, but because she'd find out eventually—she shrugged. Even scowled a little less, which made us think she was relieved. "They look well together," she said. And after a pause, "But she should fix her own clothes first, which are too tight." Then Hendrina turned back to the fire over which she melted lead. The territory beyond the Drakensberg was still in dispute, she reminded us. We'd need bullets soon. She could be condescending, our Hendrina. But only because we disappointed all her expectations.

Still, we copied our friend and leapt into preparations, mixing tins of gunpowder and salting meat and ignoring the boys entirely. When this only made them more interested in us, we suspected Hendrina of teaching us how to lure a man. We ascribed to her all sorts of knowledge she had no reason to possess as she strode earnestly across the veld, trampling the bitter flowers with some new purpose in mind. Hendrina spoke only of the logistics of the crossing, which were complex. As if any of us cared.

The worst part about our friend was how often she was right. When we emptied all our belongings from the wagons on the steepest sections of the cliff to walk the items over the sharp precipices ourselves, we could not help hating Hendrina. We suspected that if she had not gone on so, the wagons would have fit through the narrow paths that had been chosen and not needed dismantling. Instead, we lugged chests and churns and stoves and mattresses, though it was summer and our lightest linen clothes scratched raw our skin.

We blinked then when we finally saw Natal, convinced exhaustion had summoned a mirage. Blue rivers stitched green meadows to shaded valleys that stretched out all the way to the ocean that led to India. Somehow we fancied that Hendrina was responsible for the perfection of Natal as well, and as always we forgave her everything.

All that remained was to find a way down. We could not just hook the wagons back onto the oxen since they would careen over the steep slopes and crush the beasts. So we transferred the back wheels, which stood almost as tall as a man, to the front and tied great logs from the beech trees our menfolk chopped in their place for brakes. The oxen still struggled, notwithstanding our improvements. They fell to their knees. One broke a leg. But on the first day, only a single wagon shattered its disselboom, and most of us called the expedition a success.

For weeks, we camped beneath the Drakensberg. Our cattle extended five miles along the Tugela River, our tents spread so that for once we did not hear our neighbors fart. The ploughs and spades and picks we'd lashed to the sides of our wagons seemed almost sensible in this landscape of wild syringa and feather-tipped cotton trees. When they thought we were not watching, our mothers even fingered the seeds they'd brought for mealies and sorghum and wheat. It was hard not to believe that this was our Promised Land. Although many of the men still thought we had miles to travel before we'd harvest again. They wanted to head north, fearing another war. Others trusted the governor enough to stake out the choicest territories to farm. Not that the northerners in Potgieter's camp ever left. Not that Maritz's men watered a single seed. Each circled his future cautiously.

Then one night as we slept, a man from another camp cantered into our midst, screaming, "They're here! The Zulus are here! They've killed everyone!" Recognizing that now was not the moment to demand details, we leapt from our beds, pulling on kappies and shawls with one hand while the other reached for the gunpowder and bullets and muzzles of our father's flintlocks, hanging over our beds. We gathered branches from the thorn trees to cover the spaces between the wagons, which our fathers swung slowly and with much cursing into a laager, ready to fight. Our mothers poured the gunpowder into the barrel of the snaphaan, followed by a plug of wadding, then a slug and a second plug, with the same fingers that would have pressed the apricot pip into the earth.

A roar of thunder shook the earth beneath our wagons, but there was no rain. This, one of the details that stuck in our memories years afterwards. The rest of the night unraveled so that it was only together that we could reconstruct the battle we'd all fought.

The menfolk primed their barrels and shot and shoved their guns back into our hands and we joined our mothers in reloading the chamber while they fired again with the second rifle that lay at their feet. In the sparks from their shots, we glimpsed the conditions in which we fought, which were somewhat less than encouraging. Dingane had an army of fifty thousand men and it seemed that every one of them was sprinting towards us, assegai in hand. So we thrust the guns back and forth, until the barrels were so hot our fingers burned and we feared the gunpowder would explode in our hands. But the Zulu warriors fell. Their brothers climbed over the mess of intestine and bone and continued to hurl their assegais, but they sunk to the ground as well. With our knives, we slashed at the hands and the legs and the heads that reached through the tears in the hides protecting our wagons from flame, and limbs tangled and piled high. Tannie Oosthuisen snatched at her trailing shawl, and we laughed at such care in the face of filth. Our skirts had soaked up all the blood.

We were not without our own losses. An assegai ripped through Oom Bezuidenhout's gut and he slumped over, holding the shaft quite tenderly, as if confused as to why it poked from his spleen. When Hendrina's mother stepped forward with her knife, a black rammed her through with a spear, too. But the grim look on his face froze when he dropped to his knees with an axe lodged in his skull. Small bits of brain matter splattered on the grass. Behind him, Hendrina breathed deeply in and out. Then she reached for her father's gun with both her hands and when it would not move beneath his weight, she pushed at him with her foot and yanked.

The rifle was too long for Hendrina, but she held it steady even as she yelled to Nella to get the gunpowder or they'd all die. Nella screamed. A gaping hole of teeth and tonsil had devoured her pretty, fat face. When Hendrina fired, the gun slammed her shoulder so hard she fell onto her ass. Hendrina rolled to her knees and ripped the gunpowder bag from her sister's hands and filled the rifle and fired again. This time she swayed back to steady herself but stood upright. She passed the flintlock to Emmelina, who, still sniffling, reloaded just the way she'd been taught.

Eventually, Nella quit hiccuping and Hendrina lost all feeling from her shoulder to her elbow as she fired again and again through the waves of men breaking over them, each weaker than the last. Then the sun burned through the morning mist and baked the mud and shit and lifeless flesh before us so that the whole valley reeked. We were exhausted and sore and starving and our dresses had dried stiff, and that was how we knew the battle had been won. The women gathered their supplies and joked about who'd reloaded fastest, who'd sliced off the most hands.

Later that day, we discovered that the first trekker camp had been massacred after Dingane murdered Retief and his company. Our mothers and fathers were shocked. But nothing was so amazing to us as how Hendrina had fought.

While we pulled the Zulu dead away from our camp, fearing disease and a cover for future attacks, we filled in the details: the arc of her axe, the smoke stinging her eyes, the blisters that burned her forefinger and palm. With each telling we knew more until every one of us could have corrected Hendrina herself on the particulars of her bravery.

Not that we had the chance. Hendrina was burying her parents. Karel dug a grave beneath a nearby mimosa and the predikant Smit said a prayer for their souls. Hendrina tried to shovel dirt over their bodies, too, but her right shoulder was blackened and stiff from the bruise of the rifle's butt. So instead she sat on the mound, as if, for once, there was no work to do. Although now more than ever there were slugs to cast and bodies to burn, wagons to tar and prayers to be said.

All morning and all afternoon Hendrina lay there. She only stirred in the evening when her sister appeared with the ox jawbone and knuckles that served to represent the family's wagon and livestock in her games, and then to argue over the route these pieces should take over the strange earth. The sun cracked on the tips of the mountaintops. Our friend was a voortrekker; she believed in setting a course.

No one thought much of Hendrina afterwards. We were busy preparing for war, which mostly consisted of arguing over tactics and praying to the Lord. We were growing sick of the voice of God, which in our minds sounded like the red-nosed Erasmus Smit, who was not even a proper dominee. In fairness, Hendrina mimicked the motions of her parents—beating her brother long enough that he would scream, plaiting her sister's hair—so it was easy to forget that the Bezuidenhouts were dead.

But eventually our parents bored of wrangling over which dongas to avoid and which streams the Zulus could ford and turned to the question of our friend. Many words were spoken over a pipe late at night. The men mostly agreed that the children should be taken in by a wealthy family—the Martizes for example—who would be repaid with whatever the Bezuidenhout livestock produced. Certain men said she should marry, on account of it not being decent to live single like that. Certain men, it was noted, were all single themselves.

When Karel made the mistake of relaying the council's intentions to Hendrina, the whole camp heard words young women weren't supposed to know. We also heard Karel yelling: *What would she do if Dingane attacked? How could she handle her kaffirs alone? She was only a girl.* We were relieved when Hendrina held a knife to his throat and he shut up—although she should have thanked him for the warning. In Hendrina's defense, while our mothers tried to teach us manners, what we learned between the wars and the walking into foreign territory was how to survive.

We expected a show then from Hendrina. Our Boadicea, charging the front lines, shawl tied tight! So we were disappointed when we learned that she had not cornered Vrou Maritz with a glint of moonlight on the cleaver in her hand but had *bathed* with the woman. She'd soaped her body in the bushman's river and chattered on about how hard it was feeding three extra mouths with so many cattle gone. How remarkable it was that the Italian widow fared so well, she who'd led her family's wagons on the trek. And Hendrina had asked Tannie Maritz whether this wasn't what she planned to do, if—God forbid—her husband died? Surely, she wouldn't pass on everything to her sons and live on their forbearance, like a beggar in her own clothes?

"If you don't mind," Vrou Martiz said when she was through. "I prefer to bathe alone."

But then Vrou Martiz talked to our mothers and our mothers talked to our fathers, and soon everyone agreed that Hendrina would be just fine. They'd been younger than our friend when they'd started running a house, our mothers said. She would figure it out, as they had done. It was an ominous surrender to Hendrina's great will. We should have been pleased for her.

What envy we carried for her freedom vanished as Hendrina battled to survive on her own. Hendrik was missing, so Hendrina had to pen the beasts herself and then make food. Dinner was so late that when she called the servants to the campfire to hear her read from the family Bible, the way her pa had done, they'd long since gone to bed. One of many small mutinies. They were slow to respond and quick to forget what she'd asked. And Nella could not help pointing out everything else their parents would have done. "I'm not Ma!" Hendrina cried once, grabbing her sister's shoulders and shaking so that Nella's head jiggled back and forth. "She's dead!" Nella nodded at Hendrina as though she were a fool.

Hendrina rose an hour earlier, then an hour earlier again. She quit worshipping at the predikant's sermons and reading from the Bible before bed. Nella glared at her all night.

So we thought Karel just dashing to march into camp and offer his hand in marriage. He'd sought Meneer Maritz's approval, which, we agreed, exhibited great sincerity. Perhaps even love. And while we noted Magrietha's red eyes and how the puffiness to her face made her look fat, we did not gloat at her misfortune. Instead, we eyed Karel and Hendrina sidelong as they walked alone together—and then as Karel stamped off the way he'd come. Magrietha, the slut, wiped the snot from her face.

We were horrified. Had Hendrina mentioned the gossip about Karel's refusal to go on commando? Maybe she'd mocked his new *nekdoek*, which had a dandy gingham pattern we suspected Magrietha had selected. One by one, we whispered that our friend had too much pride. She'd fought. She'd won. Her insistence on living alone was showing off.

But this final sloughing of safety seemed to have sparked some peace in her soul. She reached an agreement with her brother, who was granted his freedom so long as the cattle survived. The servant, Emmelina, cooked and sewed and cleaned as though nothing had changed. Nella didn't quit acting holy, but she did compliment her sister occasionally on the tidiness of their affairs. And our mothers, too, began helping our friend. We suspected they were grateful she'd not snapped up one of the few unmarried men.

But the story of Karel and Hendrina's love was not so easily brought to an end. One autumn morning, as the first spokes of frost laced the grass, Karel appeared at Hendrina's wagon. She needed to learn to shoot, he said. "Good."

"I shot good enough at Blaukraans," Hendrina pointed out.

Karel said, "You couldn't miss."

That Karel could not only forgive Hendrina for spurning him but love her still seemed to us terribly romantic. For the rest of our lives the sound of bullets ricocheting off rocks in the smoky half-light would seem the height of seduction, our own courtships disappointing for not being tinged with the smell of sulfur. Though Hendrina pretended she did not care for the attention, she flaunted her prizes of dassie and bok. She could not piss without her father's gun slung across her back. It was a strange way to woo a woman, all right, but Hendrina was insistent that she was no ordinary girl.

We didn't want to believe then that Karel, who had risen so high in our estimation, was following the cowardly Potgieter back over the Drakensberg into the veld. How, we asked Hendrina, could the man who'd stolen his own family's cattle to join a new nation abandon it at the first sign of distress? What we meant was: how could he leave her?

Karel's love for Hendrina lent our lives mystery. Our own romances were garden variety. Ordinary boys visited our fathers to talk hunting and cattle and war. We took unremarkable walks along the Tugela so they could recount everything they'd killed. Occasionally, we kissed. Sometimes, more. We could agonize about these suitors for hours, sure. We tested out the sound of our new names and argued about our adopted families. But one love affair was the same as the last. We'd never seen anything like Karel and Hendrina before. "He'll regret it," we announced.

"Maybe I will, too." Hendrina had decided to join him on the trek. She did not want to stay in this valley where her parents lay dead in the ground. She could smell the bodies in the burnt air.

They left as the weather warmed and the snow on the peaks of the Drakensberg melted, feeding the rivers so that the currents ran cold and fast. From the peddlers who traded ivory in the Bay of Delagoa, we heard that the journey was hard. Mud swallowed wagon wheels whole. The beech forests of Natal petered out into silver thornbushes and grass and the occasional squat baobab. They burned cow shit in their fires at night. "Like Jews wandering in the wilderness," the peddlers said. But they found land, finally; fig trees gesturing against a wide blue sky. They set out farms and forded dams and carefully unpacked their seeds and pits to nurse orchards on the sour grass. "It's hard there. They won't survive long." The peddlers scratched at red wounds left by tsetse flies. They did not know our Hendrina.

Karel built a house of mud and reeds, the walls covered in mist, the floors tamped down first with clay and cattle dung, then later peach stones that he'd crushed. Hendrina slept in her wagon until Karel built her a plot as well for her neighboring land. Nothing so grand as his dwelling, which had separate rooms and an overhang for the kitchen fire when it rained. But neat, with its own wood door carved from the iron-stemmed mopani tree. An ox skull served as a stool on her stoop.

And that's all travelers would say of our friend. "She threatens to shoot everyone!" They shook their heads when we laughed. "Not even a cup of coffee, hey!" That was Hendrina, we claimed. Unkindly, but not without a measure of pride.

For years we imagined the life she and Karel led, settling on the details until we no longer needed to speak of her; we could feel our Hendrina elbowing around in our chests. By then we'd gotten older as well, and we had our own lives in Natal to talk about. We'd married, born children, raised farms that were being threatened by the British again. We argued over whether we'd have to hoist our belongings into wagons once more to cross the shadow of the Drakensberg.

Then the British raised their flags in Durban and our commandos slunk home on horseback. We lashed out at our husbands, yelling about God and honor and courage and right, because we'd planted such pretty gardens, built such tidy lives. *If Hendrina were here*, we said. Which was a shock. We'd gotten used to her silence, nestled beside our hearts.

Now, ten years later, hauling furniture over a mountain pass that had not changed, we washed behind our children's ears, anxious to present these creatures we'd made to our friend. We wanted her to praise them. We feared they would not compare with her and Karel's kids.

But Hendrina barely noticed their scrubbed faces and well-sewn clothes, which we'd had to root out of the chests we'd carried so far.

The children beside us on the stoop itched to be acknowledged so they could run off and play. We craved a mug of coffee, a seat, some sign we hadn't intruded on her life. "I'll start a fire," she finally said, spitting out her tobacco chew.

Twenty-four and Hendrina lived alone in the same hut Karel had built her years earlier. Her sister had married a prominent burgher with a farm fifty miles south. Her brother had also wed but was on commando against Mzilikazi in the north. Hendrina's *beskuit* were chalky for want of butter. And Karel? He'd married too, she explained. Just one week earlier.

Nine years he'd lived beside her and now that she was alone he married! *The bastard!* We said. *Son of a whore!* "Oh, Karel was born of an elephant's shit. But I don't begrudge him his wife. She's a pretty thing," Hendrina said of Aletta van der Merwe. "As fifteen-year-olds are."

We were outraged. Less for her sake than our own. Their romance had for years sustained our own regrets about the men we'd married, and nourished our fantasies. That Karel had wed another woman laid waste to the possibility that our lives could be extraordinary.

But Aletta was more than pretty. She was quick to lend a hand and laugh and devised all sorts of tortures to remind Karel of herself. "I bang the pots in the morning after my husband's drunk too much," she confessed, doling out another slice of pie. "Sometimes I salt his coffee, too, if I've seen he's a lingering eye." We visited her often, never once stopping to speak to the friend of our youth, whom we hardly recognized anymore. Hendrina did not drive her wagon to parties or church and avoided every nagmaal. The hair thickened on her upper lip.

Occasionally, we heard about Hendrina from Nella, who'd grown into a sturdy woman with two fine chins. Nella said Hendrina liked to pretend she lived in poverty. Obtaining a portion of their parents' property for a dowry had been a battle hard fought. And Hendrik should have had a farm to offer his wife, not needed his rich in-laws to grant him a plot of land. Nella herself did not pay social calls. "What can you do with a woman who refuses to go to church? I have young kids to think about," she said as if religious apathy were catching.

We nodded, knowingly. But there were days our minds wandered from the catechism. Hendrina seemed happy.

There were times we found ourselves in her hut, waiting for her to find her rusks in the dark. She refused to light candles, which took too much time to make. When she gave up on *beskuit*, inevitably because she had not baked any, we passed around a bottle of *mampoer* instead— and sometimes a pipe of the *kaffirs' dagga*—and talked. Not about our children, but the British and crops and soil, the conversations folding into one long thread we could not unravel even later in bed. "Disgraceful," our husbands said, pinching their noses at the skunk of our breath. "If the children should see you like this!" But they wouldn't. We couldn't remember the last time we'd seen our own mothers. They lived so quietly in our houses, they'd disappeared.

Our husbands forbade us visiting Hendrina, which made us want to see her more. She was smart, after all. She'd managed to keep her cows free from river fever and had not had to sell during the worst of droughts. The servants gossiped that it was her ramshackle farm that had kept Karel's estate afloat those years. We tried to tell each other that this care for Karel even after she'd been cast off was proof of a tragic love. But we suspected that Hendrina, who understood something we would never grasp, was making a point.

The years collapsed, one into the next, and our own children soon talked of marriage and we hunted for suitors who would not beat our daughters much or who would make them rich. We hugged these almost-women to our breast and hated ourselves for being pleased that soon they'd understand what life was like. But they did not notice our attentions. Our touches barely grazed their skin. If we left the pins in our daughters' wedding dresses, if we curdled the milk in their cake, we could not be blamed. We refused to be erased.

And Hendrina farmed on.

Only once in all those years did Hendrina's routine change and that was when Aletta caught malaria. Hendrina rode into the neighboring farm for the first time in years, armed with Emmelina's poultices and herbs, and did not leave for two weeks. She and Karel took turns changing cold compresses and watching Aletta die. "Abominable," Nella said, not pleased by the gossip that spread, suggesting Hendrina may have helped the girl on her way. And maybe she did. We would not put murder past our friend. But if she had, it was not for want of a man.

Hendrina did not move into Karel's bed as they all expected. And why should she, we wanted to know. Why saddle Hendrina with another woman's children? Why condemn her to be a mother, a wife, to care for more than she pleased? Hendrina had chosen her path. And who were we, we thought, tired and sore and forever falling in love with the men to whom we were not married, to disagree? Let her be. Let her be nothing to anyone. Let her stand all alone.

Only Hendrina had learned over the years how to disappoint our expectations a thousand and one ways as well. Though she was thirty-four and too old for foolish mistakes, she began to show. "I could have forgiven her," Nella said, "if she intended to marry."

No one knew who the father was, of course. Hendrina would not let even traveling salesmen step on her property. Some said it had to be the help then. Stuck alone on a farm with a bunch of *kaffirs*, no wonder she was not admitting her sin. Others of us glanced at our husbands a moment too long, curious if they remembered Hendrina the way she'd been as a girl. If they thought of her still.

At the nagmaal, which as always Hendrina did not attend, Karel slurred his words. He wanted to know if we'd heard anything, anything at all. "I've looked after her these years, you see. I want to know what I did wrong." We patted his hand as though we pitied him. But really we thought he ought to be ashamed; he'd failed. How pathetic it was that in the end he was not to blame.

That's how we thought of the father of Hendrina's child: a man to blame. Whoever had conceived with her had committed a crime we could never forgive. Hendrina was not meant to waddle like us, you see. She was not meant to fatten in the face and knit the most delicate blankets and complain about the pain in her knees. Here was the girl who'd held her father's gun and shot against an impi of ten thousand men! Here was the girl who'd trekked across the very teeth of the Drakensberg alone! She was meant for more than shit-stained rags and leaking breasts and ordinary joy.

But who else could see that apart from us in her small house? She was fading already. Her edges blurred as she searched for that lost tin of rusks with one hand, the other resting across the roundness of her belly. Like all of us, not realizing how empty it already was. ■

GASOLINE
Guillermo "Git" Lanza

The sun means nothing. Nor the yellow flowers.
Not the monsoon shower. Not the children on the corner.
I gazed down past a bank at the turbid water
And saw in a dream my leg severed.

I saw a child near Saigon cared for by her mother.
Forced to choose between a pig and her infant daughter
She spared the pig and drowned the child in the river.
When I asked why she said *another*

Daughter I can have - a pig never.
I saw my friends again - my mad brothers -
Laughing and lighting up a reefer,
Heard myself crying in a chopper.

I stood on the bank and remembered
The dead on the hills, by the rivers.

LETTER HOME
(Vietnam, 1967)

Guillermo "Git" Lanza

Dear Dad:

Dad, I'm coming home in December.
Yes, I've shot without remorse child soldiers,
Old men and women, sons and daughters
They say to make our country safer.

I've seen Marines in body bags by the choppers.
I've heard the shouts of men hit by mortars.
I heard a friend, Mike, being tortured
Then found next day the horror

Of Mike, cock in mouth, murdered.
The war's something cruel like a lover
That kills instead of me my brothers
And leaves me here, it seems, forever.

I smell, still, the napalm - Hell's sticky fire -
And smell burning flesh. I'll remember.

Git

CHICKEN
Adam Sullivan

After we'd been dating for a few months, Anh took me to meet her parents. We showed up for dinner at their restaurant. It was late, eerie quiet, which made it feel stilted and formal. Like a job interview.

I was nervous for all the obvious reasons, but mostly because Anh told me flat out: "My parents are gonna judge you on the spot. It's a Chinese thing." It wasn't meant to terrify me, but it did.

When you own a restaurant, dinner takes place well after 10:00 p.m., when the restaurant is closed and all the customers are back at home, falling asleep to late-night TV. Her father—who did not speak to me—brought out three large platters of not-immediately-identifiable food. At least, not to me. I thought they might be vegetables—rare, exotic vegetables they didn't sell at the Stop & Shop. I didn't want to seem uncultured, though, so I didn't ask. Anh picked up on this and whispered in my ear: "Chicken."

Like many Asian immigrant families, the Sams found their footing in America by opening a restaurant, and when you own a restaurant, you buy your products wholesale. For example: "chickens," as opposed to "chicken meat." The light and dark meats were separated, sliced, and sautéed into kung pao and moo goo gai pan for the customers. This dinner, which Anh was ladling onto my plate in great heaps, was the rest.

I grew up in a white Connecticut suburb, with white parents and mostly white friends. Often for dinner we'd have chicken. What we wouldn't have, though, is chicken guts. I thought about those dinners, how comfortable they were, the faintly metallic tang that was consistent across all vegetables that arrive in a can. It made me homesick then, just for a moment, and when I came out of it I realized that here and now I was the guest, so everyone was waiting. This wasn't some exotic culinary adventure for them, it was just dinner, at 10:15 p.m., and because they had manners they weren't about to eat before me, and here I was, poking the organs around on my plate, summoning my appetite. Nobody said a word. I looked to the woman who would one day be my wife. She smiled, and so I clumsily pinched a heart between chopsticks and popped it in my mouth. It tasted earthy and sweet. Like blood.

* * *

Years later, Anh and I were at the park watching Emily play. She was two then. This was all part of my grand plan to socialize her. She was our only child, and there were no plans for another, so I'd cultivated a very specific fear that she would grow up awkward, incapable of navigating social cues with other children. Anh just wanted her to play. She didn't overthink things the way I did.

Emily, however, wanted nothing to do with the other kids. She wanted me. As stay-at-home dad, I took her to the park all the time, and we had a carefully orchestrated routine. We'd start on the swings, where I'd push her for a while, and then on to the next obstacle. I would steer her away from the giant rope spiderweb and all the other things that terrified me. She'd climb to the beginning of the monkey bars and grab the first rung, but her feet wouldn't leave the platform until I was standing there, ready to catch her. I'd hoist her up on my shoulder and walk the monkey bar path as she reached from bar to bar—never really swinging, never really hanging. Safe. It was great fun for both of us. She was an acrobat; I was her safety net.

When she clambered up to the monkey bar platform this time, Anh held me back, saying only: "She needs to learn." It was excruciating, but she was right. Emily called for me, as I knew she would. I faked a phone call, and Anh rolled her eyes. Emily swung out on the bar. Fear struck her, and she dangled there, wide-eyed. Anh held my arm as I tensed like a gazelle. This was new territory for both of us. A moment passed, and when she was unable to hold on any longer, she dropped to the ground, unharmed. She looked around, ran over to us, and I scooped her up.

Emily wiggled free and ran off in search of a new challenge, and I felt my wife's big, dark eyes staring.

"What?"

"Nothing. Just, take it easy, you know?"

"Why, because I hug my kid?"

"It's just weird. Your whole family."

"How else are we supposed to show we love each other?" I realized something just then. "How come you never hug your parents?"

She shrugged. "I don't know. Why would we have to prove it?"

It sounded so callous, but it actually made sense. Their love was never in question. My affectionate family was just showing off. Suddenly it felt so hollow, and yet to not constantly demonstrate our affection was unfathomable. My love was a message far too important to rely on subtlety.

Anh is Chinese, but she was born in Vietnam. Her parents were from a town just south of the Chinese border, but soon after she was born they made the decision to flee. It was the tail end of the Vietnam War, and the world appeared to be headed straight to hell.

After a grueling three-day slog through the jungle, they arrived in Ho Chi Minh City. There was a boat; they just needed to get to it. The details of this story are fuzzy, pieced together from a handful of old memories—some from Anh's parents, others from her grandmother. There was a point where the party was crouched in the riverbed, hiding as the Vietcong marched along the road, just a few feet away. My future wife, then only two months old, began to cry. It was raining lightly, or at least it was in my mind. If they were caught, they were all dead, so Anh's mother made the decision I never could. She clutched her daughter tightly to her chest and steadied herself to take away the oxygen the baby needed for crying.

When she saw what was happening, Anh's grandmother made her stop. She assured my future mother-in-law it would be okay. Anh stopped crying, and they made it to the boat, then to India, to Connecticut, and eventually to Orange County, California.

To me it was harrowing, but over the years I came to understand it wasn't even an uncommon story; in fact I had two close friends with remarkably similar tales of escape. When there was only room for one on the boat, Thuy's mother smuggled her through in the bottom of a fruit basket. Cuong barely made it out alive. So many of my friends had near-death experiences that ultimately helped to define them as adults. Because of their childhoods, they grew up knowing how just resilient they were. They had perspective.

What I had was the exact opposite. My family never had to slog through a muddy riverbed or hide underneath a bunch of bananas. To this day, whenever I visit my parents for more than a few days, my mother will sneak into my room and gather up my laundry. The message: when you love someone, you take care of them, well past the point where they need, or even want, you to.

My Uncle Pete spent a year on an army helicopter, flying through Vietnam, returning only to learn that his younger brother, Pat, had been drafted as well. Pete quickly reenlisted, knowing that if he went back over, they couldn't send Pat, too. This too, is stitched together from my own family's faded memories and scotch-fueled confessions in the small hours of the morning. They make epic, dramatic movies about stories like these. They make sitcoms about mine.

When she was in high school, Anh brought a fifth of Jack Daniel's and, together with a friend, polished it off between classes. She awoke from her coma in the hospital, tubes crammed down her throat, IV in her arm. Her mother was hovering over her, worry lines breaking into relief as my future wife finally opened her eyes. Mom held daughter close to her chest, smothering her once more with love.

The same year, I got arrested, for skateboarding, and I was placed in an inner-city holding cell for seven hours. It was close to dawn when my father arrived. I heard his voice as he walked down the hall, and the relief was like oxygen to a drowning man. And yet, as soon as he rounded the corner, I was mortified. No one else had their fathers coming to their rescue. My cellmates saw only privilege, as though the officer would hand me my belt and shoelaces, and then it's off to Martha's Vineyard for the weekend. All I could feel was misplaced shame. I didn't hug him then. I probably didn't even say thanks.

We grew up in shadows that were impossible to fill. When it was our turn to go to war, it was no longer about freedom. It no longer felt noble. My generation had grown too cynical. War was a video game our fathers wrapped and placed under the Christmas tree. The best we could do was learn from their experiences, but even then, Anh and I seemed to glean two entirely different lessons. She knew she was stronger for having made her mistakes, and I knew I'd sooner cut off my own feet than have my daughter get a splinter.

Emily ventured over to the spiderweb ropes and was timidly working her way across the middle rung, pausing when a child would jump on to shake the macramé structure. Again I looked to Anh, but she didn't seem too concerned. As more kids jumped on, the ropes began to sway, Emily began to wobble, and I began to sweat. Anh stood there, confident, offering not her hand, but rather the knowledge of safety.

I know in my head that she is right. That when Emily inevitably topples to the ground, she will learn: *This isn't so bad. I'll know better next time.* She'll begin to understand what I never could. But some decisions aren't made with the brain.

Diving headfirst into the tangled web, I catch her head in my palm. A mouthful of cedar chips punctures my lip and wedges into my teeth, but she is safe. Blood trickles into my mouth, and it tastes earthy. Sweet. ∎

THE CALL
Laura Heffington

This guy still hadn't called me. It was around noon. "How long should it take?" I wondered. "How late in the day is significant?" A specific time had not been designated. Nothing specific was ever designated.

I had taken a bath. I had gotten dressed, but if we wound up doing something, I probably wouldn't wear that. I would change. I didn't put on makeup yet because that would seem overprepared and overthought. I was just casually hanging out in my bedroom at this point.

Now I was pinning things to a corkboard. Pictures and things. I was interested in these things, and I hoped it made me an interesting person, regardless of whether or not this guy called. His name was John.

"At least I'll have put up this corkboard, either way," I thought. "That's getting something done." Then I swept the floor. I wasn't waiting, I was sweeping the floor just like I might've done otherwise.

Maybe I should take a nap. I hadn't gone to bed until one-thirty in the morning the night before because we'd been on the phone for two and a half hours. "I wonder what that means," I thought. "He must spend quite a lot of time on the phone, if he talks to people on the phone like that all the time." I hoped it implied that I was of special significance, because of the logical fact that a person wouldn't have time to spend all day talking to various people in such a way. But we sure weren't on the phone right now, that was for sure.

So I got into bed. Actually I fell asleep right away. I started to have a dream about trying to label a bunch of photos, and I couldn't get the labels the way some lady wanted them. It was one of my frustrated anxiety dreams about struggling with a mundane task.

I was about to have a photo show at a gallery. I mean in real life, not just in the dream. John had offered to look through the photos I was thinking of using, and he had eventually gotten around to coming over and doing that. While looking through them he got a phone call from his sister, and he referred to me as a friend he was helping.

Now, though, pretty quickly after I fell asleep, the phone rang. "See?" I thought. "You let it go and then it comes. There it is." But it wasn't. It was my ex-boyfriend, Jim. He was curating the show.

"I don't like any of X's photos that he picked out. I don't understand why he picked these. Can you look at them with me?" There were two other people in the show. Neither of them were actually named X, of course.

"Okay."

I sat down at my computer and opened up the files.

I wondered if it would bother John, my being in contact with my ex-boyfriend. "He's probably not going to call anyway," I thought.

"What's this one of the girl smoking a cigarette with the thing on her head?" Jim asked. "Look at that minivan in the background."

"Yeah, it's not that good," I said.

"Look at the one with the fat dog," he said. "See it?"

"I don't know," I said. Maybe he just got confused . . . you know, sometimes when people are making important decisions, they use different criteria than they usually would because they're trying to do an extra-good job on the decision, and it messes things up."

"Look at this one of the people in the powdered wigs with the remote control," Jim said. "I hate it."

"Actually I think that one is really good. I think it's the best one yet." I glanced at the clock. "At least it kind of makes you ask a question," I said. "You don't know what's going on." This idea, that art should prompt people to ask questions, had been taken from a conversation with John, who was a professor at an art school.

The fact that a professor at an art school was associating with me was supposed to mean that I was somehow on the same intellectual level. Continued contact was paramount to my creative self-image, which wavered continually on the brink of total collapse. There were constant decisions to be made of critical importance. Claim to know what op art was, or give him the opportunity to explain it to me? Read the Clement Greenberg article right away, or pretend I was busy doing something else first? Seeming victories were short-lived, as another opportunity for failure was always around the corner.

"Do you wanna grab lunch?" asked Jim. We were good friends now. Close enough that when I first started hanging out with this guy, I had told Jim about it because he knew us both.

"I get it," he had said. "He's smart, and he's interesting. It makes sense."

So far so good.

"Except," he had said.

"Shit," I thought. "Here it comes."

"Except I think there's something wrong with him. I don't know if he can do interpersonal relationships."

"That's okay," I'd said. "I'm not even trying to do anything here. I'm finished trying to do things." This was a thinly veiled dig at Jim, which he chose to ignore.

"I don't think I can get lunch right now," I said. "I'm too busy."

"Okay," said Jim.

I got off the phone. I looked at the clock. Then I went downstairs and looked around for a while, trying to imagine how my various knickknacks and furniture would appear to others.

"This is pathetic," I thought.

It was now 3:10 p.m. Should I ask what was going on, if he still wanted to hang out? No way, I decided. I'm not the type to go chasing after some guy, asking what he's doing. I'll go for a walk.

It was about ninety-five degrees outside. I tried to stay in the shade of the buildings. There was a travel agency and a movie theater. "Maybe I should see a movie," I thought. But I didn't do that. After the theater was a head shop. In the window was a poster of a girl in short cutoff jeans shot from behind and surrounded by big bushels of pot leaves. Her ass was perfect, which seemed weird for someone the poster was implying was a major marijuana enthusiast.

After the head shop was a yoga studio. Someone had vomited in front of it. YOGA! it said on the window. Inside I could see about ten young, thin, attractive women carrying rolled-up mats under their arms and bottles of alkalized water.

I was terrible at yoga. In college I took a yoga class to get a PE credit and by the end of the semester I was the only person who hadn't made any progress, except for a handicapped lady with a bad leg who barely even participated. I skirted the vomit and continued on.

I looked at my phone. Nothing.

Then there was a juice store with sloppy paintings of ill-proportioned fruits all over it. At one point, John had said we should make a book of photos of this sort of thing, which so far had not happened. But for now it seemed like a funny thing to show him, plus maybe he would tell me what was going on and whether we were still supposed to do something. I took a picture of it on my phone and texted it to him.

"Hahahaha," he replied.

That was it.

I walked on because, anyway, I liked walking. It was something I would do regardless.

After this was a restaurant I found irritating because people were always lining up all over the sidewalk and getting in my way, and then the waitresses were always petting dogs without washing their hands afterwards.

Next there was a CVS drugstore, on the corner of Figueroa and 60. Leaning against the wall and sitting on the concrete was a drunk man without shoes. He looked like he'd been there for awhile and had gotten a lot of sun. Another man was looming over him saying, "I'm going to KILL you, motherfucker! And then I will drink a glass of scotch and smoke a fat cigar over your DEAD BODY!"

The other one didn't respond. He looked exhausted. He scraped at something on the leg of his pants, then gazed off into the distance.

I crossed the street and passed a deteriorating video rental store and a school where people learn to draw blood.

Then there was a fortune-teller's place of business.

Tarot, it proclaimed on the sign. Palmistry. "Those people are just cold readers," I thought to myself (this was a term I had learned in a psychology class). All they do is say vague things like, "I'm sensing someone has died in your life," because that applies to everyone, mostly. "Is it an older person?" they say, and if you don't look impressed, they change it to, "someone who was wise beyond their years."

"They don't even tell you what's really going on," I thought.

What a rip-off.

I checked the time again. "Screw this," I thought. "I'm just going to call and see what's going on. I'm not going to wait around all day. Be direct, that's the best policy. Why not?"

So I stopped next to Big Mama's donuts near some old guys playing checkers on a cardboard box, and I dialed the number. It rang four times, and then he answered.

"Hey," he said. "What's up?" It sounded like he was yawning.

"Nothing," I said. "I've been doing some stuff. Getting some stuff done."

He didn't say anything. A guy with a tattooed head on a lowrider bicycle wheeled past, and then a bus pulled up and let out a lady with two children. The children had a big bag of Cheetos they were toting along between them, each gripping one corner.

"What's going on?" I asked.

"I'm pretty tired," he said. "I was thinking about taking a nap. What are you going to do?"

"I'm going to kill you, motherfucker," I said.

"What?"

"Nothing," I said. "It's something some man was yelling at a homeless person on the street. 'I'm going to kill you, motherfucker. And then I will drink a glass of scotch and smoke a fat cigar over your dead body.'"

"Oh," he said. "Hahaha." ∎

AFTER PICKING UP MY SON FROM KINDERGARTEN
Fred Dings

"The child is father of the man," the great Bard said,
and sometimes father of the father, I might add.

We were in the car today and stuck in traffic
as it rained. "Dad, Dad," he said breathlessly,
as if he'd run from a distant village with an urgent message.
"Look, rain snakes!" he said, pointing to his window
where raindrop runnels wriggled down head-first.
And then, before I'd had a chance to marvel at
my little Bard of the Children's Garden, he quickly pointed
outside and said, "The rainbow's like a big feather!"
Then I thought about a giant bird of light as we sat
at another traffic light.
                              After that, at home,
he showed me art he'd drawn at school. I asked him why
the water had an eye and all the trees were yellow.
He replied, "Because the stream is looking at me
and my teacher said the trees eat light."
                                          My son,
you are a spring rain rinsing my dusted sight.
You awaken my habit-eyes that have learned to sleep.
Your life is poetry. Take my hand. Lead me to your lands.

For Sue the Magnificent !

. Dave

THE SHORTEST PATH
THROUGH A MAZE
David Harrell

Scott sat in the last chair of his bachelor slum house and rumpled his cat's ears. Such familiarity was ordinarily punished, but Cyrano's tattered head stayed lopsided with contentment; loneliness had improved his personality.

He had tried to introduce Cyrano into Gail's household just before the wedding—cautiously, out of concern for Gail's young tomcat, Marshall. But on their first meeting it had been Marshall who danced, stiff legged and arrogant, while Cyrano cowered beneath a rocking chair. Terror of the neighborhood: what had happened to him? As a result Cyrano had been placed in protective isolation at Scott's house, and the weekend honeymoon had been slightly marred for Scott by the thought of his lonely, dispossessed cat.

Scott leaned back and pictured Gail's two-story suburban home with its cedar siding (a bit weathered, though; what a job that would be to stain!). He was anxious to assume the manly duties of repairing, maintaining, and defending—not simply to prove himself worthy, but to dispel any impression on the part of Gail's parents and siblings that he was an opportunist. Already there were whispers of disapproval, according to Gail. Her parents treated Richard as though he'd been bereaved, inviting him over for weekly sob sessions. Or were they, Scott wondered, strategy sessions?

Scott and Gail had chosen to be married at the district court, inviting only Doug, Scott's friend of twenty years, and Doug's wife, Sara, to serve as witnesses—along with Gail's kids, of course, Andrea and Jeremy, ages six and ten. *They* had witnessed; and Scott wished he could see the event through their eyes: images upon which their lives would gradually render a verdict.

"Instant family!" Doug had teased. "It doesn't seem quite fair—no two a.m. feedings? No colic?" Scott was taken aback. Had he stolen a blessing?

The ceremony had offered a surprising touch of mystery. The wisecracking judge who'd taken their money in the front office had emerged from the rear of the darkened courthouse chamber, wearing the dignity of a black robe. Despite their brave disdain of convention,

Scott and Gail had both been moved, though not in the same way—their first marital dispute. Did *consideration* mean sensitivity to another's feelings, as Gail believed, or the payment that sealed a contract, as Scott maintained? In any case the judge's last words were clear enough: *don't let me see you back here.*

* * *

Scott and Gail had met at the consulting firm where they both worked, he as a programmer, she as a part-time graphic designer. Smart, quick, funny, she greeted him in the hallways with a wry grin, as though to say, *I am not as you see me here.* One afternoon she breezed into the corporate library just as he was opening a dusty programming treatise, *The Shortest Path through a Maze: A New Algorithm.* He glanced up and nodded.

"Anything good?" Her tone was light. She was daring him, Scott believed, to say yes.

"Hard to know. You're talking to a man who reads cereal boxes."

She raised her eyebrows and ducked down to see the title. "Ah. Just what we needed. Not a moment too soon, if you ask me."

Scott laughed. "Well, for those lost in mazes—particularly those who've tried the old algorithms—it *does* offer hope. Or it did ten years ago."

She shrugged and offered a mock-brave smile. "Some of us are still lost, these ten years."

He considered this carefully. Before he could respond, she executed a curious heel-and-toe turn and left him standing there, treatise in hand, wishing she'd stayed.

This incident became a running joke and evolved over time into their exact legendary beginning. Scott found excuses to walk past her cubicle, then dispensed with the excuses. He discovered he could make her laugh, that sweetest, most intimate of powers. They traded favorite books. They exchanged notes.

In Gail's scrupulously neutral portrayal of her husband, Richard, an engineer, Scott was certain he saw a modern-day Alexey Alexandrovitch Karenin. Controlled, soft-spoken, supremely rational, Richard was a torment to their fidgety son, Jeremy, but a slave to their precocious daughter, Andrea. If Scott felt any qualms, they stemmed not from the civilized violence he was preparing to do Richard, but from the puzzling question of why Gail had married him in the first place. When he pressed her, she hesitated before saying, with a rueful smile, "I suppose I traded myself for kids."

"Is that what you want your kids to understand?"

She turned away.

"Gail—"

"You have no right," she said, speaking with difficulty, "to judge my decision."

But he *had* judged her decision. What she didn't understand was that he had found her innocent. True, she had made a loveless marriage; but it was no crime to take a wrong turn. The crime, he thought, was to persist in the error.

* * *

Scott's right leg was asleep. Murmuring apologies, he worked his hands under Cyrano's uncooperative body and lowered his cat to the bare floor. When he could feel his leg again, he hoisted the easy chair by its coffee-stained armrests and carried it to the heap of castoffs in the driveway: mismatched furniture, paperbacks in cardboard boxes, brick-and-board bookshelves, cheap kitchenware; all headed for the Salvation Army. Gail had teasingly suggested that if he kept his furniture, the marriage was off. Seeing his junk through her eyes, he felt an odd mixture of shame and relief to be plucked up and scrubbed clean.

He corralled Cyrano, surveyed for the last time his empty living room, and maneuvered through the front door—using precious seconds of Cyrano's trust to lock it. Between the house and car, Cyrano progressed from denial to panic and finally, once inside Scott's Honda Civic, quiet despair.

Scott drove the residential streets of Lakewood Heights slowly, to allow the poison to be drawn from his spirit. Cinder block homes lined the streets seemingly without end, differing only in the color of paint each owner had seen fit to apply. The town had been built to satisfy, inexpensively, a hunger for suburban living at the end of World War II. Covenants now enforced the style of what must have seemed, on paper, a version of the American dream. Each and every parcel boasted a backyard large enough to contain a swimming pool or a tennis court, if one had the ambition. But by and large, Lakewood Heights now told a story of poverty, a sigh of defeat within a single generation. A few homeowners had resisted heroically: one of Scott's neighbors had installed aluminum siding, purely to conceal the graceless cinder block. (Now *that* was a low-maintenance home.) But Scott doubted anyone was fooled by the mask.

One of his first home improvement projects had been to clear the trackless blackberry jungle from his backyard. He'd spent an entire weekend with a gas-powered brush cutter, staggering and slashing and cursing until the hardened stalks lay at his feet. The woman whose lot adjoined his across the alley beckoned him to his back fence to confess it was the first time in twenty years she'd seen his house. Now that he had sold the place, to a young woman with scared eyes and two young kids, he supposed the jungle would rise again.

When they reached the freeway, Cyrano emitted a cry of reproach. "I know what you're thinking," said Scott. "You trusted me, right?"

* * *

Scott's brother Theo lived in a decent neighborhood not far from the university. A few months earlier, the house across the street from his had been torched, one of a series of arsons. As Scott snugged his tires against the curb, he saw the burnt remains for the first time. The blackened roof beams and rafters stood open to the sky, exposing the home's intimate interior of beds, dressers, framed pictures. Would he, in a moment, see the occupants going through the motions of their lives, snacking, watching TV, dozing in their underwear?

Theo had acquired his house as a bank repossession in the recession of '81, not long after his own marriage had foundered. But he was handy with tools and seemed glad to have an abused home to heal. Scott had to give his brother credit: he'd created his own durable, if costly, peace.

Holding Cyrano against his chest with both hands, Scott approached the front door and kicked gently. Theo opened it and stood holding a putty knife, flecks of white on his wrists.

"Hey, Theo."

"Scott and Cyrano! So this is it, huh?"

"Last chance to change your mind—"

"No, no. I'm ready." He bent down to Cyrano's level. "How're you holding up, kid?"

"He's in shock, a bit. Are you in the middle of something?"

"Naw, just the usual problems in this place. One thing leads to another. Tried to paint the bathroom and noticed some water damage around the base of the shower, so I wiggled the tiles along the edge and the floor came up in my hands. Come on in."

Scott poured the unhappy Cyrano out of his arms and the cat immediately began, with quick, nervous movements, to reconnoiter the living room. Theo nodded approvingly. "Typical cat."

They transferred Cyrano's belongings—food dishes, favorite toys, and carpet-covered pedestal—from the car to Theo's living room.

A terrible sadness threatened Scott's resolve. Life was full of omens—you had to mute them to keep your sanity. He reminded himself that Gail had been willing, after all, to accept Cyrano, saying (with the breezy confidence he admired), "Oh, he and Marshall will work it out. One of them will end up in charge."

As they stood watching the jittery cat, Theo put his hands on his hips and gave Scott a sidelong glance. "How's it going?"

"Oh, fine." Scott struggled to be honest. "I guess I'm not sure how it's supposed to be going."

Theo nodded.

Scott, being the youngest in his family, now expected advice. But Theo merely said, "A little luck's involved."

Scott nodded as though he understood. He cleared his throat. "Thanks for taking Cyrano. He was the one thing I felt bad about."

Theo shrugged. "It had to be done."

* * *

Scott guided the Honda along the curvilinear streets of Gail's neighborhood. Authentic suburban fathers, watering their lawns, glanced up as he cruised by but did not challenge him. The driveway in front of Gail's house held a space, his space. Their decision to stay put had caused some distress, not for him, but for Gail: the place was tainted by years of grinding her teeth, putting up with Richard's righteousness. Of this Scott had no firsthand knowledge, of course, observing only that in fighting the divorce Richard had been careful to portray Gail as a bad mother as opposed to a bad wife. This had sickened her, and still did, as though each night her ex stuck another pin in her voodoo likeness.

Scott hesitated at the front door, debating whether to knock, and at last turned the doorknob. He found Gail sitting cross-legged in the middle of the living room, surrounded by stacks of glossily veneered particleboard, studying a diagram with the assistance of Marshall. She flashed Scott a defiant grin. "Caught me. I wanted to surprise you with a new dresser."

"I *am* surprised."

"I mean *assembled.*"

"You need a man for this job."

She put a finger to her chin. "Hmm, where could I find one?"

"You have me. Anyway you're holding the diagram upside down."

"*You* try reading it," she cried, flinging the sheet at him, "you're so smart." She rose with a single, lithe movement and stomped theatrically toward the kitchen—pausing at the doorway to purr, "Will you be long?"

"I will not." He turned to the sheet of instructions and read: *Attach long top support rail (part D) using the short barrel bolt (part H) inserting into barrel nut (part J).* He aligned the diagram on the carpet and Marshall immediately sat on it.

"Think you're being funny," he said.

"What?" Gail called from the kitchen.

"Nothing—this is harder than it looks! Where are the kids?"

"They're at Richard's. He's supposed to bring 'em back around dinnertime."

He felt a trace of disappointment and suppressed it. This was the last weekend before they had to return to work, after their three-day honeymoon; he'd hoped the kids would spend the night with their father. He was still unnerved by the nonstop job of parenthood.

The dresser absorbed all his attention for the next hour and gave him, in the end, a little thrill of accomplishment, duly applauded by his wife. Gail took him by the hand to inspect the various divisions she proposed for their bedroom. Would the right side of the bed be acceptable? This was pure courtesy, their preferences having been established in *his* bed. The bathroom counter? And so on: her creation of space to make him feel at home. The new dresser was installed, and from his stack of boxes in the garage he took unworthy bachelor garments to fill it.

Dinnertime came and went, but no kids. Gail fretted; Richard had indicated "portentously" that he had something to discuss. The kids were always wired after being with their dad. In Andrea's case this took the form of what Gail called "chronic princess syndrome." From Jeremy there invariably spilled forth, within minutes of Richard's departure, a torrent of complaints about his sister's deviousness. Scott had the weary feeling that Andrea would forever define Jeremy's life.

"This is so typical of Richard," Gail said furiously. It was now seven thirty. "Why don't we go grab some dinner for ourselves? He must've fed 'em by now."

"You stay. I'll pick up some burgers," said Scott. "If we both leave they'll have to wait outside."

"That's his problem."

Hearing Richard get in trouble made Scott feel expansive. "Let's eat, at least. Hang tough."

* * *

Scott returned to find Richard's BMW in the driveway next to Gail's car, with Andrea and Jeremy sleepily piling out. He parked the Honda in the street. As he approached the BMW's gleaming trunk, he saw Gail advancing from their doorway toward Richard.

"Right on time," she said. "That's where Scott parks, actually."

Richard closed the door of his BMW, being careful not to slam. He was trim and broad shouldered, disproportionately so. His eyes shifted toward, but not quite to, Scott.

"In the future, would you mind parking out on the street?" said Gail.

Richard smiled. "Actually, this brings up what I wanted to discuss with you."

Gail was silent.

"I hadn't intended that anyone live here but you and the kids. My purpose in allowing you to stay in our house was for their sake, primarily, so their schooling wouldn't be disrupted." He waved a hand at Scott but kept his eyes on Gail. "Now that he's here, I would expect you to cash me out."

"I'll have to check the decree," said Gail. "I thought I had two years."

Andrea and Jeremy stood beside their mother, grinning uncertainly.

"Andrea and Jeremy, would you please go inside for a minute?" said Scott. He crossed the driveway to Gail to enforce this suggestion. Reluctantly the kids edged through the doorway and he closed the door before turning to Richard to say, "I didn't think we should discuss this in front of them."

"You're not discussing it," said Richard.

Gail said, "What I do with this house—"

"*Our* house," said Richard.

Gail bit her lip. A protective impulse, and a wicked one, moved Scott to say, "You'll get your dough, Richard. No one's suggesting otherwise."

Richard's lips tightened. He said to Gail, "We'll discuss this again in private."

Scott could not resist. "Will the kids be invited?"

Gail touched his arm.

Later, in bed, Gail said: "I want to cash him out as soon as possible."

Scott sighed. "The decree gives us two years, like you said. This isn't a good time to open our veins for Richard."

"I can't stand dealing with him. I want this settled."

"I feel like you're playing the role he wants. The guilty party."

"What does *that* mean?"

"Gail, fight back. He's obviously a man who needs to believe he owns the moral high ground; why should we make it easy for him?"

"I don't *know,*" she cried. "I don't know what you're trying to say. Why should I feel guilty?"

He was surprised, mortified. "That's the opposite of what I meant, Gail. I'm sorry. Let's talk tomorrow."

* * *

Scott awoke early and unwillingly. He listened to Gail's innocent snore. She'd told him *he* snored, but all she had to do was nudge him and he stopped. Even his unconscious was well-behaved.

Gail gave a little cough and stopped breathing. An insight, revelation? But this was followed by a moan—a sound of pure dread from deep in her chest. Then a series of shivery breaths.

"Gail," he whispered.

She kicked convulsively.

"Hey." He shook her shoulder.

She started awake, blinking at him. "I'm sorry."

"Are you okay?"

"Oh, God. I think so."

"Sounded awful."

"You were being mean."

"Was I? Sorry. I didn't know I had a role."

"You were mad because you had to give up your bachelor house and bachelor cat. Especially your cat—you said if one of them had to go it should be Marshall, because he's a wimp."

"Not true! Marshall's a great guy, a gentleman. You *know* I love him."

"But you miss your tough smelly bachelor cat."

"Well—I did feel bad, until Theo took him."

"I *knew* it."

"But Cyrano's got it made now. Theo's a soft touch."

She frowned. "You're a soft touch too, at least with animals. It's humans you're rough on."

"Can you please forgive me? For what I did in your dream?"

Gail gave a wicked laugh. "I might. But I want to know something. Do you like children?"

"Yes."

"Do you like *my* children?"

"Yes."

"How much?"

"Lots. It's just—we don't know each other very well yet." He pictured

Jeremy and Andrea, trying to put his finger on it. "I'm not sure they have much use for me."

Silence.

Gail said, "You know what? You don't need to report every single misgiving."

"Right, you're right. I just meant——"

She rolled toward him and stopped his mouth with her own. He inhaled the warm fragrance of her hair; after a moment, his hands found the small of her back.

* * *

Over coffee and blueberry muffins they discussed a second mortgage, maturely agreeing that sooner was better than later to cash Richard out. Scott promised to do the dirty work, dealing with loan officers, jumping through their hoops. After calculating a new household budget, his cheered-up wife stated that if they wanted a post-honeymoon fling, it would have to be now.

Scott spent the afternoon raking the yard, scooping out rain gutters, trying on the job of husband. After the lawn's cover of dusty red and brown leaves had been collected into four burial mounds, he leaned on his rake handle to cool off. Soon, half of all this will be yours, he thought. Gail was right: something out of kilter had been fixed.

From their neighbor's house floated sounds of domestic crisis, shocking in the autumn air. A furious maternal voice cried, "Oh no, what have you done? I *told* you to be careful!" Scott listened, afraid of having to judge whether the voice was out of control. At the same time there was an undeniable pleasure at finding anguish beneath the neighborhood's polished surfaces. "You are simply *not* paying attention!" the female voice continued. "I am so sick and *tired* of cleaning up after you!" Pause. "I am *not* giving you another full glass!" Judgment and mercy. Don't spill this one, kid.

He bagged the leaves and gave the front and back lawns one last trim.

In the evening, Gail got a call from a friend: there was a sale at the mall.

"Hang on a sec, Kris." She covered the mouthpiece and pleaded with her eyebrows at Scott. "Am I available for a midnight madness sale?"

"Go," he said. "Shop. I'll babysit."

"Are you sure? This is crazy. I can't ask you to do that."

"I live here, remember? We'll be fine. I'll fix popcorn. We'll watch a movie."

Gail chewed her lip; uncovered the mouthpiece. "Kris? Meet you there in an hour."

Jeremy, Andrea, and Scott clustered around Gail by the coat closet as she prepared to leave. "Will you guys be okay?" she asked, looking at Scott.

"I wanna go too," said Andrea.

"Good idea," said Jeremy.

"Can I, Mom?"

"No, this is Mom's night out. I should be back before bedtime. Why don't you and Jeremy see what's on TV?" This triggered a race for possession of the TV controller.

"I'm nervous," she admitted.

"Don't worry. I just have one question. When's the true, bottom-line bedtime?"

She hesitated. "Well, I suppose nine for Andrea, nine thirty for Jeremy."

"Okay."

"I won't be long."

"Be long! Go out there, have fun, and try to think of some way you can make it up to me."

"You're so . . . contractual."

Scott watched her pull out of the driveway. When he returned to the family room, Jeremy and Andrea were already arranged on their sacred halves of the sofa, their attention divided between the tube and territorial maneuvering.

"*Stop* it," yelled Andrea. "Jeremy hit me."

"Keep on your own side," warned Jeremy.

"Jeremy, no hitting. That goes for you too, Andrea. We can have a nice time tonight, but if you keep hitting each other I'll send you both to bed."

They subsided. He sat between them in time to see a talk-show hostess, her expression torn between empathy and voyeurism, gush, "How did you *feel* about that?"

"Oh, it exuberated me," replied her guest, to a chorus of whoops and whistles from the audience. He or she was identified as JESSICA, FORMER CON ARTIST WHO NOW POSES AS A TEMPERAMENTAL ACTRESS ON DAYTIME SOAPS.

"Jesus," said Scott. "Aren't there any movies on?" He grabbed the TV guide and scanned it. "Hey, how about this? *Invaders from Mars*—in color, even. Scared the hell out of me when I was a kid—"

"I like this," said Jeremy.

"Me too," said Andrea.

So they watched as Jessica's good-natured dupes were introduced, grinning as though they'd been in on it, eating up the applause. The talk show was followed by a docudrama featuring rape, murder, and pillage. The latter made Scott so uncomfortable he suggested a video, eliciting groans from his charges.

"Can we at least have some popcorn?" asked Jeremy.

"Damn, I forgot. Popcorn comin' up." Stop swearing in front of the kids, damn it. He put a bag of Jiffy Pop in the microwave and pushed "Popcorn," luckily one of the few foods the designer had felt sure of. After a few seconds there came the first muffled *chuff.* Not like the cast-aluminum skillet of his youth, which had produced a satisfying ping! when the kernels ricocheted inside. As the fusillade from the microwave intensified, he rummaged in the freezer for ice. Might as well score some points here. He filled three tall glasses with ice cubes and topped them up with Coke. Gradually he became aware that the popping had ceased—but not the microwave. When he yanked at the microwave door, black smoke poured out.

"Christ."

The smoke detector went off. Andrea, convulsed with laughter, flopped across the line of demarcation. Jeremy promptly hammered her shoulder.

"Jeremy, cut it out," called Scott. He fanned the smoke detector with a kitchen towel.

"Tell her to stay on her own side."

"I *did,*" Andrea bawled. But she aimed a kick at Jeremy's knee, and he slugged her thigh.

"All right, that's it," said Scott. "You can both go to your rooms."

They stared at him through the haze. The smoke detector refused to quit; for a brief moment, Scott considered smashing it.

He dropped the towel in the sink and faced Jeremy and Andrea. "Let's go."

But they waited until he crossed the family room and reached for their arms. Jeremy evaded him and stomped off through the kitchen, pausing to say, "Your popcorn's done."

"It's not *fair,*" Andrea quavered. She shook off Scott's hand and padded after her brother with an air of solidarity.

From the kitchen doorway he watched them trudge upstairs. He opened some windows; after a moment the smoke detector fell silent.

He channel-hopped awhile, too depressed to endure a single commercial or its muted pantomime. It was eight thirty. Should he make sure they were really in bed? Part of Jeremy's crankiness, it occurred to him, must have been because he was tired; he was a crasher. Andrea tended to stay up late, angling for private treats, warm milk, songs. Bedtime was just another phase of the day for her.

He heard footsteps in the hall and Jeremy, scowling in his pajamas, appeared in the kitchen. "Could you make Andrea stop singing? I asked her and she just keeps on."

Scott sighed. It seemed reasonable enough.

Upstairs, Andrea's bedroom door was slightly ajar, the light from her reading lamp just visible. She was singing something he didn't recognize; perhaps she was making it up on the spot. Jeremy paused at his own bedroom door, which faced hers, to raise his eyebrows. "Okay, you go on back to bed. I'll ask her to be quieter."

"Tell her to shut up."

"Go on, Jeremy."

He knocked softly on Andrea's door. "Andrea?" The tuneless song flowed on. He entered and found she was, at least, in bed, propped up with pillows, surrounded by picture books and stuffed animals.

"Andrea, I'd like you to stop singing now. You can stay up and read awhile, but your singing is keeping Jeremy awake."

She grinned but continued singing.

"Andrea, I mean it. If you can't stop singing, I'll have to close your door."

She interrupted herself long enough to say, "Mom lets me keep it open," and resumed.

He stood at her doorway, hand on the knob. "Make up your mind, Andrea."

She ignored him. He stepped into the hall and pulled the door shut.

A pause, as though to take a breath. And then the singing—benign, in retrospect—turned into a furious scream that followed him all the way downstairs. He took a seat in the TV-less living room and leafed through a magazine. Fifteen minutes crawled by. Damn it! Who'd have thought she was this stubborn? Evidently this was music to Jeremy's ears; no complaints. Scott gritted his teeth. Test away, Andrea; you're taking a fall.

He heard a car door slam outside, and Gail burst in, packages dropping to the floor, her face flushed.

"What in God's name is going on here?"

He stood. "It's not as bad as it sounds. I'm being tested, I suppose."

"What happened?"

"Andrea wouldn't stop singing, and she was keeping Jeremy awake.

I told her I'd have to close her door if she didn't stop." He shrugged. "She didn't stop."

"She can't stand to have her door closed."

"Well, she should have thought of that."

Gail covered her face with her hands. "I *knew* I shouldn't have left. It just felt wrong. How could I have been so *stupid*?"

Surprised and hurt, he shrugged again. "It's to be expected, isn't it?"

She uncovered her face and started up the stairs, two at a time, using her hands for balance.

"Gail—"

But he couldn't express the idea, unneeded until now, that she should not relieve him of duty in front of the troops.

The screaming abated. After a moment Gail returned, smoothing her hair with her left hand.

"I think she'll be all right now," she said. "Can we talk in our bedroom?"

Scott followed her, depressed by a sudden vision of the lesson they were teaching Jeremy and Andrea. As he closed their bedroom door he said, "This is ridiculous. She was fine, Gail. It was all calculated."

She spun to face him. "She's a little girl. It was a minor problem and you mishandled it."

"What did you tell her, anyway?"

Gail glanced away. "I just calmed her down. I opened her door a crack."

"Saved her from her evil stepfather? Is she singing again?"

"You make her sound like a demon."

"She's not a demon, but she's not an angel, and neither is Jeremy. They're human. They're both a little spoiled, if you want my opinion."

"I don't."

"Then what am I doing here?"

Gail sank to their bed and curled away from him. In the silence, the air seemed to thicken. After a moment Scott sat beside her and touched her hair, but his hand felt weak, ghostly: as though she'd dreamed him, and was just waking up. ■

THE HOUSE SPEAKS
Leona Sevick

There was a time when we were happiest on our own.
From the moment the sun fingered the faux wooden slats
of the blinds and she stretched, arms overhead, to the moment
when in bed her book tipped forward onto her chest, signaling
it was time to put her glasses on the bedside table next to the
water and flick off the light. The lavender smells of her showering
and the soft squeaks of her wiping the bathroom mirror made
me smile. Attending to whatever it is that keeps her from me
throughout the day, I was patient, still. But once she came through
our side door and put down her bag and books, hung up her keys
and pulled her shoes off, placing them carefully into their slot
on the hanging rack that we both love, she was mine. We chopped
vegetables for curry, drank a little white wine (not too much--maybe
a glass or a half more), ate slowly and washed up. Evenings she'd
curl on the couch to watch our favorite shows, and I would watch
over her, content. Don't tell me we weren't happy because I know
we were. The years have passed, and with them came the others.
Rarely do I find us alone again. Now I know they're gone when
the dishes pile up in the sink. The cobwebs form their lonely nets
at the floorboards, and clothes hang everywhere. Sometimes I
find her staring off into the distance or sleeping on the couch. We're
just no good on our own anymore, and I'm learning how to live with it.

MISTAKES WERE MADE
Ian Randall Wilson

Yes, mistakes were made. One family chose New Orleans for a vacation. Another went north. How different the outcomes will be. The one up north, no sense speaking of them. They're enjoying sun and great food. The other, well, the world is an enormous place, and when the rains come, no one can really tell if it's a summer shower or the start of a deluge. The rain in Maine is very different from the rain on Lake Pontchartrain. If her daughter had come up with such a little rhyme, the mother would have applauded, telling her how smart she was. But the mother was in no mood for anything light. She had been checking the news. The radar said a storm was upon them, but weather can prove more fickle than a little boy in his first ice cream shop. The way her little boy, when confronted with all those flavors, started to cry. Wasn't it possible that the massive high pressure zone filling the screen with its lurid red might veer off and avoid landfall entirely? They've been predicting weather since the 1880s with little success. If you look out your window and it's raining, then it's raining. The walls protect you from the wet; a barrier that can't be breached, right? Drains to the sea purge off all the water. No real need to worry. Man has conquered nature with the devices built by his hand. If you look outside and it's raining, it's raining. That much any idiot knows. No need for a degree in meteorology—is that even a science?—to stand outside and get soaked.

Meanwhile, so much calls upon our attention. So many times we want to do something else, to be somewhere else. The mother thought this every moment she was with her family in New Orleans. Other families were somewhere else—in the north. One somewhere else—up the bayou (because in Louisiana somewhere else is always up the bayou)—Mayor Ray Nagin played a villain in an independent film, his first acting role. How the lines rolled off his tongue. This might be the start of a whole new career; still it took him twenty takes. The family vacationing in New Orleans spent part of their time on Bourbon Street, the wife on crutches trying to negotiate the uneven sidewalks, each plant of the rubber-tipped crutch jarred all the way up her arm. The father held his daughter and son by the hands and seemed oblivious to his wife's struggle. But even if he had seen—oh, he had seen—what could he do? Carry her on his back? He had only two hands and they were occupied right then with the hands of his children. There weren't that many years left before his son and his daughter would shake him off, would not want to have their hands held or be hugged or kissed. He heard it from friends at work. One minute she's your little girl, coming into your lap. The next, she sets up, as the literature states: *an interpersonal no-touch zone eventually extending to six feet of the space around her*; beware of entering unbidden. They become monsters, the people at work said. Where do the little girls go?

A thousand miles away, FEMA Director Michael Brown turned at different angles in the mirror, showing off his brand-new summer suit. He had heard from the National Hurricane Center, but he wasn't too concerned. He had decided his principal obligation was to convey a "positive image of disaster operations"—that was his charter. The family stopped for coffee and beignets, the children getting powdered sugar everywhere. The wife was happy to sit down, putting her crutches on the floor.

The governor actually took some action, holding a press conference, directing agencies to prepare for the storm and stand by. But she sent a legal form to President Bush instead of picking up the phone. Mistakes were made. Her letter didn't actually tell the president what her state needed in the way of rescue boats, potable water, food. Bourbon Street was unusually empty, according to what the husband had read, and the family wondered where everyone had gotten to. It's not as if rain was an uncommon thing.

These were actions and official actions—or inactions. Because mistakes were made. The residents of St. Rita's Nursing Home in St. Bernard weren't ever going anywhere, then or later, no matter what the news was saying, no matter what it looked like outside. Most were parked in the common room and couldn't walk, lolling in their wheelchairs, staring at the TV that was always on in an imitation of life. In the Ninth Ward, Paul Merely pulled out his life jacket, which had gotten a little tight since the last time. He'd been through Betsy and Camille, what was one more come down his way? It wasn't as if rain was an uncommon thing. Cecil Jones took another drink. Marvin Laroue, he lay down to take a nap. Just people in New Orleans; none the family had met. People in New Orleans, living their lives—Phillipe Ledoux, Joyce Norman, Damien Common, Herman Falcone—names that would get on a list and that list would eventually go on for 1,826 more names (according to the final tally); that will be in the future, of course.

Mistakes were made. In the days before the storm made landfall, the wife should have been watching where she was going. She should have been watching when she stepped off the last riser, what she thought was the last riser, but what turned out to be not the last riser at all, the ground farther away than anticipated. Sprained the ligaments in the ankle, the doctor said. Have to get around on crutches for at least two weeks. Two weeks of a two-week vacation on crutches in a place she didn't want to be to start with. The doctor said it was necessary to keep the weight off the foot and let things heal. So she stumped around, keeping that left foot off the ground as best she could. It was exhausting, trying to use the crutches.

Mistakes were made. The son didn't watch the screen door slam and it caught his fingers. Nothing broken, but a bad bruise. The doctor said, This is getting to be a habit with you people. Is everyone like that out west? Hey, you've heard that joke about California: the land of fruits and nuts. Her smile was more like a grimace; oh, the pain. Her boy was black and blue, but nothing broken. Let it rest, the doctor said, though for a little boy it was tough to rest because he was always trying to hold on to things with the bad hand, yelping when he did.

"This is a death house," the wife said.

"Stop being melodramatic," the husband said. "Let's go out and maybe we'll run into a krewe."

"Why, oh, why, did you bring us here?"

Mistakes were made. They should have vacationed somewhere else. The husband should have listened to his wife when she said she wanted Disneyland. The kids wanted that, too. Mickey Mouse. The Main Street parade. Fireworks, with a few "reasonably priced" nights at the Dally Inn Anaheim, only ten long blocks or so from the main gate, courtesy breakfasts included. Where stairs were built by licensed contractors and each riser was the same height. But mistakes were made. They cut the jaunt to Bourbon Street short and came back to the house where they were staying north of Claiborne Avenue in New Orleans, right there in the Ninth Ward.

"It's a lovely neighborhood," the friend from work who lent the family the house had told them.

The friend was lending them a house that had been in his family since the Civil War, a house that looked like it had been built in the Civil War—a bombardment, the wife thought. Then she thought that was unfair of her. The house was in a neighborhood that, frankly, seemed a little bit down at the heels though the grounds of the house were well tended and the paint on the walls relatively new. In the topography of the city, the house was in perhaps the lowest of the low-lying areas. Who studies topography when they come for a visit?

The family sat in the living room of that little house, while the people who could leave the city were leaving. The ones who couldn't, well many of them were walking to the Superdome, carrying what little bit of food they could round up. Or they were staying put, sure that they had been through it before and could get through this one because the damn weathermen might be wrong. It wasn't like rain was uncommon. The storm could veer off, and everyone that ran would feel like a fool.

Mistakes were made. Maybe if the Corps of Engineers hadn't let the levees rot from underneath. Oh yes, did you not know that was the reason for the breach? Or one of them? Or none of them, because mistakes were made, not by anyone in particular. The mistakes themselves had created their own mistakenness. Maybe if an evacuation plan had been in effect? This is blame again, isn't it? Or that bastard Bush, if he hadn't let the whole city drown. Wasn't that a lovely shot of him at the window of the plane moving down to take a closer look at all that rack and ruin.

A husband. A wife. Two children, boy and girl. The trip the husband had always wanted. Not at Mardi Gras—they couldn't afford that—but wasn't it always like Mardi Gras in New Orleans?

How about if the city weren't built below water level and hadn't been drowning periodically for three hundred years? First the Indians and then the French and then the Spanish and then a mix of every race and color and creed. Hurricanes sweeping through sometimes twice a year, sometimes not for five. Levees built higher and higher. Swamps drained. The water always breaking through.

Why did the husband have to have another of his genuine ethnic experiences, staying in exactly the city's most unluxurious part? So he could say he experienced things like a true resident of New Orleans. He tried to make the wife understand this when they spent a night in a lighthouse in Maine. When they stayed at five of the houses along the underground railroad's route. The kids should have experiences, he told her, while they were young. Genuine experiences.

How about if they'd packed up and left as soon as the storm was reported? How about if they hadn't moved upstairs?

They had gone to bed on a Sunday night and everything seemed all right. They were up first thing Monday and suddenly the waters were rising. The wind shrieking. The dog barking. Where was the dog? Where had the dog gotten to? Surely up was the right direction. Who could think in all that tumult? It was so early in the morning. One minute the living room was dry and light, the next, water up to their knees. Up to their knees then up to their thighs. The wife on her crutches, her ACE-bandaged foot dripping.

"It's cold, Daddy," the son was saying.

The daughter looking shocked. The rain in Maine is very different from the rain that falls on Lake Pontchartrain.

They had to go up, above all that gray, cold, increasingly cloudy water. Up where the husband thought it would be safe and secure. Except here was another of those mistakes in the making: Up and into the attic with no light and no tools. Up and into the attic with no way to cut through the roof sheathing. No water. No food. No cell phone.

* * *

There are two chairs in the attic, and if the adults stand on them, their heads come right up to the roof line, which smells of tar and must and mold. The electricity is out and it is dark. The father says it will be all right. He keeps saying it like a mantra, like he's chanting, like he is safe and warm and dry where they live out west. But he is not safe and warm and dry. Still he says, they'll be all right. They'll be all right. He has to believe himself. He has to believe that they will survive the rising waters. That help will come—though no one knows they are in the house except for a few neighbors who are struggling themselves and the friend who loaned them the place.

The winds are so loud he can't hear himself think, doesn't know what to do. He bumps into a trunk. Maybe if he turns it on its side, he can put the little girl up there. Anything to raise them above the water, keep them close to the roof. They're above the second floor. Surely the waters can't rise that high?

The little boy is in the attic as is the little girl. The wife has not yet made the climb. She hangs back, unwilling to risk what she fears as entombment. One step at a time, the husband urges her. The first floor is submerged and the waters continue to rise.

"How do we get out?" the wife asks. "How do we get out if we go up there?"

Leave it to her to try to be practical in a moment of emergency. The kids don't know which way to turn. The boy's hand hurts. The little girl can read the fear. The father says they have to get above the water.

"Then why don't we go out the second floor windows and let the waters carry us up to the roof? It has to be better outside than in."

The husband and the kids are going to the attic. That's his decision.

Somewhere outside a transformer explodes. Buildings pull off their foundations. Anything not battened down starts to float away. The entire world is moving.

"Is this like Noah?" the little girl says.

Who can think? The air is saturated and heavy. Each breath a faulty bellows. How did they get themselves into this? The water creeps higher.

He's made his decision. That's a summary of the entire marriage, and she's gone along. Two children when she only wanted one. A house out west when she wanted to live somewhere else.

The water is murky and cold and full of greasy green streaks. It's coming up, halfway up the wall of the second floor now. In a few minutes, the decision will be forced upon her. To stay is to give up. To stay is to drown. Either she goes up—into the attic—or out one of the windows of the bedrooms, and takes her chances outside.

She was never a gambler, a risk-taker. Her children are in the attic. She must go to them. She knows it is the wrong decision. She passes her crutches to her husband, who grabs them. She hops onto the first rung. Her ankle can hardly bear the weight. She braces for pain, each step an exclamation of breath. The sharp exhale. She tries to get on her good foot as fast she can.

Now she is in the attic and stops to recover her breath. When she was a young girl, she took a Sunday school class where the teacher talked about moral dilemmas. What if four of you are trapped in a mine with only enough air for three? Do you kill one to save the rest? Do you steer the runaway car toward the young woman on the bridge in order to let the five workmen live? Do you kill the crying baby so it doesn't tip off the soldiers coming to destroy the village? Who do you push out of the overloaded lifeboat in order to save the rest? How passionate they got in the class that day, trying to figure out the right answer.

The husband has managed to maneuver two trunks into the center of the attic, right below the rafter's peak. He places the chairs next to them and helps the children onto their perch. Anyone can see this is hopeless. The runaway car is steering toward them. The mine is running out of air. The lifeboat is overloaded. Hopeless. Because the trunks are not high enough. Only two feet off the floor and if the water rises (when it rises?), what help then? The father hopes that two feet will make the difference between survival and decease. Hope is the little beacon up ahead, the dying light that beckons.

The wife is up on one of the chairs, swaying, working to keep her balance there in the dark. The waters are rising. Every time she leans toward the bad ankle, a jolt through her leg like a hammer blow. The waters are rising, cutting off the second floor and coming in now through the opening in the floor. The rate at which the waters rise cannot be believed. As if the world grows more compact about them, she can feel the attic air compress.

Both parents are up on the chairs, the children on the trunks. The little boy is quiet. The girls is snuffling, too frightened to say anything. The children know that something is terribly wrong and that their parents are afraid no matter how much the father cajoles them and tells them it's an adventure. Who goes swimming in an attic in the dark?

The waters rise, coming halfway up the wall, rising and rising. The wind shrieks. Too dark to see, they feel for one another. The husband keeps his hands on the children. The wife tries to stay balanced on her crutches on top of the chair. Higher and higher the waters rise, cold and greasy around their legs.

Then there is only a foot of space above the water line, the mold and tar smell intense, the adults straining to keep their heads above water. The father holds up his children to keep them breathing.

"Help," he says to his wife. "You have to hold one of them."

She can barely hold herself, pain stabbing her foot. Her good leg cramps. She nearly falls off the chair, but rights herself. She manages to keep breathing that terrible fetid air. With every breath the space shrinks.

Is it the mine scenario? Is there only enough air for three? Or two? Or one? Who will be the one thrown out of the boat?

The children can no longer stand on the trunks and they're trying to keep their heads above water. The husband is holding them up, but it's exhausting.

Suddenly her chair tips over. In an effort to take the pressure off her foot, she shifted and the chair is gone. There's nothing beneath her now. No support. No structure. She has to tread water with her one good foot. She feels herself slipping away. The darkness calls her. Water, cold.

"Tired, Daddy," the little girl says.

The wife understands. She is tired, too. It would be so much easier to just let go and let nature have her. Some people say drowning is peaceful, if you accept what's coming.

In a breath she could disappear. She is at once all the problems between them, the Mother of Nothingness with her bandaged foot unraveling. Her husband is clinging to life for all of them. He will not suffer their destruction by deluge. In the face of the final immolation, he is urging them to hang on. She closes her eyes, willing herself somewhere else, and when sight is restored, he has somewhere found an axe.

"On the wall," he says. "Clipped to the wall. It was there all the time."

With little leverage and only the force of will, he starts chopping, but he has to let the children go and they dip below the water.

"Grab them," he shouts.

She swims to her left and kicks enough to lift her daughter, but not the son. With her bad leg, she can only manage one.

"Grab them," he shouts again, swinging the axe as divots of wood sheathing and tar go flying into the void.

And then at last the hole is open and he is forcing his daughter through. He is grabbing his son and getting him out and onto the roof, the boy coughing and sputtering, trying to take in a lifetime of air. Then the husband climbs up himself and leans in over the hole. He was a man born to make openings. She realizes that now. He offers his hand, reaching in and as far and deeply as he can. In the light from outside she sees a change come over his face that makes something cold rise up from her feet to her chest because she understands that he can leave her there and stay with the children on the roof. His expression fixed and permanent like an old man who watches winter rain and understands just how thin the blood becomes. ∎

COMET POND
Pamela Gemme

They've parked the station wagon so that
no one will see me from the road.
Dad picked up coffee and corn muffins,
on his way from his right to work, he wants a shotgun wedding.
Mother keeps the car door open to watch me,
while she drones on to my father that the coffee
is black and she wanted cream.
They pontificate over adoption I won't give my baby up.
Despite Jesus, I bet they wish I get an abortion.

My big belly is like a hot
air balloon above the flume.
They are mad at me, but they take me to swim at Comet Pond
in hopes I will be washed of my sin.

Pollywogs at my feet,
Little pond harbor me;
a wayward girl from a white house falling apart. I float like some
inflatable whale
warming in the morning sun, dreaming the pond becomes my
golden
dome.
My boyfriend is the black swan. My belly doesn't bother him
My belly is a pond my body made. I want to have a girl.
I want her to sing *Mockingbird*.

They tell me I won't finish high school.
I study biochemistry.
They tell me; that welfare is a shame;
I won't collect welfare
They scold me that I'll never have a home,
I will live my life with them.
I know they bring me here
out of love.

I SEE A LONG JOURNEY
Joan Frank

I understood everything for a brief period, some while ago.

To the best of my ability to convey this: I really did.

I was driving home, alone, in the morning, after the previous night's reading in another city, at some distance: the drive would take a couple of hours. The reading, my last for this particular book, had gone reasonably well, and I had no immediate, further public presentations to angst about. I felt light and free, relieved to move back into the autonomy, privacy, and comfortable, interior brooding that defines the cycles of my days.

November weather was unstable, dramatic. Cold rain hammered my car like thousands of nails when I set off, soon giving over to great piles of dark, mottled clouds: these moved tensely above the tangled pile of freeway overpasses, the banked, grimy buildings of a passing city. It was a colorless, ugly morning by any definition, but I had good coffee and good music. And now, unbound by formal obligations, I felt a flood of affection to finally see the familiar, low hills hover into view as I neared home; to see cows and fields and splintery old farmhouses in the distance. On the radio, the classics station began to play Rachmaninoff's Piano Concerto No. 2, and the instant, rich passion of its opening phrases seemed to perfectly describe the movement of weather and earth around me.

Then something happened.

As I gazed at the flow of landscape and traffic, as the music built and swirled and surged—the signal events of my life floated calmly forward and panned across my mind's gaze for review like some gentle film: I could pick out, at will, any moment, however tiny, any face or setting along the continuum of my past; I could inhale the very *smells* of the places I'd known. Infancy: staring uncomprehendingly, on all fours on the carpet, as my kind Uncle Joe, seated across the room, held out his hands to me, coaxing *Come on! Come on*! Childhood: Desert air, cactus blossoms, the chlorinated local swimming pool, the tooth-tugging sweetness of a Snickers bar, the rough, lined paper tablets we learned to write on at grade school, the green lunch ticket that got hole-punched each day, the sterile pungency of the nurse's office. Mother's death. Moving to Sacramento. Teenaged loneliness, bewilderment, listening to the radio late at night as if each song carried a coded message of rescue. Young adulthood: College, West Africa with the Peace Corps, crucial years in a Brigadoon-like Hawaii. Father's death. Migration back to the San Francisco Bay Area; a disastrous love affair. Middle age, graduate school, writing's taking hold.

Good marriage. Friends' deaths. Sister's death. Sister's sons' new babies.

The images moved in measured procession past my mind's eye, a magic lantern.

At the same time, the passage of time itself (as I assume lay minds understand it) became for some reason utterly clear and apprehendable, even *visible*—together with all the generations of human life that had unfolded since we emerged from water, over inconceivable swaths of time.

I swear I am not making this up.

I could see it all—at least, so it felt. I saw time as an endless set of waves, marching in long lines toward shore to break over humans again and again in eternal, stately rhythm: Suffering, wild joy, raw birth, wretched death. Wars, terrorism, turmoil. Beauty, mystery, exaltation. I could range backward and forward infinitely over the full panorama— horror to sublimity—without effort, as if my mind's eye were a dial. Whether it was the music, the majestic, roiling weather, the strong, good coffee, or a combination of these, I saw, knew, understood.

It felt bracing, yet calming. Inevitable as air.

Like weather, it was what had been and what would continue to be. The suffering was inextricable from the joy and boredom and senselessness, and in that blessed interval of clearly grasping this, I felt a deep stillness. The vision conveyed its own perfect, ongoing inevitability. I was able to let go of anguish for my dead—both recent and distant—for the nightmare state of my country and world, for the unanswered valor of human heroism, human stoicism, the excruciating unsolvability of everything. At the same time, I understood quite clearly that I would soon fall back into blinkered, human striving. The shape-shifting clouds, the plaintive imploring of the concerto's piano; its urgent, utterly modern questioning, as if it were pacing a room with accelerating intensity, turning at length to open its arms in exasperated wonder—*Now, I ask you!*—and those glowering clouds' haughty answer: *Yes, this.* I understood that I will continue to desire, anguish, struggle, imperfectly love those beings in my orbit. I understood, too, more concisely then than ever before, that eventually I will cease, leave those beings and this world. That they will in their turns desire, anguish, struggle to make the best of the time given them and to love the beings in their orbits; sometimes failing, fearing, getting lost or hurt, until they too leave this world and their own beloveds, who will in their turns struggle.

Nothing more, nor less.

Do cats or dogs or birds think such things? Gorillas, dolphins, lizards?

The violins sang *This, this.* The piano rushed and crashed and pooled alongside them.

Filled with a kind of awed attention, accepting for the first time in my life what had always before to me been pretty much unbearable, I wondered whether I might have stumbled upon a state that Eastern spiritual disciplines seek. Whatever it was, I felt grateful for even a breath's worth, and hoped I might later be able to remember any of it.

It turns out that I *can* remember it—maybe not quite to the degree I felt it while driving, underscored by the churning, purling Rachmaninoff. Something about the act of driving, the isolation in a moving vehicle, heralded and even *narrated* by the music, enters the bloodstream— becomes a permanent part of it.

I remember enough, clearly enough, to marvel—and to feel deeply thankful.

I have thought many times about this strange glimpse into the infinite during a simple drive home. A good image for the encounter might be a famous old anonymous woodcut, which first appeared in an 1888 French book about weather. It depicts a humble shepherd (or priest, or preacher) who's managed to wriggle his head and shoulders through the seam at the horizon dividing land from starry heaven. Practically dropping his walking stick in amazement, he beholds the brilliant operating secrets of the universe—the gargantuan, intricate gears and wheels of the cosmos. (Except the awestruck wanderer is not driving a 2008 Toyota Scion.)

Now whenever I happen to catch the strains of the Concerto No. 2—
and I don't tend to go hunting for it, because who wants to normalize the
miraculous, or push their luck—the Cosmic Glimpse (yes, it sounds like
a comic book from the sixties), with its overpowering, wheeling-watchwork
comprehension, rushes back into my chest: vibrant and mighty yet also,
always, strangely soothing. And when I think about it more I consider
that a case can be made for time itself as the ultimate place we inhabit,
albeit very, very briefly.

When we talk about living somewhere, I have noticed, we generally
sound as though we mean "carrying on this way in perpetuity." Of course
that's the dream, the story we tell ourselves. Our lease on inhabitable time
is stunningly short. Yet while we are here, in the midst of our little arc,
most of us think and act as though it will last forever. (It's mainly older
people, I notice, who are able to bring themselves to say, "We will probably
live here—this village or town or city, this house, this apartment—until
we die.") In fact time is the vastest real estate we know—not that we can
genuinely claim to know it, in the intimate, thoroughgoing sense of that
word, let alone possess it. We speak of seizing time, seizing the day, but
it might be more accurate to say that time is seizing us. Or rather that
time coexists with our temporary presence in it, as if we were short-lived
guppies in an implacable river. I don't imagine I will ever understand the
physics of time, the science of time, of wormholes, spiraling, or (hand
over heart for *A Wrinkle in Time* author Madeleine L'Engle) tesseracting.

I do know that some comprehensions seem to have to pick their
moments to enter us to stay. They have to be spelled into our hand, if you
will—in the manner of Helen Keller's suddenly grasping the concept of
water, thanks to Anne Sullivan's patient, repeated ministrations. I know
now, sharply and viscerally, that what time we have in which to dwell in
these humble bodies—thinking, moving, speaking and singing, loving,
suffering—is inexpressibly finite. And though most of us are able to
sense, on rare and incandescent occasion, that "some things are eternal,"
we tend to lapse quickly back to grosser, daily concerns. It's too much.
Most of us, exempting "saints and poets maybe" (bowing twice to you,
Thornton Wilder) aren't built to hold such knowledge at the forefront
of thought every minute. Most of us must marshal waking awareness
for the survival tasks, marking out our turf. (This, too, soothes us.) To
remember now and then that we float, for a flashing moment, in the
illimitable space of time will for most of us be the best we can do. And
until the final hour, when (perhaps?) the lens opens all the way before it
shuts forever, that will have to be good enough. ■

GOODBYE, KELLERMAN
Linda Downing Miller

I'd invited Kellerman up from Indianapolis for a visit but then the election. My wife wouldn't have him in the house. The Kellerman I knew was large-hearted, his only drawback, excessive enthusiasm—dangerous in bars late at night, surrounded by the wrong team's fans—but on the whole, kind of an asset in our college years. In my fifties, my marriage was more important. And Kellerman had made the mistake of showing his political hand online: a clear lack of upset, a too-quick call for optimism.

How to break it to the K-man that he'd been disinvited? He wasn't the kind to take a hint or no for an answer. Lying wasn't optimal, not my nature to do it well, and my wife abhorred the mildest deception. Bettina wanted me to confront Kellerman, to explain exactly why he was no longer welcome in our home. She said we needed to help him understand why his position was indefensible. Regardless of how openly and tolerantly and charitably he conducted himself and his own affairs—not that we had current exposure—his vote had huge and terrible ramifications for others. I saw her point, but I wasn't sure it was my place to convince Kellerman of anything, beyond the fact that our weekend plans were now off. I knew I might fail to accomplish even that if I talked to him live.

I drafted an email, ironic in light of recent events; it got me thinking about the FBI and a series of off-color, off-topic jokes, so I deleted the email and settled on a text, brief and true.

"Conflict's come up December 3 weekend. Have to cancel our plans."

We had a round of back and forths, Kellerman inquiring into what was up, hoping things were okay. How were my folks doing at the nursing home? Was there a problem with putting him up at our house? He'd grab a cheap Airbnb and we could still do a tour de bars like old times. I thought about it for a second, but Bettina was too volatile about everything, and I was on her side, I was. I told him my folks were fine. They hadn't a clue what was going on in the world anymore, but they remained with it enough to play poker every Tuesday, Thursday, and Saturday at Sunset Plains. The running game, with its ongoing tally of plastic chips, had become their only interest in life from a conversational standpoint, as far as I could tell.

Anyway, to squelch Kellerman's continuous follow-up, I finally had to suggest that something was going on with Bettina's health . . . something she had to get taken care of, nothing serious, but I wanted to be available to help; she'd be resting up over the weekend. The implication of female trouble is usually enough to throw any guy off, and Kellerman was no anomaly. "We'll do it another time. Best to Bettina."

A small lie, successfully managed. I put Kellerman out of my mind. The skipped visit was a disappointment, but on the other hand, he took a good amount of energy, and I hadn't been feeling all that energetic. Work had gone off playbook; the IT project team I was managing kept missing deadlines, and I didn't know enough about the new security technology to push things any faster. The election results hadn't helped anyone's motivation in my division. I looked forward to a solitary weekend on the couch watching football. Bettina would be downtown Chicago with friends—some "chocolate tasting" for somebody's birthday, some wine and art thing afterward. She took an overnight bag when she left Saturday morning. One of the ladies with a "weekend condo" in the Loop had offered to host anyone who preferred not to drive at the end of the evening.

If Bettina was disappearing, why did it matter whether or not Kellerman darkened our door? Why wouldn't I be perfectly free to tour the bars with the K-man? If you have to ask . . . Look it up, why don't you? The word "normalization" might be relevant.

So noon Saturday, there I was, settled into the old lumpy futon couch we kept in our basement, a couch that wasn't all that comfortable but that had the advantage of looking onto the biggest of our two TVs. Bettina disliked TV on principle, so the fact that we owned two, one larger than a toaster oven, was a victory of sorts for me. The old futon came from a studio apartment of Bettina's before we'd met. Frugal right? And a man-cave-appropriate couch would have been too big to fit down the narrow stairway.

The Walleyes won the coin toss and scored on first possession. I cheered for my alma mater and high-fived our pine paneling. Before I knew it I was sitting back down with an open IPA, cold against my palm. I'd consumed three quality beers by halftime, my team stalled and losing ground 7–21. That's when the doorbell rang.

On a weekend, it was likely to be some kid selling candy for a self-centered cause, or a couple of smiling Jehovah's Witnesses expecting to change someone's world view with twenty minutes of gentle proselytizing. This person was persistent. Three long rings. I girded myself for a fourth; instead I heard Kellerman bellowing, "Reggieboy!"

Maybe it was the IPA in my bloodstream, but the long-dormant nickname and the tenor of his muffled bellow brought a pair of joyful tears to my eyes. It was something, feeling any spark of joy those days. I took the stairs two at a time, reckless in my condition, and flung open the door without a thought for Bettina. Kellerman stood there in his green-and-brown jersey. The weather was weirdly warm for December. Blocking the numbers on his chest was an enormous floral arrangement.

"For the lady of the house," he said, brandishing it. Then, "Go Walleyes!"

It was instinct to high-five. As we made contact, Kellerman bobbled his one-handed grip on the flowers. Both of us fumbled for them, catching our hands in the stems. The vase did a slow-motion slide onto the concrete, missing the doormat by a few critical inches. Shards of glass scattered against Kellerman's sturdy brown boots.

He crunched closer to the threshold. "Damn. Where's your broom?"

We trooped into the kitchen. I filled the small side of the sink with water, and we abandoned the flowers there.

"How's the wife?" he asked in an unusually subdued tone.

The mention reminded me I wasn't supposed to have let Kellerman in. That I might be normalizing something simply by standing there with him. Should I pretend Bettina was resting upstairs and try to get rid of him as quickly as possible? For some reason, maybe the prospect of rooting for the Walleyes with someone who cared, I took a different approach.

"The hospital kept her overnight for observation. I'm headed back there in a couple of hours." It was a stupid lie, so many potential weaknesses.

"Where are you watching the game?" Kellerman asked.

I could fill a couple of pages with highlights from the second half, but suffice it to say, if you missed it, you missed a pinnacle in Division II football. The Walleyes fought back to 17–21. In the last thirty seconds, Adnan Abeyzi hurdled a Grizzly linebacker and ran sixty yards for the win. Kellerman and I fish-danced around the basement twice. The Walleye coach praised Abeyzi, who praised an unfamiliar higher power. We sobered for a moment, no doubt thinking of the president-elect's campaign promises. A commercial touting a cure for toenail fungus came on.

I muted the TV. "I should probably check in with Bettina."

"Go ahead, go ahead." Kellerman thudded back into the futon. "Geez. This thing has about as much give as a two-by-four."

"It has sentimental value for me and Bettina," I said, which was halfway true.

I held the railing on my way up the stairs. How many beers had I had? I found my phone on the kitchen counter and texted my wife, "Having fun?" She sent a smiley face and the words "chocolate coma."

"I'm good to drive if you need a lift over there," Kellerman said from behind me. "You guys recycle?" His arms were full of empties.

I slid out the bin, hidden behind a panel of maple since our kitchen remodel. While Kellerman unburdened himself, I considered coming clean about his problematic presence. His doughy face was so straightforward and unsuspecting, though. Who'd want to crush that, especially considering the news that face had processed earlier in the year? Being told there's someone else, and his name is Chad. Being told we're dropping your product line; HR has the details on your package.

"Sorry about crashing your wife's recovery weekend," Kellerman said. "I figured—why not drive the flowers up myself? Save the $14.50 delivery."

"Gas has gotten cheap," I agreed. After a second's hesitation, we high-fived.

"How are things back in Indy?" I asked.

"Not much to talk about. Trying to do some networking. LinkedIn, Match.com. I switch off." He gave an extended, Kellerman-style burp and pulled out his keys. "Should we head to the hospital?"

"Bettina said she has a few more tests . . ." As I was floundering further into my lie, the phone rang—the landline I still had, mostly to deflect solicitations and surveys. The caller ID said Sunset Plains. I picked up.

Five minutes later, I was in the passenger seat of Kellerman's SUV, literally heading for the Sunset, where my parents had apparently barricaded themselves in a utility closet. Somehow they'd gotten the impression their poker winnings could be cashed out before year-end—for a partial refund of their substantial LifeCare Investment™. Stonewalled on a payout, they were shouting "no more runaround" from behind the closet door. Staff were concerned about the air circulation in there. And potential dehydration.

"Your folks have spunk. Gotta love 'em," Kellerman said, after I'd explained the situation. "It's about time somebody demanded accountability."

My own sympathies rested with the Sunset Plains personnel, charged with the impossible task of keeping people happy when their conditions were so obviously declining. If someone had told a white lie to keep things running smoothly, it was understandable. Maybe not commendable.

I glanced at Kellerman; in profile, his face looked less vulnerable than it had in my kitchen. I cleared my throat. "Bettina actually thinks . . . Bettina and I feel . . . with the last election . . . We think each voter is particularly accountable for his or her vote, for the candidate's views that vote implicitly endorsed."

I was surprised to hear the word "implicitly" popping out of my mouth. I must have picked it up from Bettina or the ethos.

"It was a rough one," Kellerman said. "But I think we'll all come out of this for the better."

"Who do you mean by 'we'?"

"Everybody. Everybody, Reggieboy." I waited for the K-man to say except Muslims. Except undocumented immigrants. Except people who aren't straight and white and male like us. He didn't. I waited for my voice to ask him about those everybodies. It failed to. We arrived at Sunset Plains with our friendship unchallenged. The sun was indeed dropping behind the sprawling brick building, tinting the surrounding prairie pink and deepening the green of the front lawn.

"Nice digs," Kellerman said. "Your folks really need that payout? Guess they deserve it, though, if they played for it fair and square." He followed me through the handicapped entrance.

I started toward the receptionist; she waved me on with an expression that managed to convey both recognition and censure. I visited monthly, or tried to. It was an ongoing battle between guilt and depression, avoidance and contact.

About fifteen yards down the wide front hall, a small crowd of senior citizens, some in wheelchairs, clustered around a closed door. One lone staff member in blue scrubs stood among them, one smooth brown face in a sea of withered white. Kellerman and I proceeded toward them.

"It doesn't even smell like pee in here," he announced.

I didn't know the staffer standing sentry at the closet. Her name badge said Janine. "How long have they been in there?" I asked. "I'm the son, by the way. Reggie Hutchens."

"Glad you could make it," she said. "I'd guess it's been a couple of hours. We unlocked it, but they've got your dad's wheels jammed against the door."

I put my face to the crack, too tight for visuals. "Mom? Dad? Come on out. It's me, Reggie."

"Who?" Mom's voice sounded close.

"Our useless boy," said my dad. "Stuck us in here in the first place. No thanks."

Some lady behind me muttered "useless boy" and chuckled. "No thanks," said another heckler in a regal tone.

"Mr. and Mrs. Hutchens!" Kellerman called.

"That can't be old Lionel Kellerman can it?" my dad asked. "My God! Is that Lionel Kellerman?"

Kellerman grinned. He leaned in close. "It's me, Mr. Hutchens. Come on out and say hi."

Inside the closet, a creak and a scrape. Then Dad's voice again. "Now wait a minute. You aren't in league with those liars and cheats out there are you? I don't know about this."

"No, I—" Kellerman pushed on the door; it gave half an inch and bounced back.

"We're cashing out," said my mom. "We were promised we could cash out. No more runaround!"

"Mrs. Hutchens," Janine said. "I'm afraid that was a misunderstanding. Or someone's idea of a joke." She looked hard into the crowd behind me; no one appeared obviously guilty when I followed her stare.

"She had a royal flush today," Dad said.

"I had a royal flush!" Mom yelled.

"That's a nice piece of luck," said Janine.

"Mrs. Hutchens. Come on out and visit," Kellerman said.

"I don't know you."

"Sweetie," said Dad. "It's Lionel Kellerman!"

"Poor thing," said an onlooker.

I muscled in front of Kellerman and pushed at the door. "Dad! Mom! There's no cash coming to you. You've paid it all into this place. They're taking good care of you here. Now come on out."

No response.

"How much did you win?" Kellerman asked.

"Almost ten thousand," Dad said.

The crowd around us murmured words of awe and doubt. Kellerman whistled in admiration. "Come on out, Mr. and Mrs. Hutchens. I need you to give me some tips I can try at the casino."

Whispering behind the door. The sound of wheels on vinyl tile.

Janine motioned us aside and carefully widened the crack until she could step into the closet. "Let's get you two to your room."

The crowd parted.

* * *

Somehow during Kellerman's visit with my parents, he got them to become themselves, or as close to themselves as I'd seen them since before they'd checked into Sunset Plains under protest. The three of them engaged in a tedious and animated discussion of poker strategy, followed by an actual conversation about the election. I learned the staff had facilitated a trip to the polls for able residents. My dad chose "the outsider, the business guy." My mom scribbled in the arrow for "the woman, the smart one. I remember that!" They made these revelations with eager intensity into Kellerman's doughy face.

I tried to point out that the two of them might as well not have voted; they'd canceled each other out. My dad talked right over me, "Wrong. Our votes counted. It just so happens I picked the winner this time. Right, Lionel?" Kellerman and my dad high-fived. My mom smiled graciously. They couldn't get enough of him, "old Lionel Kellerman." If it weren't for Janine warning them that dinner service was ending in twenty minutes, we might never have gotten out of there.

In the hallway, Kellerman hugged both my parents with the zeal of someone who wouldn't be back. He wished them well and reiterated his optimism for "the better" to come. Their bent figures receded down the hall, Janine powering Dad's chair and my mother beside her, while I thought about the worse ahead of us.

* * *

The first bar I spotted from the passenger seat of Kellerman's SUV was a brown-painted relic with glass block windows and a sign proclaiming He Ain't Here. I pointed at it. Kellerman pulled over. The inside of the place matched its exterior, a mounted television the only adornment, a handful of "he's" in orange jerseys lined up to watch. I sat at the other end of the bar. Kellerman trailed me. A bartender with a comb-over, and a bushy beard he wouldn't know as hip, approached.

"A shot of tequila and a Budweiser," I ordered, after eyeing the pitiful options on draft.

"Make that two Buds," Kellerman said. He began enthusing about my parents, how "amazing" they were, "considering, you know, their age and all."

The afterburn of the liquor down my throat finally restored my voice, or something like it. I thumped my shot glass on the beat-up bar top and gave Kellerman a hard push on his Walleyes jersey. "You and my father have elected a madman to office. A misogynist. A racist. A narcissist. You've endorsed those qualities by voting for a man who demonstrates them. Without apology."

"No," Kellerman said, as if I'd somehow misheard him. "I voted for a businessman who isn't afraid to shake things up in the government. He wants to make America—"

"You're either stupid, or you're a liar."

Kellerman studied his beer as if it had gone bad. The bartender lingered nearby, drying a pint glass for much longer than it was likely to be wet. Somebody scored a touchdown on TV; the orange jerseys cheered. We all stared at the screen until a commercial about erectile dysfunction came on.

"Do we need to go pick up Bettina?" Kellerman asked, monotone.

"She's not in the fucking hospital," I said. "She just hates you. We hate you. You've ruined our nation."

I left Kellerman there, his doughy face confused and wounded. No doubt he would eventually recover, probably slide down and join the fans in orange jerseys, maybe root for their team, maybe root for the opposition, depending on whom he knew in the game and how it hit him.

I trudged along the edge of the road until the Lyft I'd summoned came along and found me. When I crunched onto my own front porch sometime later, I did my best with the dustpan and broom, but the super moon had come and gone, and the porch light hadn't worked since a late summer storm.

* * *

Swearing woke me in bed about 2:00 a.m., a string of epithets coming up the stairs.

Bettina flipped on the harsh ceiling light and threw a pair of shoes into the corner. "What the hell happened on the porch? I thought my feet were killing me before I got home." She sat on the edge of the bed to inspect the soles of her feet. I rolled closer. Even squinting, I saw blood. She scowled at me. "I take it you had a few beers?"

I confessed to some overconsumption and shared a short version of the day's events, trimming how long it had taken me to fully enlighten Kellerman. "I thought you were staying in the city tonight," I said.

"Veronica voted for hate." Bettina's expression was a poignant blend of regret and resolve. She pressed a tissue to each foot and gingerly shuffled to the bathroom to wash and bandage her wounds.

I intended to stay awake. I had a vision of making righteous, restorative love with my wife, but the day, the week, the month, the year had worn me down too far I guess. In the end, I drifted off alone. ∎

EASTER SCENE
Benjamin Harnett

The neighbor kids
have painted an Easter scene
on their window: white rabbit,
green grass and trees,
a red sun.

This last fact seems
to have bothered them. They
write an apology,
in enormous block letters,
taking up a third of the entire
pane: "We don't
have any yellow," and
an arrow, to explain.

But the iron-oxidizing red
the glassy smear of it
as it thins at the edges,
this is right for Easter.
Apology is right too,
I think, blood sweating
from the shoulder
as I carve the lamb.

EUTHANASIA CONVENT
Bradley VanDeventer

There is a place in Eastern Europe where you can go to kill yourself. Now, everyone knows that the act of suicide can be perpetrated anywhere in the world. But in between the Black and Caspian Seas—or on a cliff overlooking the Danube, where others propose—you can receive all the help you need.

The place is only open in the summertime. For the rest of the nine months of the year, preparations are made for the next suicide harvest.

There are initiation rites that one must perform to gain entry into the place, said to be so complex as to border on the incomprehensible. Some say that one performs the actions on a subconscious level and that a man or woman not even having the slightest of suicidal impulses will end up there and become suddenly glad of his or her presence.

I know nothing of those rites, though I know that I probably should. See, I have been there. And as far as I know, I am the sole person to have escaped with his life intact. I was no older than eleven, and I have never figured out how I got there.

I bring this all up because there are two nations that have recently launched investigations over scores upon scores of bodies turning up in their respective capitals, since the onset of summer. The corpses appear to have undergone death in a vast array of methods, ranging from overdose on painkillers to being shot by a line of muskets. The forensics experts have not found anything to string out any plausible theories as far as motives go.

The bodies get dumped in the darkest places of the city, be it Yerevan or Bucharest. Each cadaver is carefully wrapped in linen and appears to have been anointed and administered extreme unction. While the number of corpses that have turned up remains relatively small when contrasted with, say, casualties of a military operation, or a tragic mishap in public transportation, the bodies trickle in on a weekly basis. Sometimes there are twenty to be found; other times, three. But the numbers are too disturbing to be the work of one sick individual who would take a giddy pleasure in confounding the authorities.

I am afraid to go to Armenia and Romania and tell the police what I know of the place that I'm sure is directly involved. Also, I don't think it would be of any use. As I said, I was very young at the time. Curiosity as to why a man from suburban Holland would travel across Europe to offer information concerning an endless parade of killings would probably earn me not only more than a little skepticism, but suspicion. I'm convinced that those deaths are all suicides. Holland is one of the few countries on earth that at this time allows euthanasia. This can be attributed to one of two things: considerable empathy or considerable indifference.

My father, Max Keegstra, was a sales representative for a soft drink company. He is now retired and lives in Amsterdam with a wife younger than me. He and I are estranged, so it's not at my disposal to write or call him and ask what he remembers about his four-city business tour over thirty years ago, that time when he took me along and I got lost.

* * *

I remember walking across a vast, green pasture that sat in a valley. It was one of those rare, perfect days in which it is sunny and warm, yet a generous wind is blowing. I've always loved the wind because it seems like another presence is in place: it blasts solitude away with its slight, ear-chafing music, whipping everything about in pleasing patterns.

I walked on and on until I came to an enormous, centuries-old building fitted on all sides with crosses. I thought I had arrived at something like Xanadu, but I found out it was a convent when a blindfolded woman in a cowl answered the giant wooden front entrance and bade me enter.

The woman slowly shut the door behind me, squeezing out the sunlight. She then approached me and asked me a question in a language that to this day remains unknown to me. It could have been Romanian or Armenian, who knows. I gestured that I did not understand. She motioned for me to stay put, and that she would be back. She then disappeared down a hall. While she was gone I began to walk around and survey the place. I could tell that it was a house of God by the votive candles and crosses lining the walls. Holy Bibles in Morocco leather lay scattered about on the floor, on chairs, on tables. Upon closer inspection, I realized that they were all open at one of the four gospels. Also scattered about were copies of *Meditations*, by Marcus Aurelius, whose name I could make out in the Latin script.

I began to hear footfalls coming my way from the hall, so I scampered back to the entrance. Instead of the one woman coming back, about ten nuns dressed in similar brown sackcloth scurried toward me. All of them had hoods thrown over their heads and brown sackcloth blindfolds covering their eyes. I was struck by how quickly they maneuvered without the aid of sight. One of them came up to me and knelt down, her face in front of my own. She had pale skin and appeared rather young. I could see tresses of blond hair just behind her cowl. She asked me in perfect Dutch if I was in pain. I said that I wasn't, that I was just lost. She told me that pain and being lost are the same thing and that I did well by coming here.

She then told me that they were the Divine Order of Sisters for Assisted Suicide. I didn't know what that all meant. So she told me. She did so in such a way that, to this day, the concept of suicide does not cause me to shudder, when the rest of the world holds it to be an abomination. I told her that I didn't understand why somebody would want to do that. She explained that some people experience so much pain that it becomes unbearable. I told her that that may be true, but that nothing hurts more than death going to work on a body. She said that it was not so. And it was then and there that she began to show me around the convent.

She insisted on holding my hand, in fear that I might cause harm to myself in a way that I hadn't wanted to. She guided me through a door that led outside. We walked down a cloister. To the left of us were numerous doors that led to chambers. The very first person whom I saw voluntarily going to his demise was a middle-aged man in a business suit. One of the blindfolded sisters had led him into one of those places. Minutes later, the sister emerged from the room, quietly shutting the door. She crossed herself, clasped her hands together, and walked back to the side entrance from which we had come. I asked the Dutch sister what the man was doing in there, and she said that he was ending his pain. She said that there was a chair that he sat in and a crown that he placed on his head. Hooked up to the crown were electrodes, which he would turn on with a switch within arm's reach.

The very first chamber that I got to peer into was called the Whipping Parlor. The sister told me that it was used but rarely, since it involved a lot of pain and time. There were strange leather tentacles draped over racks—cats o' nine tails, sjamboks, rattan canes, cudgels, scorpions. In a corner of the room, facing the wall, sat a sister, rocking back and forth as she read a Bible with her fingertips. In the opposite corner sat a dormant, crude robot. Its head dangled between its knees. We left that place.

We came then to the Gallery of Toxins. Here the method was by the inhalation of things like sarin, VX nerve gas, and Zyklon B. This, too, while not left unused, was an unpopular chamber.

I asked her if they, the sisters, ever had a direct hand in the proceedings. She said no, as that would be murder, which was wrong.

I asked the sister to show me a place that was widely used, and she led the way to a courtyard, still holding me by the hand. She asked me what had been troubling me in life. I said that nothing had. She said that it was common for those visiting the convent to be in denial, and that it was not only normal, but that it was an indicator of my intentions: my uneasiness was in itself an affirmation of my aversion to discomfort and pain, and a willingness to end it all.

As soon as we got out from under the arched pathway of the cloister, bird chirping and wind-whipped fallen leaves decorated the large courtyard with an acoustic perfume that complemented the blue sky above. We walked across rock gardens and over wooden bridges arching over gently flowing creeks in which schools of shimmering goldfish swam in rhythmic harmony. We zigged and zagged around large trees before coming upon a clearing where the bird chirping and rustling leaves could no longer be heard. The lush green grass under our feet suddenly gave way to an ashen terrain.

The sister let go my hand and pointed. Standing there in front of us was a Grenade Tree. I made toward it but she stopped me by snatching my hand back up. She told me that I must be absolutely certain that it was what I wanted. I didn't know what she was referring to. Strips of bark had peeled off the trunk. A few fallen twigs lay scattered among the ashen dirt. Hundreds of grenade pins were littered about. The fruit of destruction hung from the branches, nestled among the green leaves, waiting to be plucked. They came in various sizes. Some were tiny, no more than buds. These were not to be plucked because they would yield up nothing, save a poof. They had yet to develop the cross-hatch pattern associated with pineapples and the green specimens one finds at army surplus stores. As for the fully matured fruits, they were live, hanging fat and ripe from the branches by their pins, which would drop to the ground a few days after being separated from their fruit. A sister in sackcloth was some ways beyond the tree, raking the ground, cleaning out remnants of flesh confetti left behind from previous pluckings. (Years later I learned that Zen Buddhists diligently raked their own sand gardens, but that they were content to mystify the human mind with those koans of design rather than obliterate it.)

My guide told me that the sister tending the Grenade Tree would begin to water it as soon as she finished raking. I asked her how the tree got to be there. She said that the sister had planted it years and years ago, by laying seeds into the soil.

She then led me through another cloister and out to a stretch of asphalt, where there stood eight motionless robots with muskets pointed at a blood-stained wall. This was the voice-activated Automaton Firing Squad, awaiting the command to fire by the very one to die. I asked my guide about the bodies, never having seen one during my entire stay. She said that there was a man (of God, she emphasized) who came once a week and piled up the bodies into an oxcart, which he then rode into town. Since all the sisters were blind, which was a requirement to be a disinterested member of the convent, the best they could do to clean up the place was put the bodies on garlanded gurneys and wheel them out to a storage room that sat hidden in a copse of trees some ways beyond the valley. A visitor to the convent could not enter a designated area until it had been adequately scrubbed and left entirely free of any sign of violence.

I asked if she thought any of this was bad. She said no. I told her than my mother had told me that the Bible says that one should never take one's own life, that it was a sin, a depreciation of the ultimate gift of life. She said, Not so. She then produced a copy of the Bible and showed me a passage in Matthew where Jesus is working miracles on the seventh day and for that is berated by the Pharisees. In response, Jesus says that the Sabbath is made for man, and not vice versa. The same with life, she explained. It is made for man, and not the other way around. Life is a gift, and all gifts are to be done with as the recipient of the gift so chooses.

As she showed me the Self-Serve Guillotine and Death Spa, my guide told me that the sisters at the convent considered themselves daughters of Marcus Aurelius, the sagacious Roman emperor who, during the second century, waged war with the Sarmatians, a barbarian people constantly harassing the eastern border of Rome's Thracian province. Wise, humble, and gentle (to a fault, some do say), Marcus Aurelius had always been empathetic toward the pain and suffering of others. He was therefore a proponent of the right for a person to voluntarily leave this world. She began to weave filaments of Stoicism and Neoplatonism into her monologue. A certain Heraclitus claimed that the fire of the mind ascended back into the ether to begin nature's cycle all over again. One Plotinus professed that the nous—mind, or intellect—returned through the various astral planes back to the monad. Suicide was not anathema in Eastern religious thought. The sisters at the convent were essentially bodhisattvas, forgoing their own chances at leaving the earth so that they could help others do so as efficiently as possible. Hindus condoned suicide, too, calling voluntary death *mahasamadhi*, or "great contemplation."

But I thought there was a tinge of hypocrisy and callousness on the part of these sisters. Not only were they unwilling to end their own lives, but they failed to understand the pain involved in some of the more drawn-out methods at their convent, like the Whipping Parlor and the Asphyxiation Vault. But the Dutch sister insisted that between "gradual" and "instantaneous" there existed a difference of degree rather than of kind, and that in the end none of that would matter anyway.

There was a certain point in my stay at the convent when I began entertaining the idea that I had stumbled upon a realm of archetypes, where the world's mythological dramas played out. The forces in control of the universal clockwork received everything from a snub—when unbelievers refuse to acknowledge their very existence—to a full-fledged display of faith, when the pious and literal-minded take absurd descriptions at face value. I felt the truth lay somewhere in between.

She took me to the Boutique of Hand Cannons, where guns of all shapes, makes, and calibers were kept in pristine condition. A sister sat in a rickety chair in the middle of the chamber, doing her daily polishing of the armaments. My guide told me that the sister cleaned each one of the guns inside and out, working the racks on the four walls clockwise. At the time, the sister had a shotgun in her lap. The shiny gunmetal of the weapon contrasted with the brown sackcloth of her cowl. Once aware of our presence, she held the gun out to me from where she sat. She began to stand up, ready to give up her work for whatever it was that she expected me to do. I backed away, trying to rip my hand free from my guide, who calmed me down, telling me that there was no hurry.

That's all I remember. It took me years to realize that the shotgun-polishing sister may have been my own personal guardian angel looking out for me, ready to quell any unbearable pain that may come my way. It did not mean that I was to do myself in with a gun, or even that I was to do myself in at all. She may have been a projection of my subconscious, an innermost defense mechanism against the intolerable agonies of everyday life. Some of the few people who have heard rumor of a so-called euthanasia convent say that these kinds of beings are benevolent astral counterparts. Others say that they are demons and that the convent is a real place, and is a lower level of hell, alive and kicking and plugged in right here on earth. To me, demons and angels are the same thing. The effects wrought by evil are embraced years after the fact, meaning that so-called evil is just an agent of change, sometimes even progress, whose birth pangs may be so laborious as to be considered malevolent. Just as Jesus was guilty of a Byzantine form of suicide, with Judas and Procurator Pilate as unknowing accomplices, we are all guilty of suicide just by recognizing the fatal phenomenon of Time.

Yet others, noticing that only the affluent ever gained entrance into the mysteries of the convent, suggest that the place is a business run by a shady couple from Belgrade. It is true that charges of tax evasion have been leveled against this couple, and that their paper trail shows an itinerary that skates across all six habitable continents. ∎

POWER OUTAGES
Juan Parra

My Dad played the guitar.
My mother lighted candles and tiptoed with her eyes closed.
These sequences of power outages and music went on for
  a long time.
One minute I was naming the dogs that licked Saint Lazarus'
  knees,
The next I was screaming for my life, submerged in darkness.

It was the twentieth power outage that month.
My mother no longer tiptoed but glided gracefully across the
  living room
Candle in one hand, eyes tightly shut. My father strummed the
  guitar and sang
Of angels crucifying communists, or oranges falling in love
  with naughty lemons,
Or the satire of Stalin's portrait in our empty refrigerator. But
  on some nights,
He sang feebly like a child turning old as parasite conjured
  dark magic,
From the carcass of the homeless dog who always sought to
  look you in the eyes.

I sat in front of them,
In a world that now seemed too normal for the abnormality
  of light
In the tear, that night shed. Father strummed the guitar.
  Mother perfected her glide.
I sat in front of them, each night, more and more in love.
This went on for a long time.

NOTES ON CONTRIBUTORS

D.M. ADERIBIGBE is from Lagos. His chapbook *In Praise of Our Absent Father* is part of APBF New Generation African Poets Chapbook Series, and he was a 2017 OMI Fellow at Ledig House. He's received other fellowships and honors from the Ucross Foundation, Jentel Foundation, Dickinson House and Boston University, where he received his MFA in creative writing as a BU Fellow and also received a Robert Pinsky Global Fellowship. His poetry appears widely in journals in the US and UK and was recognized with a 2017 Pushcart Prize Special Mention.

BRYCE BERKOWITZ's work has appeared or is forthcoming in *Best New Poets 2017*, *Ninth Letter*, *Third Coast*, *Passages North*, *The Pinch*, *Sugar House Review*, *Hobart*, *Barrow Street*, *Permafrost*, *Eleven Eleven*, *Tampa Review*, *Hawai'i Pacific Review*, *The Laurel Review*, *The Southampton Review*, *The Fourth River*, and others.

CHRISTOPHER YOHMEI BLASDEL is a shakuhachi performer and ethnomusicologist who lived and studied in Japan for over four decades. His major publications include *The Shakuhachi, A Manual for Learning*, and *The Single Tone, A Personal Journey into Shakuhachi Music*. He writes both in English and Japanese and was awarded the prestigious Rennyo Award for Japanese non-fiction in 2000. He has also released a number of CDs of both classical and contemporary shakuhachi music. Blasdel presently is an adjunct lecturer in Japanese music at the University of Hawai'i, Mānoa. "The Serpent's Dance" is based on his personal experiences while performing gagaku Imperial court music for the yearly On Festival at Kasuga Shrine in Nara, Japan. This short story is his second piece to be published by *CQR*. "An Exchange of Fire," an essay detailing the tragic disappearance of the poet Craig Arnold, appeared in *My Postwar Life* (Chicago Quarterly Review Books, 2012). More information on Blasdel's activities can be found at www.yohmei.com.

BEVERLY BURCH's work has appeared in *New England Review*, *Willow Springs*, *Salamander*, *Tinderbox*, *Mudlark*, *DMQ* and *Poetry Northwest*. Her first book, *Sweet to Burn*, won the Gival Poetry Prize and a Lambda Literary Award. Her second poetry collection, *How A Mirage Works*, was a finalist for the Audre Lorde Award. She is a psychotherapist in Berkeley.

STEVEN CARRELLI is a visual artist and writer living in Chicago, where he teaches in the Department of Art, Media and Design at DePaul University. He earned an MFA in Painting from Northwestern University and a BA in Studio Art from Wheaton College. He received a Fulbright Grant to Florence, Italy, as well as grants from the Ruth and Harold Chenven Foundation, the Chicago Department of Cultural Affairs, and the Union League of Chicago. Carrelli's paintings and drawings have been exhibited nationally in numerous solo and group exhibitions and have appeared in many publications, including the *Chicago Sun-Times*, the *Chicago Reader*, and *New American Paintings*. His work is included in the collections of the Illinois State Museum, Elmhurst College, Northwestern University, and DePaul University, among others. He recently completed a public mural commissioned by the City of Chicago, and he has recently created a public sculptural installation, funded by the National Endowment for the Arts and the National Trust for Historic Preservation, installed in June of 2018 in Lockport, Illinois. His writing has also appeared in *Crab Creek Review*. Carrelli's work is represented by Addington Gallery in Chicago.

WAYNE CONTI has placed stories with *Open City, Brooklyn Rail, Mr. Beller's Neighborhood, Pindeldyboz* and *Anderbo*, where he has been a Contributing Editor. He is currently working on a novel. One of his stories was adapted for radio by KVMR and was played on public radio stations around the country. A degree in classical languages lead to a time as a computer programmer in several major banks prior to his current situation as the proprietor of Mercer Street Books in New York City. He has spent ever so long living in a 4th floor walk up in Greenwich Village (rent stabilized). He is focused right now on such authors as Marcel Proust, Kafu Nagai (though he doesn't know a word of Japanese), Willa Cather, Charles Baxter, Tobias Wolff and Robert D. Hare.

HEATHER COUSINS grew up in the small town of Bear Lake, Michigan. She studied anthropology at Bryn Mawr College and then received degrees in creative writing from Johns Hopkins University and the University of Georgia. She has one full-length book of poetry, *Something in the Potato Room* (Kore 2009), and one chapbook, *Freeze* (Codhill 2013).

COREY DAVIDSON has a Bachelor of Arts in Psychology from the State University of New York at Plattsburgh. In college Corey ran away from adulthood, problems, and responsibility as fast as he could, but in so doing twice achieved All-American honors in cross country. An avid sports fan, his favorite teams are the New York Football Giants and New York Yankees; it follows that his first published story should appear in a Chicago based literary journal. Corey's favorite writers are Thomas Pynchon, Philip K. Dick, and Theodore Geisel. And although a man of intense literary interests, the author is most at peace with the universe while smoking southern-style BBQ at his home about twenty miles south of the US border with Canada. Corey is married with three children.

DOUG DIBBERN's first book, *Hollywood Riots: Violent Crowds and Progressive Politics in American Film*, won the 2016 Peter Rollins Prize. He has published scholarly essays on Howard Hawks, Fritz Lang, and the Hollywood Left, and more creative essays on movies for *The Daily Notebook* at Mubi.com. He has a Ph.D. in Cinema Studies from New York University and teaches there now in the Expository Writing Program.

FRED DINGS has written three books of poetry, *After the Solstice* (Orchises Press), *Eulogy for a Private Man* (TriQuarterly Books), and *The Four Rings* (currently under review). His work has appeared in *The New Republic, The New Yorker, The Paris Review, Poetry, TriQuarterly, World Literature Today*, and many other periodicals. He currently teaches in the M.F.A. program at the University of South Carolina.

NOAH DOBIN-BERNSTEIN is a union organizer living in Chicago. His stories have appeared in *Lunch Ticket Magazine, Every Day Fiction* and Akashic Books' "Mondays are Murder" series.

ANDREW FAGUE wrote his first formal poem about the 1985 Chicago Bears, and it was immediately recognized for its potential to be turned into an elementary school rap video. Later his skits were turned into a musical about saying no to drugs. Turning inward and living in a small town in Guatemala, he had a quinine-enhanced dream of Friedrich Nietzsche solemnly handing him a work of some kind while being derided by all around them. He's now pretty sure that work was Nikos Kazantzakis' *The Odyssey: A Modern Sequel*, and the past twenty years— graduate studies in poetry, waiting tables, cutting tile, running a day care, then teaching literature, composition, mythology, and creative writing at various colleges on the West Coast—have been a voyage of leaving and returning to the southern border of the Northwest, where he now lives with his wife Meghan and two children and teaches at Cabrillo College and UC Santa Cruz. Beginning with the sun and the moon, he has been re-orienting with the fundamentals and following his writing into the realm of desire, keeping in mind Walter Payton's words: "Running the ball is like making romance." His poems have been appearing in *Catamaran.*

SHAWN FAWSON works and resides on Whidbey Island in Washington. Her book *Giving Way* won the Utah Book Award for Poetry in 2011. She holds an MFA from Vermont College of Fine Arts.

JOAN FRANK (www.joanfrank.org) is the author of seven books of literary fiction and a book of collected essays. Her pending book of four novellas, *Where You're All Going,* has won the 2018 Mary McCarthy Fiction Prize, and will be published by Sarabande Books in early 2020. Her last novel, *All the News I Need,* won the 2016 Juniper Prize for Fiction. Her book of essays, *Because You Have To: A Writing Life,* won the Silver *ForeWord Reviews* Book of the Year Award. A MacDowell, VCCA and Ragdale Fellow, Joan also reviews literary fiction and nonfiction for the *San Francisco Chronicle.* She lives with her husband, playwright Bob Duxbury, in the North Bay Area of California. joanfrank@comcast.net

PAMELA MORNEAULT GEMME is a poet, political activist, and a child protection social worker. She lives in Boston, Massachusetts. Recent or forthcoming publications include *Haiku Journal, Protest Poems.Org, Heliotrope, Anthology, J Journal,* and *Eclipse Literary Journal.* Pamela recently won Poetryinplace.com contests in the city of Newton, Massachusetts.

TONI GRAHAM is a native of San Francisco. Her most recent story collection, *The Suicide Club,* received the Flannery O'Connor Award for Short Fiction. Graham teaches at Oklahoma State, where she also serves as editor and fiction editor for *The Cimarron Review.*

BENJAMIN HARNETT is a historian, fiction writer, poet, and digital engineer. His works have appeared recently in *Pithead Chapel, Brooklyn Quarterly, Moon City Review,* and *Tahoma Literary Review.* His story "Delivery" was chosen as Longform's "Story of the Week." He holds an MA in Classics from Columbia University and in 2005 co-founded the fashion brand Hayden-Harnett. He lives in Beacon, New York with his wife Toni and their pets. He can be found most days on Twitter.com: @benharnett. He works for *The New York Times.*

DAVID HARRELL lives in Washington state. After graduating in English literature at the University of Chicago and driving a cab in Seattle, he earned an MPA in public policy at the University of Washington and began a career in public service and consulting. He was admitted to graduate school in economics at UW but did not last long, perhaps because he could not stop auditing undergraduate writing classes on the side. Subsequent fiction-writing programs at Lake Washington Vocational-Technical Institute and the UW Extension led, eventually, to an MFA in fiction from UW. This is his first published story.

LAURA HEFFINGTON was born, and still lives, in Los Angeles. She broke an uninterrupted chain of professional musicians reaching back five generations, although she eventually made a career of photographing them instead. She did join a band for a year or so, but got tired of carrying equipment around and staying up late. She attended California State University and graduated summa cum laude with a degree in psychology, which proved to be of no direct professional relevance whatsoever. No one has ever asked to see her transcripts or her Golden Key Honor Society pin, but she continues to hope that these achievements might come up in conversation one day, since the pin cost $16. She also painted sideshow banners for awhile, and worked at a textile design company, back when such things were done on paper with paint instead of on computers. Her photo book, *Architectural Tour (and Elements of Design)*, was published in 2015, and showcases structures of limited visual appeal in her beloved hometown of Highland Park. She has one son, one daughter, and one axolotl, which is a type of endangered amphibian from Mexico.

FLORENCE HOMOLKA's creative writing has appeared in *Fiction International, Epiphany, NC Review, Big Sky Journal, Bangalore Review* and others. She serves as a professor of English at CUNY's Borough of Manhattan Community College. She has also written for *Avenue, New York* magazine's publication *IN New York*, and *CITY* magazine.

RICHARD HUFFMAN completed undergrad work at Eastern Washington University. His graduate studies in Sociology and Creative Writing were completed at San Jose State U. His short stories and articles have been published in *Catamaran, The Reed, The Chicago Quarterly Review, Good Times* newspaper and elsewhere. He has written a gritty Western Historical novel and is working on a novel about race relations and love's vagaries in the aftermath of the Vietnam war. He is a Vietnam Vet and was an active participant in The Black Panthers movement in the 60s and 70s. He now lives in Santa Cruz with a dachshund of questionable character.

Anthony Hecht once said of his own poetry that it travelled down the "Via Negativa" — what one critic called "murder, mayhem and madness." Git Lanza's work takes the same road. Born, raised and educated in the United States, **GUILLERMO LANZA** currently lives and writes in Bogota, Colombia.

LARA MARKSTEIN is a South African born New Zealander, who currently lives in Durham, North Carolina. She graduated with a Bachelor of Arts in English from Harvard University, and received her Masters in Fine Arts from the MFA Program for Writers at Warren Wilson College. Her work has appeared in *Glimmer Train*, *Agni* Online, and *The Michigan Quarterly Review* among others. Lara currently serves as the Program Officer at the UC Berkeley Center for New Media, where she gets to help run such awesome events as the Art, Technology, and Culture Colloquium and the History and Theory of New Media Lecture Series.

BEN MASAOKA was born and raised in Los Angeles, third generation Japanese American. A late 1960s graduate of alternative high school, he earned Science credit for growing a single corn plant behind the classroom building. Suffering from major gaps in essential knowledge, such as the names of capital cities and most Presidents prior to 1960, he bounced around the Pacific triangle of LA, Hawaii, and Seattle for many years, finally to settle in Seattle where he currently lives and teaches high school. He is married, has three children and an old black cat named Kuroneko. He has enjoyed a life-long interest in the martial arts and currently practices with whiskey drinking descendants of whiskey drinking Taoist warrior scholars. Martial arts, he believes, are a lot like writing. As for writing, he prefers a simple yet vivid style. He hopes to retire soon and keep bees on his overgrown property in suburbia. This is his first published work of fiction.

KAREN MCPHERSON has published one chapbook *Sketching Elise* (Finishing Line 2012) and a full-length volume of poems *Skein of Light* (Airlie Press 2014) and her poems (and translations from the French) have appeared in numerous literary journals including *Descant*, *Beloit Poetry Journal*, *Cirque*, *Cider Press Review*, *Zoland*, and *Potomac Review*. *Skein of Light* received an Honorable Mention in the 2015 Eric Hoffer Book Award in the poetry category and her poem "Provenance" won First Place in the Oregon Poetry Association spring 2015 contest. She is also the author of two critical monographs and a book-length translation of poetic essays by a Quebec poet. Her website is www.kmcphersonpoet.com.

Originally from Spain, **ISIDRA MENCOS** has lived in the US since 1992. She holds a PhD in Spanish and Latin American Contemporary Literature from the University of California, Berkeley, where she taught Spanish language, literature, and creative writing for twelve years. Her book of short stories, *Juego de voces*, was published by Ediciones Navegante (1997) and an awarded academic book, *Mercè Rodoreda: An annotated bibliography*, was published by Scarecrow Press (2004). She recently switched genres and language and is now writing memoir in English. Her essays "The Dress" and "The Thin Black Taste of Summer" have been published in *The Penmen Review* and *Front Porch Journal* (2017). Isidra has been a featured blogger on *BabyCenter,* the *Latino Community Foundation, Viva Fifty*, and the *Huffington Post*, among others. She's currently writing a book-length memoir entitled *The Conquest of Pleasure*, which tells her journey from repression to liberation, mirroring Spain's transition from dictatorship to democracy.

LINDA DOWNING MILLER's short stories have appeared in *Water-Stone Review, The Florida Review, Fifth Wednesday Journal, Fiction International*, and *Crab Orchard Review*. Her story "Threat Response," in *Water-Stone Review* 20, was previously selected by Edwidge Danticat as one of two runners-up for the 2016 Kore Press Short Fiction Award. Linda's personal essays have been published in the *Chicago Tribune, Chicago Parent*, and other places. She lives in Oak Park, Illinois and leads creative writing classes in Chicago at the Newberry Library, the Center for Life and Learning, and elsewhere.

ANDREW MULVANIA is the author of one collection of poems, *Also In Arcadia*, published by The Backwaters Press in Omaha, Nebraska, in 2008. Recent poems have appeared in *Hudson Review, Southwest Review,* and *Waccamaw,* and new work is out in the latest issue of *Smartish Pace*. He has twice been a writer-in-residence at the Chautauqua Institute and was awarded an Individual Creative Artists Fellowship in Poetry from the Pennsylvania Council on the Arts. He was a professor of English and Creative Writing at Washington & Jefferson College from 2005-2014, and currently teaches writing at Moberly Area Community College in Columbia, Missouri.

TERESA BURNS MURPHY is the author of a novel, *The Secret to Flying* (TigerEye Publications, 2011). Her work has been published in several literary journals and anthologies, including *Amazing Graces: Yet Another Collection of Fiction by Washington Area Women, Dreamstreets, Evening Street*

Review, Gargoyle Magazine, The Penmen Review, r.kv.r.y, Slippery Elm Literary Journal, Southern Women's Review, Stirring: A Literary Collection, THEMA, The Tower Journal, and *Westview.* Originally from Arkansas, she currently lives in Northern Virginia. To learn more about her writing, visit her at www.teresaburnsmurphy.com.

NATALIA NEBEL is a writer and translator (Italian to English) whose fiction, book reviews, interviews and translations have been published in a variety of literary journals, including *Fifth Wednesday Review, Burnside Review, Great Lakes Review, Free Verse, Prague Review, Triquarterly, Another Chicago Magazine, Newcity* and *Primavera.* She is a Pushcart Prize nominee, and most recently her story "Bats" as well as her essay "Lazurus" were nominated for the AWP First Journal Award by Northwestern University. She feels honored that "Lazurus" is being published by *Chicago Quarterly Review,* a journal that provides a crucial outlet for established and emerging writers in the literary community at large. Natalia Nebel is also co-founder and co-curator of the literary reading series *Sunday Salon Chicago.*

CHIKA ONYENEZI is a writer living in the United States. He was born in Owerri, Nigeria. His work has appeared, or is forthcoming, in *Burrow Press, Cosmonauts Avenue, Ninth Letter Magazine,* and elsewhere. He received Honorable Mention in the 2016 *Glimmer Train* Fiction Open. He spends most of his time daydreaming, and collecting wish trinket from sea waves. In addition to writing short stories, he has a novel in progress.

In the fifth grade, **FRANCES PARK** wrote her first book on an Underwood typewriter and never quite returned to the real world. She's the author of ten books published in seven languages, including the novel *When My Sister Was Cleopatra Moon* (Hyperion), the memoir *Chocolate Chocolate: The True Story of Two Sisters, Tons of Treats, and the Little Shop that Could* (St. Martin's Press) and the children's book *Good-bye, 382 Shin Dang Dong* (National Geographic Books). Her short stories and essays have been published in *The Massachusetts Review, The London Magazine, OZY, Next Avenue, USAToday.com, Gulf Coast Journal, Hawaii Review,* and *Arts & Letters,* to name a few. For her work, she's been interviewed on NPR, The Diane Rehm Show, Voice of America, Radio Free Asia and *Good Morning America.* Her essay "You Two Are So Beautiful Together" earned a spot on *The Best American Essays 2017* Notable List.

JUAN PARRA is a Cuban American poet whose work has featured in both national and international reviews. He and his wife share their home in Miami Beach with one extraordinary toddler. He has a BA in English and is currently working on completing his first volume of poetry titled *Flu in the Time of Allergies.*

ROBERT LEONARD REID is the author of five books, four works for the theater, and more than one hundred magazine articles, short stories, and essays. His new book, *Because It Is So Beautiful: Unraveling the Mystique of the American West* (Counterpoint Press), a collection of nineteen essays on the American West, was a finalist for the 2018 PEN/Diamonstein-Spielvogel Award for the Art of the Essay. A prolific songwriter and busy keyboard player in both high-minded houses of worship and sleazy dives, Reid has written and staged three satirical revues and the 24-song *Bristlecone Mass.* He has received two Artist Fellowships in Literary Arts from the Nevada Arts Council and a Silver Pen Award from the Nevada Writers Hall of Fame. He lives in Carson City.

JIM RINGLEY is a writer and painter who grew up on a small farm in rural Arkansas. After college he moved to Boulder, Colorado to study at Naropa's Jack Kerouac School of Disembodied Poetics. His essays have been published in *The Sun, The Threepenny Review, Catamaran, The Chattahoochee Review,* and others. His artwork can be seen in collections of the Spencer Museum of Art, the University of Colorado, the San Diego Art Institute, and the Savannah College of Art and Design. He is the recipient of a Residency Fellowship at the Millay Colony for the Arts, New York. Jim Ringley currently lives in San Luis Obispo, California, home of the world's first motel.

MICAH RUELLE is a queer midwestern poet residing in the Kansas City area. She holds an MFA from Texas State, a CPTS from Oxford's Wycliffe Hall, and a BA from the University of Central Missouri. She has been published in journals such as *Cutthroat, Profane, About Place,* and others.

LEONA SEVICK's work appears in *Verse Daily, Little Patuxent Review, North American Review, Potomac Review, The Journal, The Florida Review, Fifth Wednesday Journal, Crab Orchard Review, The Normal School, Atlanta Review,* and other journals. Her work also appears in the anthologies *Circe's Lament* (Accents Publishing 2015), *All We Can Hold* (Sage Hill Press 2016), and *The Golden Shovel Anthology: New Poems Honoring Gwendolyn Brooks* (Univ.

of Arkansas Press, 2017, foreword by Terrance Hayes). She is the 2017 Press 53 Poetry Award Winner for her first full-length book of poems, *Lion Brothers*, and the 2012 first place winner of the Split This Rock Poetry contest, judged by Naomi Shihab Nye. She was a semi-finalist for the 2015 Philip Levine Poetry Prize and a finalist for the 2016 Ciardi Prize. Her chapbook, *Damaged Little Creatures*, was published in 2015 by FutureCycle Press. She is provost at Bridgewater College in Virginia and can be reached at leonasevick.com.

RICHARD B. SIMON's first gig as a rock writer was interviewing Butch Trucks of the Allman Brothers backstage at the Fillmore. He covered the Dead Kennedys trial, the earliest hearings about something called Napster, and many, many great concerts. He's interviewed presidential candidates (well, one), Black Panthers, heavy metal guitarists, rappers, authors, filmmakers, members of the Grateful Dead (numerous), roadies, sound engineers, noted rabbis, a few handfuls of rock legends, and plenty of regular people, too. You can catch him in the Metallica documentary *Some Kind of Monster*, so long as you don't blink. He also teaches writing, and is the lead author and editor of *Teaching Big History* (University of California Press 2015), a pedagogy for teaching the history of the universe, the solar system and Earth, the evolution of life, and the story of humans. And he co-founded the underground psychedelic rock festival the Frisco Freakout. After many years spent as an expatriated New Yorker in San Francisco, he fled the tech boom and is living as a climate refugee in the Pacific Northwest, where there is less rock and roll, but more water. He teaches Creative Writing, Big History, and other subversive things at Western Washington University.

THEADORA SIRANIAN is a graduate of the MFA Program at the University of Massachusetts, Boston. Her poetry has appeared in *DIAGRAM*, *Meridian*, *Best New Poets*, *Ghost City Press*, and *CONSEQUENCE*, among others. In 2013, she was a finalist for The Poet's Billow Pangaea Prize, and in 2014 was shortlisted for both the *Mississippi Review* Prize and *Southword*'s Gregory O'Donoghue International Poetry Prize. She currently lives and teaches in Brooklyn.

MARJORIE SKELLY's cross-genre book, *The Unpublished Poet: On Not Giving Up on Your Dream*, was endorsed by former Indiana Poet Laureate Norbert Krapf and published by In Extenso Press. It consists of essays, short stories, and poems. She has won first place awards from Poets and Patrons, the Jo-Anne Hirshfield Memorial Poetry Contest, and the

Palatine Public Library. She has twice reached finalist status for the Word Works Washington Prize for a poetry book, and twice reached finalist status in the Gwendolyn Brooks Open Mike Poetry Contest in Chicago. One of her short stories, "Standing in the Dark with My Family," was given finalist status three times with *Glimmer Train*, and another short story, "The Day her Feet Stood Still in 1968" was given an honorable mention twice, also with *Glimmer Train*. Her short story "Pass the Candied Yams" won second place in a National Organization for Women Short Story Contest. Marjorie has taught writing at several universities, poetry writing (revision) at Harold Washington Library, and poetry and fiction writing at Eisenhower Library, all in the Chicago-land area. Most recently she taught a class on the history of Handel's *Messiah* at both Eisenhower and Highland Park Libraries. She is also a singer and has sung with North Shore Choral Society and Edgewater Singers, and has twice sung in the Jazz/Gospel version of Handel's *Messiah* known as "Too Hot to Handel." She lives with her husband Jim and her daughter Maggie in Chicago.

SETH D. SLATER has contributed to *Bird's Thumb, Metonym, Le Scat Noir, The Tishman Review* and *New Madrid*. Slater received a *Glimmer Train* honorable mention and was a recent AWP finalist for best novel excerpt. Slater is completing his MFA in Fiction at San Diego State University where he teaches Writing and Rhetoric.

Inspired by Hispanic religious icons, folk art and the wild orchard behind her Northern New Mexico childhood home, **ELEANOR SPIESS-FERRIS** has become a widely exhibited artist nationally as well as internationally. She has received numerous fellowships and grants, including an Arts Midwest Fellowship grant and several grants from the state of Illinois and the city of Chicago where she now resides. The Art Institute of Chicago awarded her the Vielehr Award during the 80th Exhibition of Artists of Chicago and Vicinity. Spiess-Ferris has shown her work in many one-person exhibits and group exhibits throughout the United States at universities, museums, and commercial galleries: these include venues in Oklahoma, Indiana, Michigan, Wisconsin, Missouri, California, Colorado, New Mexico, Washington, Texas, South Carolina, and Illinois to name a few. Internationally, she has exhibited in India, Spain and France. Reviews of her work can be noted by James Yood in *Art Forum* magazine, by Garrett Holg in *Art News* and by Margaret Hawkins for the *Chicago Sun-Times* to mention a few. A retrospective of her work will be shown in 2019 at the Illinois State Art Museum in Springfield, Illinois. The exhibit will travel to the Evanston Art Center, Evanston, Illinois, in 2020.

ADAM SULLIVAN's essays have appeared in a wide variety of publications, including *Tampa Review, Monster Children, The Binnacle, Transworld Skateboarding*, and *Pregnancy* magazine. He's kind of all over the place. He is the winner of the 2010 Los Angeles Comedy Festival's Screenplay Competition, and the 2011 Atlanta Film Festival Screenplay Competition. He is currently enrolled in U.C. Riverside/Palm Desert's Creative Writing M.F.A. program. Man, getting to 150 words in a bio is tougher than he'd anticipated. One time he went on a Caribbean cruise and got second-degree burns on his leg from squeezing lime into his beers and wiping the pulp on his knee. Apparently the citrus acts like an anti-sunblock. That was a weird one. He doesn't have a website, but he probably should. Are you supposed to plug your novel? He's hard at work on his first novel. Also a collection of essays, like the one in here.

LISA TADDEO is a 2017 recipient of The Pushcart Prize. She received her MFA in fiction as the Saul Bellow Fellow from Boston University. Her fiction has been published in *Granta, The New England Review, The Sun Magazine* and *Esquire*, among others. Her nonfiction has been published in *Esquire, New York Magazine, Elle Magazine, The New York Observer, Glamour Magazine* and *The Sun Magazine*. Lisa's work has been included in *Best American Sports Writing* and *Best American Political Writing*. She is currently at work on her debut nonfiction for Simon and Schuster, and her first novel.

REBECCA TURKEWITZ's short stories, essays, and humor writing have appeared in *New South, Sonora Review, Harpur Palate, Catapult, The Toast, The New Yorker's* Daily Shouts, *McSweeney's Internet Tendency*, and elsewhere. She holds an MFA in fiction from The Ohio State University. She lives in Portland, Maine.

DANIEL UNCAPHER is a PhD student in Creative Writing at the University of Utah whose work has appeared in *Baltimore Review, Hawai'i Pacific Review, Wilderness House, HCE Review, A-Minor, Posit, Neon*, and others. He holds an MFA from Notre Dame.

MITCHELL UNTCH is an emerging writer. Partial publications include *Beloit Poetry Journal, Poet Lore, North American Review, Confrontation, Nimrod Intl, Natural Bridge, Owen Wister, Solo Novo, Knockout: Baltimore Review, Lake Effect, Catamaran, Grey Sparrow, Illuminations, Tusculum Review, The Tampa Review, Mudfish, Painted Bride Quarterly, Meridian, Chattahoochee Review, Tule Review*, among others.

BRADLEY VANDEVENTER is the author of the novels *Our Lady of the Hypercube* and *Angels with Engine Failure*. His short stories have appeared in *Angry Old Man Magazine* and other literary journals. He lives in Anaheim, California. More of his work can be found at https://bradleyvandeventer.com

LARRY WATSON is the author of ten books, among them the novels *Montana 1948, Orchard, Let Him Go,* and *As Good As Gone.* Watson's fiction has been published in more than a dozen foreign editions and has received prizes and awards from Friends of American Writers, Mountain and Plains Booksellers Association, New York Public Library, Critics' Choice, and elsewhere. *Montana 1948* was nominated for the first IMPAC Dublin international literary prize, and *Let Him Go* was nominated for the same prize in 2014. Algonquin Books will publish his next novel in 2019. His short fiction and poetry have been published in *Gettysburg Review, New England Review, North American Review, Mississippi Review,* and other literary magazines. His essays and book reviews have appeared in the *Los Angeles Times,* the *Chicago Sun-Times,* the *Washington Post,* the *Milwaukee Journal-Sentinel,* and other periodicals. His work has also been anthologized in *Essays for Contemporary Culture, Imagining Home, Off the Beaten Path, Baseball and the Game of Life, Tales of Two Americas, These United States,* and *Writing America*. He teaches writing and literature at Marquette University in Milwaukee.

WANG WEI (699–759) was a Tang dynasty Chinese poet and painter.

IAN RANDALL WILSON has published two novellas, *Great Things Are Coming* (Hollyridge Press 2009) and *The Complex* (Colony Collapse Press 2015), and two story collections. His fiction, poetry and essays have appeared in many journals including *The Gettysburg Review, The New Mexico Humanities Review, Alaska Quarterly Review, The Mid-American Review,* and *North American Review*. His first poetry collection, *Ruthless Heaven,* was published by Finishing Line Press. He has an MFA in Fiction and in Poetry from Warren Wilson College. He is on the fiction faculty at UCLA Extension. By day, he is an executive at Sony Pictures Entertainment.

YANWEN XU was born in Xuzhou, China. He now studies and writes in Santa Cruz, California.

GARY YOUNG's most recent books are *That's What I Thought,* winner of the Lexi Rudnitsky Editor's Choice Award from Persea Books, and

Precious Mirror, translations from the Japanese published by White Pine Press. His many honors include the Shelley Memorial Award, and the William Carlos Williams Award from the Poetry Society of America. He teaches creative writing and directs the Cowell Press at UC Santa Cruz.

FAN ZHONGYAN (989–1052) was a Song dynasty Chinese statesman, poet, and a founder of Neo-Confucianism.

KENYON*revi w*

e

ONE OF AMERICA'S
MOST HONORED LITERARY
JOURNALS SINCE 1939

DISCOVER US AT
KENYONREVIEW.ORG

IN PRINT
ONLINE
IN CLASS

MUSIC
OF THE
BAROQUE

It all starts here.

From opera to oratorio, suites to symphonies, it all starts with the Baroque. Join us for a season full of inspiration, including—

Vivaldi's Four Seasons (Nov 4 & 5) based on sonnets written by the composer

Bach's Christmas Oratorio (Nov 25 & 26) the holiday story in dramatic narrative, moving arias, and inspiring chorales

Holiday Brass & Choral (Dec 13-16) showcasing medieval and Renaissance music

And much more!

Single tickets start at $25, or purchase 3 or more concerts for as little as $60.

312.551.1414   baroque.org

Heddalu1@aol.com

HeddaLubin.com   greenbriarjewelry.com

THE BOOK STALL

The Book Stall is a full-service book store located in Winnetka, Illinois. Our friendly, knowledgable staff is always ready with recommendations, special orders, and gift cards for our customers. Our selection has something for every type of reader: from history to fiction, philosophy to graphic novels, and much more.

The Book Stall is known for its many special events for kids and adults. You will often find literary and best-selling authors signing their books. The store also sponsors reading groups, poetry sessions, and story-telling time for children. We're connected to the popular Peet's Coffee.

www.thebookstall.com
(847) 446 - 8880
@thebookstall

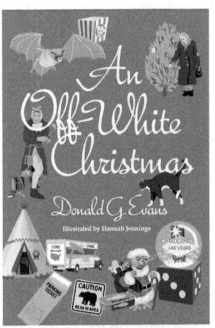

Hannah Jennings Design
HannahJennings.com

Book Covers
Illustration
Graphic Design
Book Design
Copyediting

Dippy the Wisp
She keeps stopping to change her hat.

MUNRO
CAMPAGNA

ARTIST REPRESENTATIVES

WWW.MUNROCAMPAGNA.COM · STEVE@MUNROCAMPAGNA.COM · +1 312 560 9638
Illustration: Clint Hansen

SUNDAY SALON CHICAGO IS A READING SERIES
THAT TAKES PLACE EVERY OTHER MONTH

OPEN TO ALL
FOR OVER TEN YEARS
THE SALON SERIES HAS BROUGHT WORD POWER TO
NEW YORK CITY, NAIROBI, MIAMI AND CHICAGO
ING OUR BEST LOCAL AND NATIONAL WRITERS AVAILABLE
TO A LARGER COMMUNITY

WE MEET AT CELTIC CROWN PUBLIC HOUSE*
2356 W. Cullom Ave., in Chicago
A 7PM TO 8PM ON THE LAST SUNDAY OF EVERY OTHER MONTH

EAT, DRINK YOUR FAVORITE DRINKS, MAKE NEW FRIENDS
AND ENJOY THESE READINGS WITH US!

OUR EXCELLENT EVENTS ARE ALWAYS FREE

*We will be returning to our original venue Riverview Tavern
once its remodeling is complete.
For updates please check https://www.sundaysalon-chicago.com

The Shakespeare Project of Chicago
proudly presents

Moby Dick Rehearsed
By Orson Welles

Friday, March 15, 2019, 7PM – Niles-Maine District Library, Niles, IL
Saturday, March 16, 2019, 10:00AM - The Newberry Library, Chicago

A Shakespeare company puts down their rehearsal sides of *King Lear* and curiously take up those of a new play entitled *Moby Dick*. On the rehearsal stage of platforms, the teasers overhead suddenly become yardarms with sails and a tall ladder becomes a mast. The platforms become the decks of the ship on which the cast sails through the storms and tribulations of the Pequod hunting for Moby Dick. The original production of *Moby Dick—Rehearsed*, directed by the author, Orson Welles, ran June 16–July 9, 1955, at the Duke of York's Theatre, London. This event, produced by The Shakespeare Project of Chicago, is part of the exhibition *Melville: Finding America at Sea*, January 18 through April 18, 2019, at the Newberry Library.

Produced with permission of Orson Welles, Inc.

www.shakespeareprojectchicago.org

CPSIA information can be obtained
at www.ICGtesting.com
Printed in the USA
FSHW022008291219
65565FS